Differences in
Visual Perception

The Individual Eye

Jules B. Davidoff

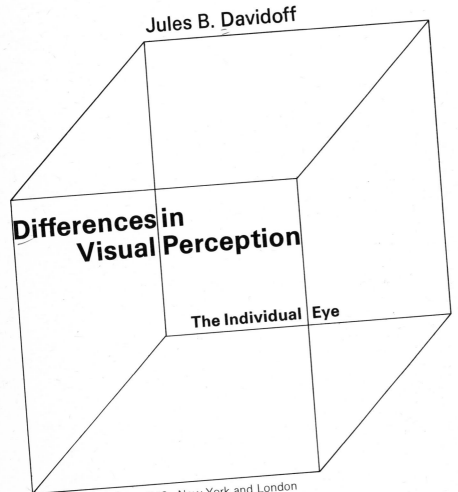

Differences in Visual Perception
Visual Perception

The Individual Eye

ACADEMIC PRESS, INC., New York and London
A Subsidiary of Harcourt Brace Jovanovich, Publishers

Granada Publishing Limited
First published in Great Britain 1975 by Crosby Lockwood Staples
Frogmore St Albans Herts and 3 Upper James Street London W1R 4BP

Library of Congress Catalog Card Number 74–10467
ISBN 0–12–204850–4

Printed in Great Britain by William Clowes & Sons Limited, London,
Beccles and Colchester.

Published in the United States by
Academic Press Inc., 111 Fifth Avenue, New York, New York 10003.

Every effort has been made to trace the source of and obtain
permission to use all copyright material reproduced in this
book. This is acknowledged wherever possible.

Contents

Acknowledgements

I would like to express my thanks to the many colleagues who have helped in some way with the preparation of this book. In particular I should like to thank those who have helped with literary quotations. Dr John Worthen supplied some of those for the section on ambiguity in literature, and Ros Castell suggested the quotation heading Chapter Four. Special thanks must go to Dr Norman Dixon for his many valuable comments on the whole manuscript. Lastly, I acknowledge the help of Oliver Freeman, for the publishers, who did his best to ensure that the book came out in a form close to the author's wishes.

Jules B. Davidoff

Swansea
October 1974

Introduction

Do people see the world in different ways? This work is devoted to a discussion of the extent to which this is the case. It would be nice to be able to present a simple catalogue of the necessary facts, but this is not possible: there must of necessity be a selection from the vast body of work on visual perception which has been recorded since the time of the ancient Greeks. Also, much of the important work to be discussed was initiated from some theoretical standpoint, and the words used to describe an event will inevitably reveal the assumptions of the person who is describing it.

With this in mind it is fitting to say a little about the assumed nature of the world and the relationship of the perceiver to the world. The commonsense view is that there is a concrete outside world with real, constant and verifiable properties. It is not possible to prove the truth of this proposition; in the last analysis it has to be assumed from a consensus of opinion. However, since it is subjectively felt that the world is a stable, verifiable place we have no concern in taking this as our starting-point. It might be thought that this would conflict with the notion of differences between observers in their perception of the world, since there is the problem of how and why such differences could arise. Yet it does not. What concerns us here is to show how, from the same visual input, different percepts may arise. Perception goes beyond the mere reception of the visual input. Historically, there has been much discussion of the difference between 'pure' sensation and the final elaborated percept. This distinction concerns us little since we are only directly concerned with the latter.

Heaton (1968) gives a phenomenological account of vision and talks about the world as being a product of perception, not the cause of it. Yet from time to time he talks about objects which are perceived as smaller or larger than they 'really are'. This apparent contradiction should not surprise us. On the one hand we intuitively feel that the world 'really is' in one form only, on the other hand we conclude that the percept will be different according to such factors as the past experiences of the perceiver.

There is a perhaps related distinction between perception and cognition. Let us take the example of a swastika. On one level, everybody will see the same shape. But as the swastika is a meaningful symbol, it will be interpreted differently, it could even be said, perceived differently, by different people.

Traditionally, the perception of incoming stimuli is considered separately from other mental processes for which such present stimuli are not needed. These latter processes are generally discussed under the heading of cognition. Arnheim (1970) takes the view that the distinction between perception and cognition is misplaced—even harmful. The processes of perception are, according to Arnheim, operations such as 'active exploration, selection, grasping the essentials, simplification, abstraction, analysis and synthesis, completion, correction, comparison, problem solving, as well as combining, separating, putting into context'. But can perception and cognition be so easily joined? If one can have the temerity to use a quotation supplied by Arnheim against him, one might make use of that phrase which Francis Galton scathingly applied to certain statisticians. He said that they reminded him of the natives of 'one of our flat English counties, whose retrospect of Switzerland was that, if its mountains could be thrown into its lakes, two nuisances could be got rid of at once'. Or, put another way, it can be concluded that just because mountains merge imperceptibly into valleys, this should not stop us talking about mountains and valleys.

The purpose of this book is to present the differences in visual perception that can occur in various circumstances when observers perceive the 'same' event. If one were trying to theorise about all aspects of perception then it would be difficult to see how this could be done without resorting to some scheme analogous to that put forward by Arnheim. The distinction between perception defined as mere reception, and cognition defined as the operations upon that which has been received, would not be useful.

To some extent the distinction between perception and cognition is a problem that is avoided in this work. Arnheim says that there is no real difference between 'what happens when a person looks at the world directly and when he sits with his eyes closed and *thinks*'. But this distinction is crucial to our consideration of perception. Perception, being here the subjective appreciation of the immediately present outside world, cannot consider imagery and thinking. Perhaps both processes depend on interpretation and both involve exploration and selection, but imagery is not tied to the *immediate* stimulation. It is, of course, quite possible to have some form of perception without there being any external stimulus present. If this work were to deal with all the differences that could arise in every situation where one has a percept one would have to deal with phenomena such as hallucinations and dreams as well as imagery. And indeed it may be the case that the causes of individual variations in these phenomena could be traced to individual experiences at some point with stimuli that *were* actually present. They are omitted here because it is desired to impose a constraint upon the word 'perception' and deal only with differences that arise in the way a person sees the world as it is presented to him. It will therefore be appreciated that much material of a cognitive nature cannot have priority here.

It is not possible to deal at great length with the individual pieces of research upon which this book is based. Because of this, references are given to original work and to review articles which the interested reader can consult for more information. Also, facts will be reported in many instances as if there were no difficulties in obtaining them. Strict methodological controls will always be necessary to obtain findings which clearly prove the point of a hypothesis which is being tested. These controls are not mentioned here unless it is felt that the perspicacious reader would be troubled by their omission.

It is also necessary to raise the question of the word to be used to describe the perceiver; in scientific journals one has the choice between calling him (or her) a subject or an observer. To call him a subject suggests that changes in his perceptual sensations are forced upon him and that he is to some extent trapped. To use the word 'observer' suggests that he passively watches the outside world and, again, plays no part in the perceptual process. Neither of these is satisfactory, but 'observer' will be used here.

The theme which runs throughout this work is the fact that the same external input does not necessarily bring about in all of us the same perception. We tend to assume that when viewing a scene every observer has the same perception. Since most of the time no conflict arises between observers, this does not seem a bad assumption. However, it is hoped to document a large number of circumstances in which disagreement does occur. It is not a question of us mere mortals being easily fooled, but a realisation that the observer takes an active part in the perceptual process. The observer does not simply sit and watch, he also takes part.

In discussing the ways in which perception differs from individual to individual we shall often resort to phrases such as 'differences in information processing' or 'visual processing'. It is a fair question to ask exactly what these processes are. To a large extent, describing those changes that occur in the visual system as 'processing' hides an ignorance of what is exactly happening. It is a useful phrase, but it may well remind the reader of processing peas. Though the comparison may seem bizarre, the word 'processing' is used in the same way: we have an input which is altered to form a final product. It is possible to spell out in detail exactly what the operations are that change the pea 'from its natural state', but it is not possible with the process of human vision. Yet we have no qualms about talking of 'visual processing', since it is a logical necessity that some operation is carried out if the perception is altered. To try to point out some of the differences in this processing system between individuals is the first stage in understanding the problems involved.

As the book begins with differences in perception which are in operation for only a short time, it is necessary to distinguish between short and long-term effects and to decide at what point 'short' becomes 'long'. This is a very tenuous distinction and no fast division can be made. The result of this, and other such uncertainties, is that particular areas of research are divided between different sections of the book, with pieces of information appearing under the various headings that seem most appropriate.

The effects which we classify as short-term differences in perception are perhaps the best understood. Many of these are standard perceptual phenomena to be found in most textbooks on the psychological aspects of vision. For example, recent work in physiology has shown a relationship between the structure of the human visual network and changes in perception. As it has been shown that there are edge-detectors in the visual cortex, we may well expect there to be some effect if an observer has these edge-detectors stimulated for some time. However, biological systems tend to recover quickly and after a short time the effect resulting from that satiation will disappear. Of course, it would be wrong to pretend that we understand all about differences in perception of a short-term nature; we certainly do not.

Our ignorance of long-term differences in perception is more basic. Since we are confronted with permanent differences in the ways in which two observers view an object or scene, the possibility of explaining these differences between individuals becomes more complicated. We are faced with differences caused by some permanent factor. On a trivial level, physical abnormalities in the visual cortex will, of course, result in differences in perception. On a less obvious level, colour-blindness seems to be linked to a genetic factor. These innate differences between observers are not always easy to distinguish from differences due to the varied experience of the observers. Anyone who has been concerned with the problem of whether the intelligence of a person is acquired or based on some innate factor knows the practical insolubility of this 'nature or nurture' issue.

However, the possibility of changes in perception due to experience requires us to consider the changes in the development of perception. This raises problems of a practical and a theoretical nature. The practical problems involved with the testing of children are varied and often tiresome, but recent methodological advances have enabled us to ascertain much about the perceptual development of even the preverbal child. Yet the theoretical problem of how these changes occur remains mostly a mystery. This great gap in our knowledge is one that must be filled if we are fully to understand the processing system we are discussing. The developmental changes in the processing system may result either from inherent maturational changes or from differences in input through experience. They may even occur from some interaction between maturation and experience. But, as has been pointed out, we do not really know the nature of the processes underlying visual perception. This being the case, the first essential is to say exactly what these developmental differences are, and this is what will be attempted in the third chapter of the book. Some indication of the processing differences may be given, but to clarify these must, in the main part, remain an endeavour for the future.

The last sections of this work bring us back full circle to a consideration of the nature of the input to the visual system. It has been argued that there is an essential ambiguity in the input from which perception is constructed. To some extent this is a view that is put forward here. But the input can only be ambiguous if there are observers to construct different perceptions from the input. Whatever the system that changes the input and differentiates one individual's perception from another's, it involves an active participation which may in the long term give us clues to the interpretation of the visual world.

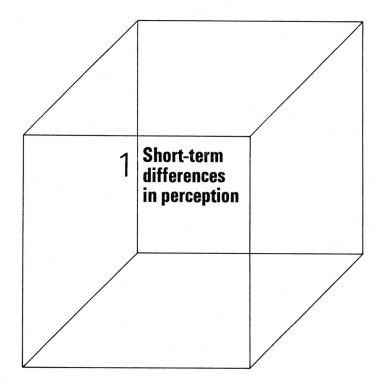

1 Short-term differences in perception

This chapter is devoted to differences in perception which are of a temporary nature. We shall consider the case where two observers initially perceive the outside world in the same way and then, because of some manipulation of the visual input or some short-term change in an observer, we are able to make one of them perceive the world differently for a short time. The division into short and long-term effects is somewhat arbitrary: it will in some cases be hard to make such a sharp dichotomy. But even if there are blurred middle cases, the two ends of the continuum are separate enough to justify the division.

In general, short-term differences in perception concern what happens after some well-defined event. It is a pity that we cannot use the term 'after-effects' to describe all these changes, but this term is generally retained for a specific set of such effects which are considered later in this chapter. To begin with we shall consider a very common short-term change in perception—that of the after-image.

After-images

If an observer looks at any bright object for about one minute, then transfers his gaze to a blank wall, he will see an image of that object on the wall.

This is called an after-image. It may well be coloured differently from the original object.

This fact, in other forms, has been known for a long time. We have all looked at the sun for too long and been able to see it for some time afterwards. Boring (1942) states that Kircher in the seventeenth century reported a friend as having a wager with a priest that he could make him see in the dark. He did this by asking the priest to stare out of a window, then look at a piece of white paper after the room had been suddenly thrown into darkness. The priest found that he did experience some visual sensation. The paper, however, is quite irrelevant. If the light was strong enough, the priest may have seen a white after-image of the initial stimulus which was followed by a blue, which in turn was followed by a green, then a reddish colour, then finally blue or green. This 'flight of colours', as it is called, is normally seen after looking at a bright white light, though other orders of the 'flight of colours' have been reported. However, the priest would have had one supporter in Feinbloom (1938) who said that these after-images are never seen without some external light being present. Berry and Imus (1935) gave seven stages for changes that occur in the after-image. They consisted of sequences of positive (like the original stimulus) and negative (brightness relationships opposite to the original) after-images.

Plate 3 shows a set of traffic lights with the wrong colours. If the reader looks steadily at the dot in the centre of the red circle of the traffic light, it will be found that the red colour has drained out of the circle. This can be proved by looking through a hole punched in a card, so that only part of the circle is visible: if the card is removed, the part of the circle fixated looks a duller red than the part not fixated. More surprisingly, it will be found that if the gaze is transferred to a grey surface or piece of paper, there will be projected on it a circle of a distinctly different colour. The colour may be faint but the red will produce a green. Conversely, a green will produce a red after-image. It is found that blue will produce a yellow after-image and yellow a blue after-image. If the whole traffic light is now fixated, it will be found that the after-image gives an approximation to the 'proper' colours.

The colour or brightness seen by an observer after staring at a coloured surface will vary according to the colour or brightness of the surface upon which he is asked to project his after-image. A green after-image will mix on a red surface to give yellow. Also, fixation of a black square will give rise to a lighter square as an after-image, even when the surface upon which it is viewed is white. (For a comprehensive review of the work on after-images, see Graham (1965).)

If the reader has any difficulty in obtaining these changes in his after-image it may well be due to his inability to fixate a spot. Though this seems a simple task, many people have to learn to do it. It is in most cases easily accomplished. Fixation is important in this task because it is only the central area (fovea) of the receptive surface of the back of the eye (retina) which is responsible for colour-vision. Generally, coloured stimuli will not be seen as anything except white in peripheral vision. Even in the central area of the retina, the various hues are not perceived equally well in exactly the same places. One has to bear this in mind, since the result of different perceptions arising from light falling on different receptors, or even on no receptors at all, would be obvious. This point will be taken up again later.

After-images depend upon the area of the retina stimulated and seem to be connected to a bleaching of the retinal pigmentation. Therefore, they would not appear to have any central causation. However, complications arise from work carried out in the USSR in the 1950s. The Russian investigators claim that it is possible to condition an after-image by classical conditioning. This is the procedure by which Pavlov made a dog salivate to the sound of a bell. In a similar vein, it was found that an after-image of a circle or a triangle was perceived after hearing a tone. The experimental procedure was to present the tone before, say, a very bright circle. This temporal association of tone and circle (hence after-image) occurred maybe hundreds of times over many days. It is said that eventually the tone produced the after-image without the bright circle actually being presented to the observer.

Using this technique one can get an observer for whom a tone now means an after-image. Presenting the same stimulus to two people can therefore result in their having different perceptions. For one, a tone will quite naturally give an auditory sensation. For the other, it gives more than that: he also has a visual sensation. Since simple association has taken place, one would expect that there are other stimuli besides a tone that could be made to elicit an after-image. Indeed, Davies (1972) suggests that another flash of light would do equally well.

Davies reports other interesting findings. The conditioned after-images were frequently said to be distorted in size and shape from the original stimulus. Since the stimulus was carefully presented to the same area of the retina every time, one has to look for some explanation. Davies considers that one possible explanation is that the observer has, during the conditioning procedure, two after-images: a normal one resulting from the bright stimulus, and another, conditioned, after-image elicited by the tone. It is not clear why this should produce a distortion in size and shape unless it is suggested that the two after-images would drift in opposite directions. Davies does put forward some evidence of this. The fact that there are two after-images may also explain why observers reported that parts of the after-images alternated between positive and negative phases. Normally, the whole figure would alternate. After-images, if viewed for some time, can break up and parts of them disappear. If this were happening to one of the after-images, then, if the two after-images were out of phase, anything that vanished from the after-image would allow that part to be seen in a different phase state.

We have noted in this discussion that continuous pairing of one stimulus with another may give rise to a curious perception, since an after-image can be produced without the original stimulus being present. But, as we have just hinted above, continuous presentation of the same stimulus will also produce unusual effects, and this is considered next.

Repeated presentations

It is a common enough experience that the continued repetition to oneself of a single word drains the word of any meaning. A 'ganzfeld', as produced first by Metzger (1930), achieves a similar visual effect. Continuous presentation of a completely homogeneous visual field is found to produce a 'drained' visual world. A ganzfeld can be produced by surrounding the whole observer with a homogeneous field of light or by wearing a contact lens of translucent plastic, or simply by cutting a ping-pong ball in half and fitting it over the eye. An observer viewing a ganzfeld filled with coloured light finds that it soon becomes devoid of all colour. Some of Cohen's (1957) observers reported that there was no visual experience at all, not even that of blackness.

The well-known Muller-Lyer Illusion is shown in Fig. 1. The two vertical lines are in fact the same length. It was found by Judd (1902) that continuous presentation of the illusion resulted in a decrement of the illusory effect. Judd found that after many trials, the illusion reduced to the stage where the vertical lines were seen as being the same length; in some cases, the illusion could even reverse. The result of a decrement of illusory effect with repeated presentation has been confirmed many times since and applies also to other illusions (Coren and Girgus, 1972). The decrement occurs without any knowledge of the illusion, observers reporting that the illusion looks the same at the end of the inspection as at the beginning. Also, it is not necessary to adjust the lines for the illusion to decrease.

The explanation of this decrement has been related to the eye movements of the observer. For example, it is known that steady fixation of a stimulus, or presenting it briefly (the eye takes time to move), results in no decrement. What role do eye movements play in these illusions? It has been suggested that the part of the Muller-Lyer which covers the apparently longer vertical line may 'draw the eye out' and magnify the length of that vertical line. Yarbus (1967) looks at this from the viewpoint of the already operating illusory effect producing the differential eye movements, suggesting that these result from the illusion rather than being the cause of it. No matter which comes first, Festinger, White and Allyn (1968) did find that this decrement in the Muller-Lyer Illusion was

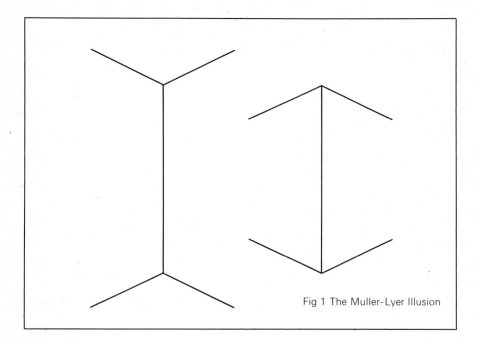

Fig 1 The Muller-Lyer Illusion

accompanied by a change in the way the illusion was inspected. However, since the illusion persists even when the eye is incapable of moving (see the stabilised retinal images below) eye movements themselves cannot be the whole cause of the illusion.

It is important to try to draw a distinction between changes of short duration and those long-term changes which might affect the way in which an observer would look at many different situations, perhaps in the distant future. If the decrements produced in these illusions are of a short-term nature, then their subsequent presentation, say a week later, would result in just the same amount of illusion as at the beginning of the very first presentation. Also, the rate of diminution of illusion should be the same. If there has been a long-term effect this will not be the case. There is little direct evidence on this point, but a short-term change is favoured.

The phenomenal changes which occur in a stimulus with continued auditory presentation are mirrored by changes in visual perception when we have continuous viewing of an object. If we provide the necessary conditions, the perception of even quite simple objects will alter and break down (for a review, see Heckenmueller (1965)). First of all the contours disappear, followed by the colour and finally by the brightness.

If a stimulus such as that shown in Fig. 2a is fixed at one point on the retina, a disappearance of part of that figure results. The shapes shown in Fig. 2b represent what the observer may see in this situation, though the parts shown do not occur equally often, or necessarily in that order.

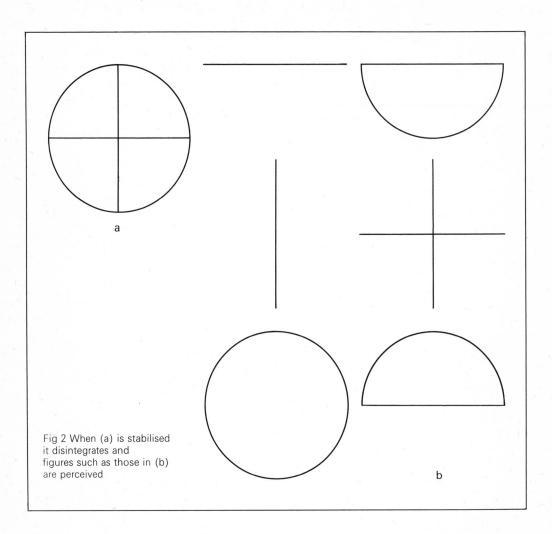

Fig 2 When (a) is stabilised
it disintegrates and
figures such as those in (b)
are perceived

It is under special conditions that these changes happen. In saying that the object should be continuously viewed, it was not explained what this meant or how it could be achieved. Continuous viewing means here that the object always stimulates the same area of the retina. The eyes are continuously in motion so that, unless some means can be found artificially to stabilise the image on the retina, it will not be possible for precisely the same area of the retina to be continuously stimulated. This, however, can be achieved by means of a contact lens arrangement, or, more simply, by flashing a bright light to get an after-image which, because it bleaches the pigment on the retina, must from necessity stay in the same place.

Let us consider the case of two observers asked to look at an object: one of them normally and the other as a stabilised retinal image. Can we say that the two observers who are asked to inspect the object are seeing the same thing? If two people were viewing different objects, say, a tree and a house, it would be considered trivial to ask why they saw different things. Similarly, if two people were to view the same house from different angles it would be no surprise if they reported seeing different things. What we would really like to show is that there are cases where the same receptors in the eye have the same input and individuals still perceive differently. Of course, when we talk of the same receptors we are referring to the mere geography of the system and not to any prior experience which may alter the state of those receptors or to any interpretative functions going on because of the receptor stimulation. Stabilised retinal images provide us with an odd case because the same receptors are continuously stimulated, which is not normal. The two observers looking at Fig. 2a, while being exposed to an identical external input, have that input transmitted to slightly different receptors—so it may be unfair to claim that they are receiving the same input. However, these effects of stabilised retinal images can also be achieved with voluntary fixation of patterns.

McKinney (1963), for example, found similar fragmentations when viewing luminous figures in the dark. Indeed, this fragmentation occurred as little as three seconds after the outset of the experiment. The disappearance of lines occurred in meaningful units. In Fig. 3, observers reported the disappearance of the H or the B rather than some odd shape. This might suggest the influence of past learning, but it could equally well be due to the ease with which one can report a B or an H and the relative difficulty of describing anything else. This applies also to the reports they note of the figure disintegrating into a 3 or 13. Whichever of these interpretations of the responses made is correct, there is no doubt that continuous exposure to such a situation can alter the perception of the observer compared to that of the first few seconds of his inspection. Despite the repetition of these findings, they still come as a surprise. It could well be thought that the more one looks at an object the more one is likely to be accurate about its shape. This does not seem always to be the case.

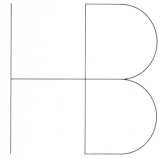

Fig 3

Adaptation

Arriving in the tropics from a temperate climate, one is at first over-whelmed by the heat and humidity, but in a very short time one adapts and these cease to be noticed. Similarly, one adapts to the coloured edges produced by spectacle lenses (chromatic aberration) and these coloured edges disappear after wearing spectacles for some time. May not some other adaptation process explain some of those effects already mentioned, and be responsible for differences in perception reported between our observers?

At many points throughout this chapter, when looking at these short-term differences, we shall consider two observers who, when looking at an object, report initially that they have the same percept. That is to say, there are no long-term individual differences in their perception. The perception of one of the observers is then altered by some manipulation. This leaves some residual effect, so that now when the two observers receive the same input they no longer report that they have the same percept.

One of the simplest examples of such a difference in perception is the adaptation which would occur to one of the observers if he went into a cinema. If one of the observers has just entered and the other has been there half-an-hour there will be differences in their perception. We have all encountered the experience of not being able to see when first entering

Fig 4 The course of dark-adaptation (after Hecht, reprinted from *Handbook of General Experimental Psychology*, Murchison, C. (Ed.), Clark University Press: 1934)

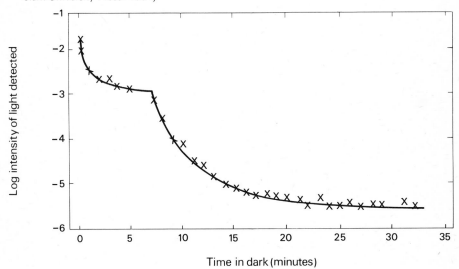

a cinema and therefore stumbling over people, while after half-an-hour or so one can see around quite well. In this latter condition, we must have adapted to the light conditions. Of course, the opposite occurs if we emerge from the cinema into bright daylight. Adaptation to light, however, is achieved quite quickly, being nearly complete after a minute or two; but it can take up to half-an-hour to be completely dark-adapted.

When the experiement is conducted between our two observers, one in and one out of the cinema, to find the lowest intensity of light that they can detect, there will be differences. Figure 4 shows us that as the observer adapts to the dark he can gradually see a light of a lower intensity. It is important to note that the scale on the ordinate is logarithmic. This means that after ten minutes there is a difference of two log-units for detection to be experienced, i.e. there is a 100-fold difference in the intensity of the light needed for perception at the beginning as compared with that after ten minutes. After half-an-hour of dark-adaptation, this has risen to four log-units (or even five), that is 10,000 (100,000) times greater. (At very low levels of illumination, Hecht *et al.* (1942) have worked out that the receptors are responding to individual quanta of light.)

The curve consists of two parts, which represents the fact that colour-vision is entirely lost at low levels of illumination. If the light our observers were watching were red, the lower part of the curve would not exist. The central part of the retina (fovea) consists of different receptors from those of the rest of the retina. These receptors, called cones, are responsible for colour-vision and have different sensitivities from those of the rods which are responsible for brightness in vision. This means that at very low levels of illumination a person cannot see an object that is looked at directly. This is known to astronomers and has, indeed, been called the 'Arago phenomenon' after the French physicist N. F. J. Arago (1786–1853), who first noticed that on a very dark night one can see more clearly a distinction between two stars that are close together while looking to the side of the pair, rather than directly at them.

Figure 5 shows the relative sensitivity of the rods and cones under the stimulation of various wavelengths of light. Thus, while a light-adapted observer may see nothing at all, a dark-adapted observer may see from a light patch of a given intensity either a coloured or a colourless patch, depending on the wavelength of the light.

Helson (1964) has suggested that many of our judgements are based on recent experience which serves as a reference point or adaptation level against which we judge subsequent events. This is because one does not judge, say, the brightness of a stimulus in some absolute way but with reference to one's experience. This can mean that in one context a light may be judged to be of a certain brightness, but if the adaptation level changes the same light may be judged to be dimmer than a much dimmer light (objectively measured) seen in the first context.

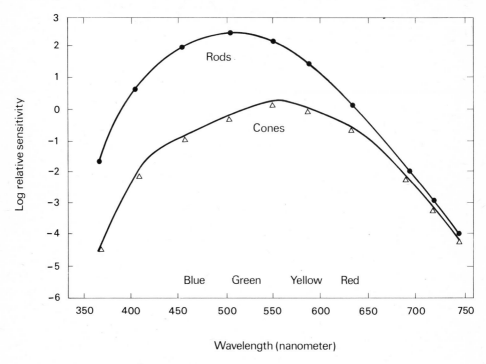

Fig 5 Relative sensitivity of the rods and cones
for different wavelengths of light (reprinted from
'Human vision and the spectrum', Wald, G.,
Science Vol. 101, 29 June 1945, 653–658)

According to Helson, the factors which contribute towards the judgement of a stimulus may have been acquired throughout one's lifetime.
Adaptation level theory encompasses a wide variety of phenomena. As
Helson says, 'an individual's attitudes, values, ways of structuring his
experiences, judgement of physical, aesthetic and symbolic objects,
intellectual and emotional behaviour, learning and interpersonal relations
all represent modes of adaptation to environmental and organismic
forces'. The most common use of his adaptation level theory has been in
trying to pinpoint the conditions under which a stimulus is judged to be
large or small. For example, it has been applied to what one might well
call the 'grant application procedure'. People presenting proposals for
grants put in inordinately high estimates in order to set up a level against
which their claim is to be judged; though, in fact, reduction of a large
percentage would still leave them the amount they really require.

The effects of an adaptation level act in a different way in an experiment
of Helson (1938). He made observers sit in a room illuminated by light
of one wavelength, say red. The walls and table in the room were covered

with the same grey paper which could, however, be of differing reflec-
tances. The paper was white, grey or black (80, 23 or 3 per cent reflectance).
Everything in the room would appear some shade of red. After five minutes
of illumination the observer judged a set of seventeen grey samples. The
observer viewing these without this adaptation would see them as going
from white to black in equal steps of lightness. What the observer in the
adapted room saw would depend on the reflectance of the paper. Greys
that had the same reflectance as the wall and table, or table covering,
were judged to be a grey of medium lightness, lighter samples to be red
and, the greater their reflectance, the greater their apparent saturation or
purity of colour. Samples of a lower reflectance, therefore darker than the
wall or table, were seen as the complementary colour (green), and the
darker the sample the more saturated the colour appeared.

What is important is that the number of greys judged to be red altered
according to the paper that was used to cover the room. If the adaptation
was achieved with the white (80 per cent reflectance) wall then only the
two lightest greys appeared to be red, the next two lightest appeared grey
and all the rest appeared shades of green. Thus it is possible to see a grey
as any shade of red or green, or indeed any shade of yellow or blue, if the
adaptation is in, say, yellow light. One might note here that we have
already seen from the observation of after-images that red and green seem
to be connected, and also yellow and blue. We can see that it is possible,
for a short time at least, to make our two observers view a standard grey as
almost any colour.

Apparently in certain states of meditation exactly the opposite to this
adaptation process occurs. It is a normal state of affairs for the perception
of an object to change with continued inspection. We have already considered the instance when two observers perceive an object in different
ways because one of the observers has been subject to continuous
presentation of the object. If both of our observers had had this previous
experience, we would expect the same, albeit altered, perception. However,
practitioners of Yoga and Zen meditation claim that they experience an
object the thousandth time in the same way as they did at first, therefore
everything is always new. This, it is said, can be achieved by concentration
upon one's breathing or upon a simple question. Kasamatsu and Hirai
(1966) report that these findings are supported by the introspection of the
observers in an experiment they performed upon Zen masters:

The Zen masters reported to us that they had more clearly perceived each stimulus
than in their ordinary waking state. In this state of mind one cannot be affected by
either external or internal stimulus, nevertheless he is able to respond to it. He
perceives the object, responds to it, and yet is never disturbed by it. Each stimulus
is accepted as stimulus itself and treated as such. One Zen master described such a
state of mind as that of noticing every person one sees on the street but of not
looking back with emotional curiosity.

Adaptation has been called an automatisation process (Hartmann, 1958) resulting in the disappearance of an object from consciousness. De-automatisation, or the reversal of automatisation, is said to occur from meditation. Deikman (1963) found that during meditation the colour of an object could even appear to be more saturated, as opposed to the normal diminution of intensity which occurs from prolonged viewing. His observers were taught meditation using concentration upon a blue vase. There were reports such as, 'The base was a hell of a lot bluer this time than it has been before'. The colour of the vase could even shift to purple.

It is normal, except in the newborn, for the adaptation or habituation to a sound or light to be accompanied by a change in physiological measures. Belief in the possibility of meditation affecting the perceived world is certainly enhanced by the finding that these changes seem not to occur when the Yoga meditates. The unusual brain wave changes which occur while meditating also appear to carry over for a few minutes after meditation. Thus there is an after-effect of the meditation process. But after-effects, as mentioned above, refer to a specific set of effects which we will now consider.

After-effects

Two people looking at as simple an object as a straight line can be made to view it differently. One can be made to see it curved while the other sees it straight. Conversely, one of the two people can be made to see a curved line as straight. All that is necessary to achieve these distortions is to make one of the two observers inspect the curved line for a few minutes.

After fixation of the curved lines of Fig. 6a for a little while, they will appear less curved. Then if two observers see the straight lines of Fig. 6b, the observer who has had this prior experience will see the straight lines as being curved in the opposite direction. The second observer will, of course, see them as straight. If the observer is given a flexible rod to adjust to the apparent curvature of the line, it will be found that the after-effect curvature is equal to the loss of curvature from inspection. Similar effects are found for straight lines tilted from the horizontal or vertical. In this case the angle of tilt diminishes through inspection. No effect can be obtained if the lines inspected are horizontal, vertical or at 45 degrees; there does, however, seem to be some connection between lines at 90 degrees to each other. Gibson and Radner (1937) noted that an exposure to one orientation produced a tilt after-effect in a line at right angles to the original. Campbell and Maffei (1971) confirmed this result and pointed out that the effect is only half as strong as the normal tilt after-effect.

These effects are only operative if the figures inspected all stimulate the the same area of the retina. But unlike many of the other after-effects we shall discuss, they do transfer to the other eye. That is to say that if one of

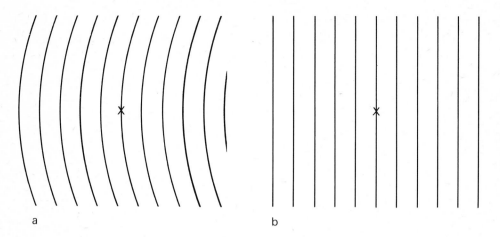

Fig 6 Fixation of the X in (a) will result in the lines of (b)
appearing to be curved in the opposite direction when (b) is
fixated

our observers looked with one eye for some time at a line tilted away from
the vertical he would find that, when he looked at a vertical line with the
other eye, the vertical line would in fact be tilted away from the vertical in
the opposite direction.

Campbell and Kulikowski (1966) noted that it seemed harder to detect
a grating (a series of black and white lines) in the presence of another
grating of similar orientation. This also works as an after-effect, as can be
seen in the amusing demonstration given by Blakemore and Campbell
(1969). They showed a person holding an umbrella on a rainy day. The
rain was made up of line segments to approximate a vertical grating. It was
possible to make the rain go away by adapting to another grating made up
of lines of the same distance apart as the rain lines. After having done this,
when the observer looked at the figure holding the umbrella he saw that
the rain had disappeared but the person and umbrella remained unchanged.
Another consequence of adapting to a grating was found by Blakemore
and Sutton (1969). It was found that if one views a grating of the same
orientation as the one adapted to, but of narrower stripes, the stripes then
appear to be even narrower than they are. Conversely, wider stripes appear
to be even wider after the same adaptation procedure. In an analogous way,
vertical black and white gratings appear brighter following exposure to a
dim vertical black and white grating, and dimmer after a bright grating has
been viewed (Over *et al.*, 1974). The effect is again orientation-specific.

A different after-effect was produced by Blakemore and Julesz (1971)
using Julesz's technique of presenting random dots to each eye which,
when fused, present a picture (Fig. 7). By correlating the dots in each of
the pictures it is possible to represent a figure in depth when the two

Fig 7 When stereoscopically fused, instead of the random
arrangements a large triangle is perceived in depth above a
background (reprinted from *Foundations of Cyclopean
Perception*, Julesz, B., University of Chicago Press: 1971)

pictures are fused. Without a stereoscopic viewing device it is usually not
possible for the reader to confirm this effect, but this is made possible by
what Julesz calls anaglyphs. A stereoscopic fusion is obtained by printing
the dot picture in red and green (Plate 1). Because each stereo-viewer
filter allows the eye to receive light from only one of the pictures, a separate
picture is obtained for each eye. The red and green pictures overlap exactly
the right amount to allow fusion.

If the reader uses the stereo viewer to view Anaglyph I and looks at the
fixation mark for about a minute, he will see two squares, one above this
mark, and one behind the plane of the mark. During this fixation the depth
effect may tend to disappear, in which case the reader should briefly scan
backwards and forwards in order to maintain the depth effect. Julesz (1971)
points out that during this fading of the depth effect, the random background pattern will appear to have regular organisational features. After
this adaptation the reader should look with the stereo viewer at Anaglyph
II. The two squares are in fact at the same depth as the fixation mark, but
it will appear that they are not. The square that took the place of the
adapting square which looked nearer the fixation point, now looks
further away, and vice versa for the other square. A longer adaptation
period will produce a greater after-effect; a five-minute adaptation
produces an after-effect of about half-a-minute. This reversal of depth does
seem analogous to the after-effect of a tilted line in that continuous
viewing of a tilted line makes a vertical line appear tilted in the opposite
direction.

McCollough (1965a) found that if black and white vertical stripes were viewed in orange light and, alternatively, horizontal black and white stripes in blue light, a coloured after-effect resulted. The vertical pattern appeared blue-green and the horizontal, orange, in normal illumination. The after-effect depended on the colour of the illuminating light and also the head position. The colours switched patterns when the head was tilted 90 degrees down to the side. This will, of course, change horizontal stripes into vertical stripes. Stromeyer (1969) stressed that this after-effect occurs because it affects some red–green mechanism. He found that if the vertical stripes were seen in green light and the horizontal in white light, an after-effect resulted with the red being seen on the vertical and the green on the horizontal. The same after-effect occurred if the vertical stripes were seen in white light and the horizontal in red. The effects of the experiment, which lasted only ten minutes, in some instances were present for as long as three days. In a similar experiment Stromeyer found that some time afterwards a 'wooden ladder, for example, was entirely tinted red and green. Next day pages of print were decidedly coloured, and even two weeks later the after-effects could be seen on picket fences in twilight'. He stresses that the effects here are different from the after-images described above, since illumination with yellow light produced a green after-effect, but the negative after-image in this case would be blue.

Stromeyer (1971) has used the McCollough effect to produce a multitude of colours. This is done in the manner of the Land (1959) demonstration, which always causes bewilderment in an audience. Land is able to produce a multitude of colours from two black and white slides of the same scene by projecting one of them in red and the other in white light. Fusion of the two slides produces many colours besides the pink one would expect. The interested reader must refer to Land's work for a full description of the procedure. Stromeyer asked his observers to watch two patterns of black and white stripes which interchanged every ten seconds. They were vertical stripes in green light and horizontal stripes in red. They did this for at least thirty minutes. The observers were then shown the pattern in Fig. 8, consisting of a 6×6 matrix of alternating vertical and horizontal gratings. The gratings were made from six different grey papers ranging in equal steps from light to dark. From the experiment of McCollough (1965a) one would expect the vertical lines of Fig. 8 to appear red and the horizontal lines to appear green when viewed under normal illumination. But more than this was seen. On the lighter bars of the grating, blues, yellows, greens and reds were all seen, as well as colours in between. The colours seen depended on the darkness of each grating. The distribution of colours, however, was uneven: it was found that purples, reds and greens predominated. A much greater variety of hues could be produced if the matrix of gratings was increased. With 100 different gratings, many more blues and yellows were observed.

Fig 8 (Reprinted from *Vision Research* Vol. 12, 1971, by courtesy
of the author, C. F. Stromeyer)

There was a good deal of agreement between the two observers of Stromeyer's experiment as to the colours seen. The major disagreement came in the description of the blues. Perhaps this is not surprising, as individual responses to colour are particularly variable at the blue end of the spectrum. However, Walls (1960) claims that light blue cannot be produced by the Land method and so there may be other reasons for the discrepancy.

It was found that if the matrix of gratings of Fig. 8 was presented as a short, bright flash after the adaptation, then in a dark room there was an after-image in which the colours 'richly glowed'. In fact some of the colours were so saturated that it was difficult to find pigments to match them.

This effect shows that, under these circumstances, colours can be made to appear where there are none. The colours, as we have seen, are contingent upon the orientation of the stripes seen and their previous colour. Held and Shattuck (1971) showed that exactly the opposite after-effect was possible. In their demonstration straight lines were made to look crooked and the crookedness was contingent upon the previous colour of the stripes. We have already noted that prolonged exposure to lines away from the vertical can produce a tilt after-effect in the opposite direction. The new departure here is that the after-effect is elicited by a colour. The observers were presented with two striped patterns as in Fig. 9a. One of the patterns was in red and black lines and the other in green and black lines. The patterns were alternated, each being viewed for five seconds, until the observer had spent ten minutes viewing the patterns. They were then shown the test field which, as can be seen, consists of a circle divided into two halves. The top half is made up of green and black lines and the bottom half of red and black lines. All the lines are vertical. However, the appearance of a test field to the observer is shown at the right of Fig. 9b. The green and black lines appear bent in the opposite direction to the green and black lines of the adapting pattern. The red and black lines behave in a similar manner.

After-effects of stimulation can therefore produce quite marked changes in perception. It may seem unlikely, but it has been known for some time (Köhler, 1920) that two observers looking at Fig. 10a can be made to see it differently. One will, of course, see (a), but the observer who has had the experience of another figure will see Fig. 10b. The figure required to effect this change is shown as Fig. 10c. The crosses represent fixation points. The rectangles of (c) are so arranged that the one on the left falls just within the parallel lines at the left of (a) and the two rectangles on the right fall either side of the parallel lines on the right of (a) when (c) is placed on top of (a). Fixation of (c) for a little while is required, then, if the gaze is transferred to (a), (b) results.

The magnitude of this so-called 'figural after-effect' is variable and it

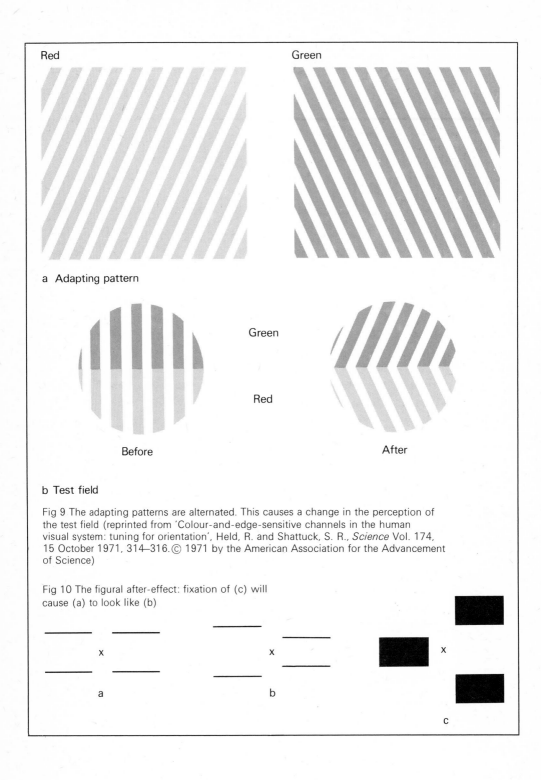

Red   Green

a   Adapting pattern

Green

Red

Before   After

b   Test field

Fig 9 The adapting patterns are alternated. This causes a change in the perception of the test field (reprinted from 'Colour-and-edge-sensitive channels in the human visual system: tuning for orientation', Held, R. and Shattuck, S. R., *Science* Vol. 174, 15 October 1971, 314–316.© 1971 by the American Association for the Advancement of Science)

Fig 10 The figural after-effect: fixation of (c) will cause (a) to look like (b)

x   x   x

a   b

c

has been shown to be dependent on many factors: for example, the distance apart of the contours. If the rectangles fall too close or too far away from the parallel lines the effect diminishes. The effect seems to reach a maximum after one minute's inspection of (c). Also, it has been suggested that the after-effect will be greater if (a) is seen for a short time. This figural after-effect has been found to be dependent on whether it is administered in a group setting or to an individual, on the sex of the observer, and on the attitude taken towards the task. It has been suggested that brain misfunction could correlate with the perception of the figural after-effect. However, the effect can be so hard to produce that Wertheimer and Herring (1968) deny its use as a clinical tool (see page 70) because of the differences produced by slight procedural changes.

Successive presentations

Figure 11 shows an interesting illusion. The circles in the centre are in fact the same size. Now we are not concerned here with all the factors which cause distortion in perception, but with the factors that can make two people have different percepts. Thus if we have the situation where two observers both have the same, although wrong, perception, it will not concern us. However, this illusion does offer us a certain possibility. In Fig. 11 it can be seen that there is an overestimation of the central circle of the left-hand portion and an underestimation of the central circle on the right. Let us consider what happens when parts of such a figure are viewed simultaneously or successively.

In Fig. 12, if (a) is superimposed on (b) so that the fixation crosses coincide, the left-hand circle of (b) will look bigger than the right-hand circle. On the other hand, if (a) is seen first, then (b) afterwards, under-estimation of the left-hand circle will result. It is not clear why this should be so, and perhaps even more puzzling is the finding by Cooper and Weintraub (1970) that the successive presentation of the central circle and surrounding circles of Fig. 11 does not change the direction of the illusion. Yet it still remains fascinating that the left-hand circle of Fig. 12 can be made to look bigger than, the same size as, or smaller than, the circle on the right.

The term 'successive presentations' means here the presentation of different stimuli one after another. Of all the effects that can be produced by successive presentation of stimuli, the most compelling is the effect of visual masking. It is not an everyday phenomenon, since it requires a certain amount of specialised apparatus for presenting stimuli for a short duration. But given that, it is quite easy to demonstrate.

If a circular black area is drawn on a white card and presented, say for 50 milliseconds (one twentieth of a second), the black circle is quite clearly visible. The presentation, after that, of a black ring which surrounds

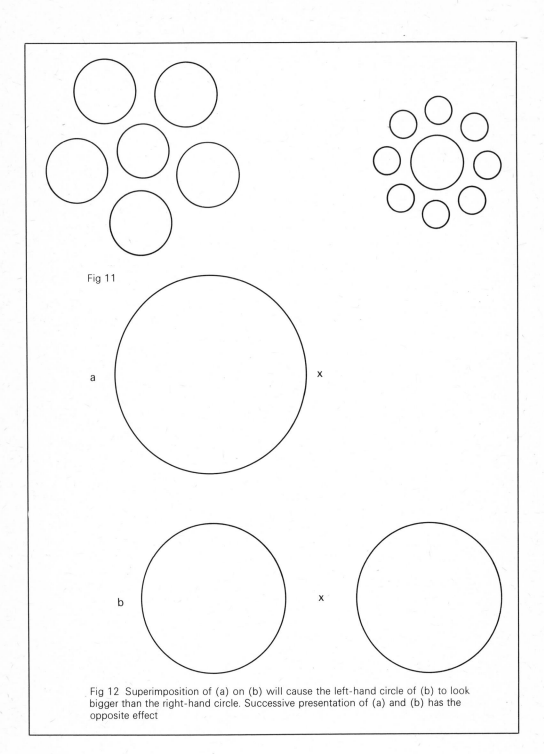

Fig 11

a

x

b

x

Fig 12 Superimposition of (a) on (b) will cause the left-hand circle of (b) to look bigger than the right-hand circle. Successive presentation of (a) and (b) has the opposite effect

the circle will not result in a combination of the figures to form a larger black circle, as would happen if they were presented simultaneously. Instead, and surprisingly, we get the disappearance of the first black circle—only the black ring is seen. The erasure of one stimulus by another is called visual masking, and this non-overlapping close proximity contour display, resulting in visual masking, has the special name of 'meta-contrast'. Metacontrast effects do not depend on the shape of the stimuli—it is not necessary to have regular figures. Indeed, Werner (1935) found that quite odd-shaped figures still disappeared as long as the outer masking figure hugged the contour.

In fact, any stimulus can be masked if another stimulus with the appropriate brightness, and near enough to it, arrives shortly after, or before, the first stimulus. As we have already noted, a line grating viewed for some time can produce an after-effect in which a similar grating will disappear. A related effect (Sekuler, 1965) can be produced by visual masking since presentation of a line grating after a line stimulus causes the line to disappear. This effect can be colour specific; Lovegrove and Over (1973) showed that exposure to a vertical red grating made a vertical red target much more difficult to see than a green or white one.

A person having the effects of visual masking explained to him may find them amazing. They can be interpreted as the present affecting the past, which is obviously illogical. Of course, this does not happen—it could not happen. But the gap between the termination of the first circle and the onset of the ring can be increased up to 100 milliseconds or so and still erase, or suppress to some extent, the perception of the first circle. To call this 'the present affecting the past' is to misinterpret the way in which the brain analyses any incoming stimulation. The timer on the machine may cause a light pulse of exactly 50 milliseconds' duration, and the time taken for the light to reach the eye is obviously negligible, but at this point we have stopped dealing with a mechanical system and have started to deal with a biological one. The human visual system takes time to operate and perhaps can only deal with the incoming information in chunks. Some limited system like this must of necessity be in operation, because the first stimulus has not, as in the normal run of things, been processed and consciously registered. This must be because of the arrival of a second stimulus.

Masking can occur with a stimulus presented before, during, or after the presentation of the mask stimulus. Forward masking refers to one stimulus affecting a subsequent one. Backward masking refers to the case mentioned above of a stimulus affecting a preceding one. The decision to call one of the two stimuli the masking stimulus, and the other the masked, refers to the phenomenal effect and not to the sequence of events. For a review of the effects and parametric studies in this area see Kahneman (1968).

The parameters of the masking situation are being actively researched, but there is still some doubt as to the relationship between the magnitude of the masking effect and the interstimulus interval (time between target and mask). Some research has suggested a U-shaped function, in other words, masking will increase up to, say, 60 milliseconds after the presentation of the target, then it will decrease. Other research (Eriksen *et al.*, 1969) suggests a maximal effect with the interstimulus interval at zero, then either a steady effect which is followed by decreasing visual masking, or a steady decline from zero as the time interval between the stimuli increases. For a review of this controversy see Lefton (1973).

A compelling and graphic explanation of what is happening could be found by 'assuming that the mask, transmitted along the same neural pathways, overtakes and substitutes for, or sums with, impulses to the target' (Weisstein, 1969). This gives an endearing image of the neural analogue of the target stimulus minding its own business, while a big brute of a mask comes up behind and rubs it out.

It also suggests that it might be possible to continue the masking process *ad infinitum*. Supposing that instead of just a target and a mask we had this arrangement followed by a second mask. Thus we could have our first black disc on for 50 milliseconds, followed, after a gap of 50 milliseconds, by the masking ring which fits exactly around the disc. This too will be on for 50 milliseconds. Then, after another gap of 50 milliseconds, this will be followed by a second masking ring exactly fitting around the first ring. The second masking ring will also be on for 50 milliseconds. Now, if we show just the first two stimuli, as we have seen, only the second is visible. If we show the second and the third alone, only the third will be seen. If we show all three, keeping the time sequences the same, is it unreasonable to suppose that we shall only see the third, because the second erases the first and the third erases the second? If this did happen, we could, in theory, sit an observer down in front of a machine which presents these stimuli and show him objects which individually would certainly be visible yet have him report that he saw nothing for the rest of his days.

In an experiment of Robinson (1966), which was essentially repeated by Dember and Purcell (1967), it was found that this did not happen. In Robinson's experiment, flashes of light were masked by subsequent flashes. Figure 13 shows the results of this study. It appears that, in the three-stimuli presentation, the first flash reappears. This recovery of the first flash in itself poses problems. Does it imply that it was held in limbo somewhere while the second flash was operated on? Or does the second stimulus not get time to act on the first, because it is already erased by the third? Whichever is the explanation, it is only possible to prevent an observer seeing the penultimate object in a stimulus sequence of which each stimulus presented alone could be clearly seen.

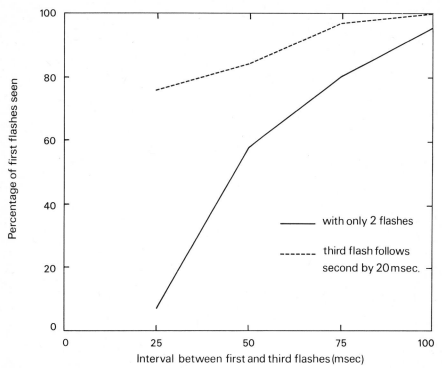

Fig 13 (Reprinted from 'Disinhibition of visually masked stimuli'. Robinson, D. W., *Science* Vol. 154, 7 October 1966, 157–158. © by the American Association for the Advancement of Science)

Another peculiar effect in this area arises when, under certain circumstances, presentation of a light flash can make a prior light flash appear brighter than it would if seen on its own (Donchin and Lindsley, 1965). Similarly, presentation of a second figure can make a prior one more clearly seen (Dember *et al.*, 1973). In this experiment, a circle cut like a pie with black and white sectors (see left-hand part of Fig. 15) was shown for a brief time. This was then followed by black rings which surrounded the locus of the first figure. If the circle was divided into a large number of sectors it was found that it was easier to see if it was followed by the rings than if it was seen alone. These experiments seem hard to reconcile with the very similar experiments which produce masking rather than visual enhancement.

The work that has been carried out in masking studies, and in other areas too, has shown that it takes time to perceive the stimulus. During this time it is possible to distort the stimulus, or, as we have seen, erase it completely. Two stimuli close together in time will normally be fused in perception. Visual illusions can be produced by patterns of intersecting

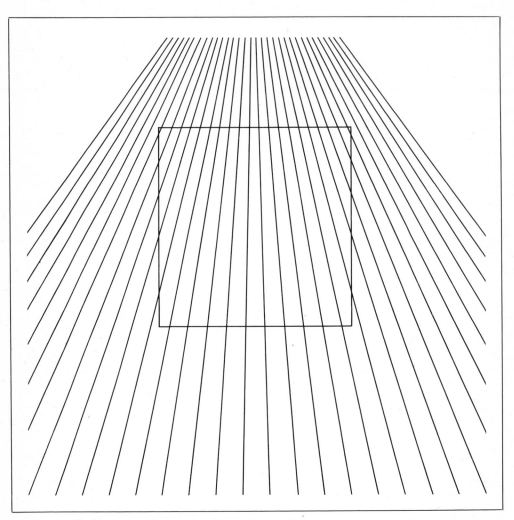

Fig 14

lines. What would happen if we were to arrange for one observer to see only the square of Fig. 14, and another observer, the converging straight lines followed by the square? In the latter case, if the two patterns were close enough together in time, and above threshold, it would not surprise us if this observer saw the square as distorted, because this is what most observers would report when viewing Fig. 14. The observer who sees the pattern in a temporal sequence would report the same distortion, as he is in fact seeing the same distortion. It takes time to process the visual information, and if the stimuli are close enough in time they will be seen as one.

An important implication of successive presentation was raised by Smith and Henriksson (1955). They raised the question as to whether the square of Fig. 14 will be seen as distorted if the lines are presented so quickly that they are not noticed. They did, in fact, report a slight tendency to view the square as distorted. The difficulty in interpreting this result is that many non-perceptual factors may be involved. Beside the ever-present difficulty of putting into words a phenomenological event, here we have the problem of relying on the observer's appreciation of his awareness of one of the patterns. If it is possible for an unconscious percept to alter a conscious percept, some theorists might want to 'make the jump' from geometric figures to more complex humanly-motivated perception (see Dixon, 1971).

According to Smith, Spence and Klein (1959) and Somekh and Wilding (1973), our interpretation of a picture can be altered in this way. Their observers were asked to give character and mood summaries of an outline face. While they were watching the faces, the word 'happy' or 'angry' was flashed on to each face at very short intervals. In fact, no observer ever reported seeing the words, yet the description of the faces clearly showed that they were affected by these subliminal cues. This could be a trivial experiment if the observers were aware of the words, so this again all boils down to the question of whether we can rely on the subjective report of the observer's state of awareness. This is an important point, but will not be discussed further at this stage as we wish to concentrate on the other effects of perception which are obviously operative, rather than on whether they can also work unconsciously.

Movement after-effects

Let us again take up the situation where two observers perceive a stimulus differently because one of them has had, just prior to perceiving the

Fig 15 Fixation of either of these displays while it is being rotated will give an after-effect of movement in the opposite direction

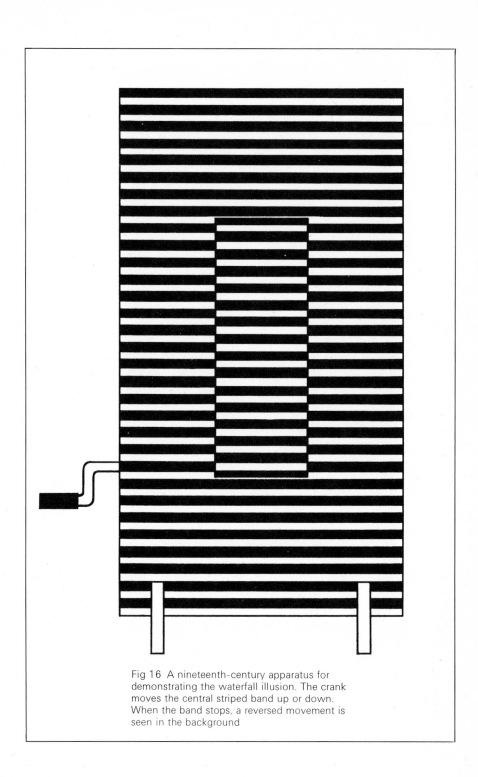

Fig 16 A nineteenth-century apparatus for
demonstrating the waterfall illusion. The crank
moves the central striped band up or down.
When the band stops, a reversed movement is
seen in the background

stimulus, some other visual experience. In this case, if one of the observers has just watched the discs of Fig. 15 rotate, then they will still appear to move even if the discs are now stationary, and this movement will seem to be a rotation in the opposite direction. They will, of course, remain stationary for the other observer.

This type of illusory phenoinenon must be one of the earliest documented. Day (1969) states that Aristotle mentioned it in his *De Somniis,* and like many other interesting psychological discoveries it has been rediscovered many times since. A similar effect called the 'waterfall illusion' is easily observed in nature. After watching a waterfall for a short period, if you transfer your gaze to the surrounding scenery it will appear to stream upwards. Figure 16 shows an apparatus for demonstrating this effect.

While watching the spiral of Fig. 15 rotate one way, it will appear to shrink, but if it rotates the other way it will appear to expand. When it stops, it appears to rotate in the opposite direction and seems either to expand or contract, depending on the direction of the original motion. Any textured object looked at after the adaptation will behave in the same way—people's noses cause particular amusement. This expansion of the spiral is anomolous as it appears to expand and stay in the same place at the same time. Holland (1965) described it as having a 'ghostly' quality. An early explanation that the effect was due to eye movements seems unlikely, as it appears to expand or contract in all directions at once. Also it is possible to obtain spiral after-effects rotating in opposite directions at the same time and, of course, the eye could not rotate in two opposite directions at once.

The parameters of this spiral after-effect have been extensively investigated. It is found that the duration of the after-effect is determined by the relative contrast in brightness between the spiral and the background, the absolute brightness of the figure, the size of the figure and the time spent looking at the figure. A maximum spiral after-effect is obtained after about two minutes' observation. The speed of rotation of the original motion affects the apparent velocity of the after-effect. It seems that there is a certain speed to obtain a maximum velocity of after-effect. A speed slower or faster than this, which is in fact a quite slow speed, results in less effect. If a disc is covered with very many small black and white squares, an after-effect is obtained from rotating the disc at very slow speeds indeed. Dixon and Miesels (1966) found that after viewing this rotating figure there was an odd squirming movement in any object that was viewed afterwards. It was a very strong effect which arose, unlike the spiral after-effect, from a disc which was hardly rotating. The effect was quite long-lasting and was more powerful if the black and white squares were randomly distributed rather than arranged in an ordered pattern. A review of movement as well as other after-effects can be found in Robinson (1972).

Wohlgemuth (1911) reported that if the observer was not exposed to light after viewing the rotating spiral of Fig. 15, then the after-effect was preserved and could be reinstated some long time after it would normally have decayed. Masland (1969) confirms this, reporting that the spiral after-effect can last twenty hours after a fifteen minute exposure. In his experiment, he used three groups of observers. The first group simply fixated the spiral while it was stationary. The second group observed the after-effect. The third group watched the spiral rotate, then sat in the dark for ten minutes, which is normally long enough for the effect to dissipate. However, when called back the next day, both Groups 2 and 3 reported the after-effect when watching the stationary spiral; Group 1, of course, did not. It may be that Groups 2 and 3 experienced the after-effect because they expected it, but this could not apply to Group 3 who had never seen it. Also, Masland reports the effect as occurring instantaneously. This is an unusual effect, but this confirmation of Wohlgemuth's report provides what must be a perplexing experience for the observers of Group 3 of Masland's experiment.

Movement after-effects can be produced in some rather special circumstances as an after-effect from a stationary figure. These involve stationary repetitive patterns such as that shown in Fig. 17. Strange effects and patterns arise spontaneously when viewing this figure, one of the most interesting being the coloured streaming effect near the centre. These effects, in this case, are perhaps more exciting than the after-effect, but we must deal here with percepts that arise because of some previous input into the visual system, rather than the illusions themselves.

Mackay (1957) found that, if the pattern of Fig. 17 was stared at for some time, what he called a 'complementary image' was observed if the gaze was transferred to a plain white surface. This appears in a form of a rosette, or has been described as resembling moving grains of rice. The directions of the lines of the after-effect are at right angles to those of the original pattern and this accounts for their alternative description as 'orthogonal after-images'. If the repetitive pattern stared at consists of concentric circles, then the after-effect resembles the pattern of Fig. 17, since these are orthogonal lines to concentric circles. Observers normally report two or more superimposed rosettes which may appear to rotate in different directions or in the same direction, in a manner out of the control of the observer. This whirling effect can easily be observed if the gaze is transferred to a random pattern of dots or to the printed text of this book. Presenting the spatially repetitive pattern followed quickly by the random dot pattern will give a brief complementary image without any lengthy fixation period. If the pattern of Fig. 17 is rotated while it is being stared at, the complementary image will rotate in the opposite direction.

Now all this is interesting and, in fact, theoretically important. These complementary images were discussed by Mackay before the determination by Hubel and Wiesel (1962) of the functional structure of the visual cortex by microelectrode implantation into the brains of cats. Hubel and Wiesel found that there were detectors in the brain for edges and lines. It could be predicted that continuous stimulation of these edge detectors would have some repercussions. Indeed, shortly we shall elaborate on these findings with respect to the other movement after-effects.

Sekuler and Ganz (1963) and Sekuler and Pantle (1967) have shown that the continued presentation of stripes in one direction, as those of Fig. 16, appears to lead to the observer's being exhausted of his ability to see stripes in that direction. This is because it becomes harder to detect a bar moving in the direction of the stimulus that has been stared at for some time: it is as if there is a 'stripe identifier' in the visual system which has become exhausted. We have in fact already suggested that the physiological discoveries of Hubel and Wiesel predict that we do have these stripe identifiers for every direction. The results of experiments such as that of Sekuler and Ganz may account for the apparent slowness of high speeds after travelling for some time on a motorway, and the extremely slow speed thirty miles an hour seems, after coming off a motorway.

It would seem from the results of Pantle and Sekuler (1968) that these identification systems for different directions are to some extent independent, in that adaptation to horizontal stripes moving vertically makes it harder to see stationary horizontal stripes but does not affect the seeing of stationary vertical stripes. We have, however, noted previously (page 12) that lines at right angles are not completely independent.

In some circumstances, complicated after-effects can be achieved using both horizontal and vertical stripes. The extremely interesting experiments of Hepler (1968) and Stromeyer and Mansfield (1970) tend to reinforce the view that the vertical and horizontal direction analysers are indeed not completely independent. Hepler noted that if the observer viewed for some time green and black stripes moving up and red and black stripes moving down, then a coloured after-effect could be obtained by presenting white and black stripes moving up or down. This produced a pink after-effect when the white stripes were moving up and a green after-effect when the white stripes moved down. Stromeyer and Mansfield found that these red and green after-effects could be produced even if the original adapting fields were of different colours. The method used was to illuminate a rotating spiral (Fig. 15) by different coloured lights. For example, when the spiral was appearing to expand, projectors illuminated the left side with reddish-yellow light and the right side with greenish-yellow light. When the spiral appeared to contract, it was illuminated only by white light. (Remember that the appearance of contraction or expansion depends on the direction of motion of the spiral.) In this experiment, the spiral altered its direction of motion every ten seconds. After ten minutes of this alternation, corresponding with changes in colour, the spiral

Fig 17 After staring at the pattern, transfer the gaze to the blank page opposite. (Reprinted from 'Moving images produced by regular stationary patterns', Mackay, D. M., *Nature*, Vol. 180, 1957, 849–850)

alternated in motion in normal white light. The observers were then asked to report what they saw. There were some individual differences reported, but generally when a spiral contracted the left side appeared reddish and the right appeared greenish. Note that these were the colours (roughly) when the spiral was expanding during the adaptation period.

These after-effects of Hepler, Stromeyer and Mansfield differ from most of the after-effects we have discussed before. In most others, with the exception of the McCollough and associated after-effects, the after-effect was in the same dimension (for example, colour or movement) as was the eliciting stimulus. In the simple movement after-effect, the after-effect is one of movement and it is elicited by a movement. In the Hepler, Stromeyer and Mansfield experiments the after-effect is elicited by movement but the after-effect is itself a colour change.

These contingent after-effects have been discussed by Mayhew and Anstis (1972) and are of considerable interest. For instance, Stromeyer and Mansfield tell us that these coloured after-effects could be elicited by movement as much as six weeks after the adaptation. We have seen above that Masland (1969) found that the conventional spiral after-effect could last a day, but generally this is the exception. Mayhew and Anstis found that movement after-effects could be elicited that were contingent upon previous adaptation to colour, intensity of illumination, spatial frequency and contour orientation. The fact that an observer can be made to see movement when there is in fact none, and that this movement is elicited by any of the factors above, warrants further discussion.

In their experiments, the observers watched a coloured rotating spiral. The background colour of the spiral changed every time the spiral changed direction, which was every ten seconds. An observer might see red when the spiral was rotating clockwise, and yellow when counter-clockwise. After ten minutes, the spiral stopped and the colours continued to alternate as before. At this point the spiral appeared to move clockwise when the yellow light was on, and counter-clockwise when the red light was on. It would be nice to leave the demonstration as simple as this, but Mayhew and Anstis made the further observation that the direction of the movement after-effect depended on the *relative* change of the colour of the stationary spiral. This they found by shining a sequence of coloured lights on to the stationary spiral after the same adaptation procedure as described above. The coloured light sequence was red-yellow-green-yellow-red-yellow-green-yellow, etc. Typically, an observer would report the spiral as moving in the following way: counter-clock-clock-counter-counter-clock-clock-counter, etc. It can be seen that after observing a red spiral, a yellow spiral triggered an apparent clockwise motion as in the original experiment above, but after seeing a green spiral, yellow triggered a counter-clockwise after-effect. Thus the contingent movement after-effect situation is quite complex.

The experimenters then investigated whether changes in brightness of the spiral could also elicit movement as an after-effect. To do this the spiral was illuminated in bright light when, say, it revolved clockwise, and in medium light when it revolved counter-clockwise. Again, after ten minutes of this alternation, the spiral was stopped and a series of bright and medium lights was projected on to the stationary spiral. The results were not so successful as for the colours, but all observers, at least, saw the stationary spiral rotate counter-clockwise when the bright light was projected on to it.

To see if contour orientation could elicit movement, stationary patterns were projected on to a revolving plain disc. The disc changed direction every ten seconds. A simple pattern of vertical lines was projected on to the disc when it was rotating clockwise, and horizontal lines when it rotated counter-clockwise. After ten minutes of this adaptation, the stripes were projected on to the disc when it was stationary. All of the observers reported that the stationary disc revolved in the opposite direction to that which they had seen previously associated with that particular pattern of lines. Thus, projecting horizontal stripes on to the stationary disc would cause it to rotate clockwise, and vertical lines, counter-clockwise.

To investigate whether adaptation to a stripe width could elicit movement, bands of moving stripes were used as in the waterfall illusion. For example, an observer would watch medium-width stripes going up, and narrower stripes coming down, for ten minutes. When presented with stationary striped patterns, most observers saw narrow stripes as going up and medium stripes as coming down.

These illusory after-effects may seem quite distinct from our normal perceptual experiences. This is perhaps most clearly seen in relation to the movement after-effect reported by Walker (1972). In this case, the perceived direction of a rotating field was contingent upon its texture. Walker arranged for his observers to view two discs which rotated in opposite directions. The discs were viewed alternately for four seconds each and for a total time of four minutes. One of the discs had on its surface a random pattern of small dots. The other had on it another random pattern, but of much larger dots. The fine (small dots) pattern always rotated, say, clockwise, and the coarse (large dots) pattern always counter-clockwise. When the observer had carried out the adaptation procedure, he viewed the fine and coarse discs when they were stationary. They appeared to rotate in the opposite directions to those in which they had previously been moving. In the case above, the fine discs appeared to move in a counter-clockwise direction and the coarse discs in a clockwise direction. Now as Stromeyer and Mansfield (1970) say about one of their after-effects: 'The advantage of this process in non-artificial situations is no-wise obvious'. However, in general, as we shall see, these illusions are more than perceptual curiosities.

Apparent movement

In 1830, Plateau invented what he called his eye deceiver or 'phenakisto-scope' (see Fig. 18), to which we now attribute Stampfer's name of 'stroboscope', coined for an instrument of his own making in 1832. The disc of Fig. 18 is mounted so that it can be spun about its centre. If turned to face a mirror, the observer, stationed behind the rectangular slots (shown as black), sees successive pictures of the appearance of a dancer in motion when the disc is rotated.

This type of movement illusion is the one most often seen by us all. We see it, of course, in the cinema. That is not to say that other illusions, such as the waterfall illusion, are not common—it would well have been known to our Stone Age ancestors as it is easily observable in nature. Also, Purkinje in the early nineteenth century could not have been the first to have made the common observation that a rotated giddy observer feels himself rotating in one direction and the environment as spinning in the opposite.

The development of the moving picture was well established prior to the investigations of Wertheimer (1912). He did, however, show the necessary conditions for movement to be seen from the presentation of two separate objects. The technique used was to show in quick succession simple geometric figures such as a line or a curve. When the time interval between object A and object B was about 200 milliseconds, the objects were seen as static and in sequence. When the time interval was less than 30 milliseconds, the objects were seen together as if they had been presented at the same time. In between, and at an optimum time interval of 60 milliseconds, there was movement.

Now, is this effect the same as the other after-effects we have been considering? We have considered two observers watching an object such as B, when one of the observers has previously been exposed to another object, such as A. This has caused a differing perception of B. In this situation of apparent movement, is Object B affected in any way? Does Object B look any different? This is a difficult question to answer; the emergence of movement seems to bring a different dimension to the perception. It is not that something has altered in our perception of B: the movement ('pure' movement, as Wertheimer called it) seems to be something separate from Objects A and B. A does not turn into B; the effect is rather of a single object moving, though neither of the objects does move. In fact, not every observer easily obtains this effect of pure movement from only two point sources of light.

The predominantly German experimenters who investigated the apparent movement of objects in the early part of this century defined various types of movement; of these, 'alpha movement' and 'gamma movement' (Kenkel, 1913) conform most clearly to the after-effect type. 'Alpha

Fig 18 Plateau's phenakistoscope

movement' refers to the change in size of an object because of its repeated presentation; 'gamma movement' to the expansion or contraction of an object as the illumination is respectively increased or decreased. In gamma movement, the object swells in all directions or closes up in all directions, as in the spiral after-effect. A review of the types of apparent movement can be found in Graham (1965) and this also deals with Korte's Laws (1915) which describe the conditions under which these types of movement are best seen. In general, apparent movement is not observed if the illumination is too low, the time gap between A and B too short, or the space between the objects too large. These factors can be balanced one against the other in order to compensate for a change in one of them.

If we place one of our observers in a situation where he is experiencing real motion, will there be any differences when compared with an observer who is only experiencing apparent motion? We have seen that one object placed near to another can be less easily seen (masked). So a flash of light presented in the path of a beam of light moving freely from point X to point Y should be dimmed to some extent. But what happens when the movement from point X to point Y is only apparent? Kolers (1963) conducted this experiment and found that the flash of light was more clearly seen by the observers watching the apparent movement than by those watching the real movement. Therefore it does seem possible to differentiate between real and apparent movement, though Frisby (1972) does argue that they are essentially subserved by the same mechanism. The illusion of apparent movement seems really to be rather a special case of differences in perception.

Transformations of the visual world

Perhaps the most complicated form of after-effect is that caused by the extensive use of some optical distorting device. In one of the early experiments of this type, Stratton (1896, 1897) wore inverting lenses to determine what would happen after a period of their extensive use and after the eventual removal of the lenses. Stratton wore spectacles that inverted the world for the waking hours of eight consecutive days. At first, the world appeared the wrong way up and there was much confusion. Towards the end of the experiment, Stratton was adjusting to the transformed visual input, and taking off the inverted lenses resulted in an initially similar maladapted state to what would have been normal visual information.

Again we must ask if this type of experiment conforms to our model of two people seeing different things when confronted by the same visual scene. In one sense it does not. One would expect two observers looking at different objects to have different percepts; similarly, it is not surprising that perception differs if one observer has distorting lenses placed in the way of his normal vision. The two observers would then have different inputs. But this would not be the case if continued wearing of an optical device produced a changing effect on the visual system. Then we could place the distorting lenses on both of our observers for different lengths of time, and they would report seeing different things while still receiving the same visual input. Also, it is possible, as we shall see, that the removal of the distorting lenses may again produce differences so that both observers, now viewing without lenses, again report seeing the world differently.

We have said that Stratton was able to adjust to an upside-down world, but the most important question to decide upon is whether the world really did *look* upside down or not. It could be that there was a genuine change in the subjective perceptual world and that it did appear the right way up. On the other hand, it could be that by practice in a transformed world Stratton had relearned the motor action accompanying the positions

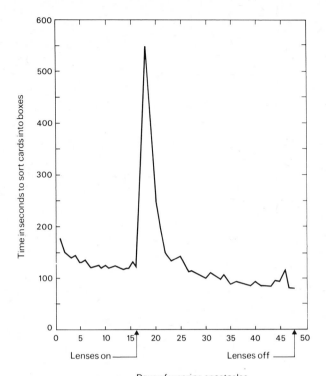

Fig 19 The effect on card-sorting of wearing inverted spectacles (reprinted from *Vision With Spatial Inversion*, Snyder and Pronko, University of Wichita Press: 1952, by courtesy of N. W. Pronko)

of objects in the new, transformed visual input, just as you can with a little practice learn to draw in a mirror, by working out which direction to move your hand, rather than really appreciating the changed visual input.

Stratton reports that while wearing the spectacles the world did occasionally look 'right side up', but he is not clear if this is always the case. On removal of the inverting spectacles, Stratton says, 'the scene had a strange familiarity. The visual arrangement was immediately recognised as the old one of the pre-experimental days; yet the reversal of everything from the order to which I had grown accustomed during the past week, gave the scene a surprising bewildering air... It was hardly the feeling, though, that things were upside down'.

In a repetition of this experiment by Snyder and Pronko (1952) the inverting lenses were worn for a longer period. Tests for motor co-ordination were made before, during and after the wearing of the lenses. One of these tasks was to sort cards into boxes as quickly as possible. This was asked of the observer for seventeen days before wearing the spectacles, for twenty-eight days when wearing them, and for four days afterwards.

Figure 19 shows the great difficulty found after putting on the spectacles. This was eventually coped with and the observer returned to pre-test efficiency. Upon removal of the lenses, there was again a slight disruption of performance. In this experiment, we have a clear account of a behavioural change, but is there a similar accompanying experiential change? Towards the end of the experiment, the observer was asked whether a view from a tall building looked upside down to him. He replied, 'I wish you hadn't asked me. Things were all right until you popped the question at me. Now when I recall how they *did* look before I put on these lenses, I must answer that they do look upside down *now*. But until the moment you asked me, I was absolutely unaware of it and hadn't given a thought to the question of whether things were the right side up or upside down'.

This is no doubt an unsatisfactory answer to the question we have posed. It is certainly true that most investigators have not concerned themselves with this, but concentrated on answering other important questions. But as we are concerned with the visual experience of different observers it is important to us and must be pursued a little further.

Kohler, conducting similar experiments, does maintain that the world can appear the 'right way up' phenomenally. This occurs after an extensive period of maladaptation when the world appears odd: places, for example, look unfamiliar, and people walking move mechanically because the up-down component, which is not normally noticed in movement, becomes very apparent. The adaptation of the phenomenal world occurs in a strangely piecemeal fashion. Thus Kohler says that an observer wearing left–right reversing lenses, may, after a while, see cars as being on the correct side of the road and their number plates as being mirror images. This, however, is claimed to correct itself after many weeks of wearing the spectacles. Moreover, these odd perceptions can help reorganise the appearance of the world. If the observer is seeing the world upside down, Kohler says that a percept of a candle burning in that way is too incongruous and causes a phenomenal reversal of the perceived world. Even stronger evidence for a change in some perceptual mechanism, as opposed to a change in motor coordination, comes from Kohler's report of what happens on lens removal. He maintains that now the world appears reversed, just as it did when the lenses were first put on. This is most important because without any distorting lenses there would seem no reason to make any correction. However, there is still the possibility of a carry-over of habits learned during the adaptation period. We shall consider this possibility, but in the last analysis we will have to rely on the observer to tell us if the world really looks upside down or not.

Studying the adaptation to the transformed visual world may tell us how normal perception develops in infancy, though most researchers in this field feel it will not. This issue will concern us in a following chapter; we should consider at this point the work of Held and his associates, who

feel that it does. Held considers that the most important factor in determining if the observer will adapt is whether or not active (as opposed to
passive) movements are carried out in the transformed visual situation.

Held and Gottlieb (1958) asked observers to view an image of a square
target which was reflected from a mirror. The mirror was positioned so
that the observers could see neither their hands nor the marks made (see
top left of Fig. 20). Ten marks were made for each corner. The observer
had to withdraw his hand between each trial. After these pre-test trials he
had to view his hand through a prism which displaced the visual input to
the right. Groups of observers did this under the following conditions:
firstly, with no movement; secondly, with passive movement; and thirdly,
with active movement. In 'active movement' the observer moved his arm
back and forth himself, and in 'passive movement' the experimenter
moved the observer's arm for him. After one of these activities, the inter-
vening prisms were removed and the observer had to repeat the pre-test
trials of marking the corners of the square. Figure 20 shows the results of
these tests.

In the post-test situation all the observers had the same external stimulation. It is clear that adaptation only occurred if active movement took place.
This does not actually prove that after the few minutes of active movement (maximum effect was obtained within half-an-hour) the appearance
of the world had altered. Many changes could have occurred. The
adaptation could be due to mental compensation, or to a change in the felt
position of the hand. However, active movement and feedback do seem to
be important factors. Held et al. (1966) have shown that this feedback
has to occur almost immediately to be effective. Delaying the visual
feedback by as little as 0.3 seconds by using a video-tape recorder made
active movement ineffective in producing adaptation.

In another experiment, Held and Bossom (1961) found that wearing
displacing prisms caused a misconception of the straight-ahead position.
The task of the observer was to position himself directly in front of a target.
The apparatus consisted of a dimly-lit target situated in a small room.
The observer sat on a rotatable chair. After several attempts under these
conditions, one group of observers put on the prisms and walked for an
hour along an outdoor path. The observers in the other group each sat in a
wheelchair and, while wearing the prisms, were pushed along the same
path for the same length of time. After this, the judgements of the straight-
ahead were changed for the active observer but not for the passive.

It has been argued that there is nothing intrinsically important about
active movement in producing adaptations: it can be thought of as just
a much more efficient way of getting any change. Certainly, it is not difficult to find experiments where adaptation has occurred without any
active movement on the part of the observer. But, if we are trying to obtain
a situation where two observers report different effects when viewing

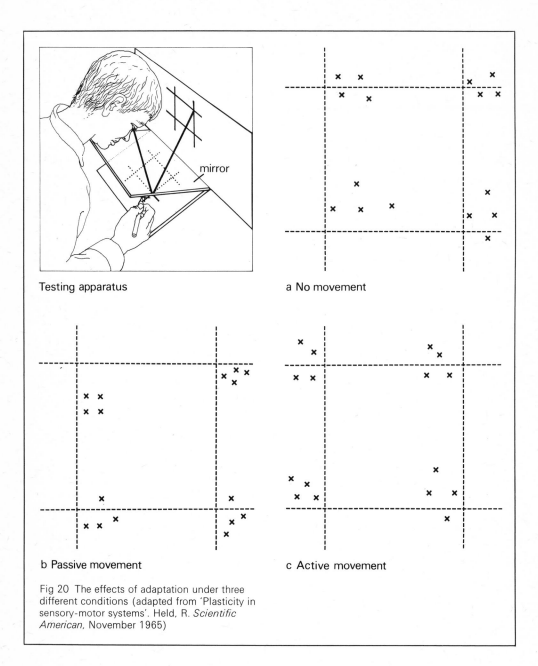

Testing apparatus

a No movement

b Passive movement

c Active movement

Fig 20 The effects of adaptation under three different conditions (adapted from 'Plasticity in sensory-motor systems'. Held, R. *Scientific American*, November 1965)

the same external scene, a good way to achieve this would be to place one of the observers in a transformed visual world in which he had to make active movements.

However, we shall return to the important question of whether the effects are due to a change in vision or to a change in proprioception (that is to say, concerned with the knowledge of the position of parts of the body). Do these reports reflect anything more than a change in the felt position of our limbs? Harris (1965) points out that if observers look at one of their hands through a displacing prism, then do a pointing task as in the Held and Bossom experiment, it should not matter which arm is used if the effect is purely visual, but could be very important if the cues used are proprioceptive. It has been found that it does matter which arm is used for the pointing. Furthermore, Harris points out that this effect (the difference between the hands) occurs with the eyes closed or blindfolded. There are exceptions to this finding for other experiments, but they have been explained by changes in the felt position of the head, or the eyes in the head.

Let us take as an example a person writing letters on a board while wearing reversing prisms so that left appears right and right appears left. When the observer first puts on the reversing prisms, a letter to the true left will be seen on the felt right. If he looks at his hand trying to write on the board adaptation begins. When he moves his hand to the left it will appear to go to the right. He sees it going to the right and its felt position gradually becomes as if it actually does move to the right. At this stage the observer may write letters backwards when asked (see Fig. 21). The judgement of

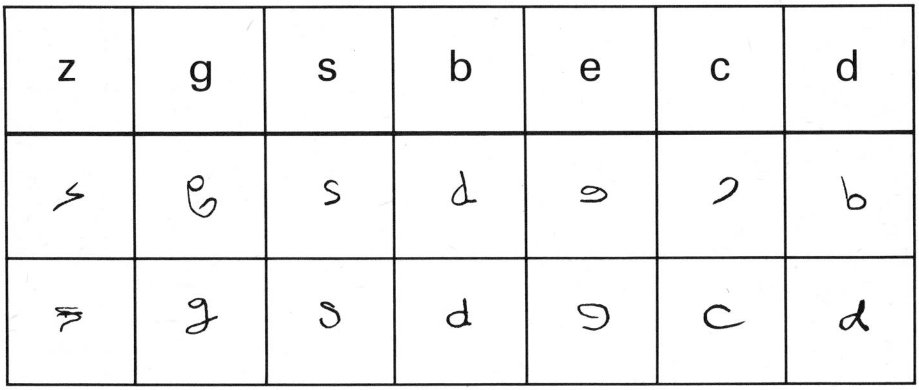

z	g	s	b	e	c	d
ƨ	℮	S	ፏ	℈	℩	ɓ
⇁	ꟼ	Ꙅ	d	℩	c	ⅾ

Fig 21 The attempts of two observers to write letters and numbers while wearing reversing prisms. Only the letter S was written normally. by one observer. It was the only letter he thought he had written back to front (reprinted from 'Vision and touch', Rock, I. and Harris, C. S., *Scientific American*, May 1967)

the right now goes along with the felt position of the hand and the true left will now be judged as the right. However, at this stage, we may get the effect, reported by Kohler, of the letters still being reversed. If the observer now learns to read mirror writing, he may be convinced that everything is now back to normal and that there is a genuine change in perception. (For a review of this work see Kling and Riggs (1971).)

This is a complicated yet convincing argument; but are there any experiments which could not be accounted for in this way? Kohler (1962) asked his observers to wear special goggles which had each lens made up of a blue and a yellow section, divided vertically. This meant that when the observer looked to the left the world had a bluish tint and when he looked to the right, a yellowish tint. In normal vision complementary light sources, such as yellow or blue, when shone on the same white surface, produce a neutral grey. Kohler asked the observer, when looking to the left or the right, to adjust a coloured patch to look a neutral grey. The amount of yellow or blue required to do this was then measured. On the first day of wearing the goggles, a great deal of the complementary colour blue was required when looking through the yellow half. Much less was needed by the sixtieth day, showing that the eye had adapted to the input. When the observer finally removed the goggles, he found that the world was tinged with yellow when he looked in the direction that would have been blue if he had still been wearing the goggles. Similarly, the world was tinged with blue when looking in the opposite (formerly yellow) direction. There seemed to be real change in the phenomenal appearance of the world associated with the direction of gaze. It could be said that when the felt position of the eye was to the left he interpreted this as requiring an adaptation for blue, so an object was seen as yellower than it really was. But this does not sound convincing, as the impression of a colour is immediate and without interpretation. This experiment differs from the experiments of Harris in that colour rather than spatial adaptation is involved. Also, one must be cautious about this result of Kohler, since neither Harrington (1965) nor McCollough (1965b) could confirm it.

Another experiment by Kohler also showed a difference in perception according to the direction of gaze. In this experiment the observer wore special spectacles that were distorting prisms at only the top half; there was clear glass in the bottom half. After removal of the spectacles, looking up produced an after-effect related to the amount of distortion. Looking down at the same object produced little or no distortion.

The after-effect caused by inspecting a curved line has its counterpart when viewing with distorting lenses. Straight lines, looked at through a prism, appear curved, though they gradually appear to straighten, and upon removal of the prism a straight line appears curved in the opposite direction. It is possible to argue, with Harris (1965), that if, after adaptation, the observer feels that his eyes have followed a straight line, when in fact they have really followed a curve, his after-effect could be predicted on the felt-position hypothesis. This may be considered unlikely and there are theorists such as Rock (1966) who feel that the visual world is itself changed, in that, after adaptation, it actually *looks* different.

The situation is complicated by the fact that any change from the conditions under which adaptation takes place causes a reduction in the after-effect. Taylor (1962) found that if, after the adaptation, the prism was removed from the goggles, but the goggles themselves kept on, there was a greater after-effect than if the goggles were completely removed. Similarly, if a tone is played during adaptation (Kravitz and Yaffe, 1972) then there is a greater after-effect when the tone is heard than without it. The conditioning here is not as strong as the conditioned after-images (page 3) as the tone does not actually elicit the after-effect.

However, the fact that in a certain type of experiment only one type of change takes place does not rule out other adaptations occurring in different situations. Hay and Pick (1966) argue that both proprioceptive and visual perceptual changes can take place, but since visual changes take much longer to be operative they are not observed in all situations. Yet the balance of the evidence seems to suggest that in most experiments with a transformed visual input, there is a re-education of the proprioceptive system for a given visual input, rather than any change in visual perception. Harris argues that this is clearly seen in the phenomenon of 'visual capture'. The felt position of a hand, when looked at through a prism, coincides with the visual position of the hand and not with the actual position in space that the hand occupies. Proprioception alters because of this 'capture' by vision.

These experiments have been considered at some length because they make clear the difficulties involved in trying to show the cause of a change in visual perception. There seem always to be other explanations, in this case mostly proprioceptive, available. Perhaps the only answer to this question of the nature of the change is to undergo the visual transformations oneself and then try to ask whether one's perception of the world is in fact altered: but then one might arrive at the same position as Snyder (above) and wish one had not asked the question.

Eye-strain

Perhaps the most common after-effect of visual experience, and also the least often discussed in books on visual perception, is that of eye-strain. The effects of eye-strain are various and include headache and even pain, but we shall be concerned here only with the perceptual phenomena associated with it.

With eye-strain, perceiving the world becomes an effort and there is a difficulty in changing focus from one object to another a different distance away. There may be a temporary blurring of vision or sense of confusion. Generally, the automatic processes by which we have normal vision are lost, and the conscious manipulation of them is accompanied by a different appreciation of the visual scene. Stutterheim (1937) reported a patient as saying that the effect of eye-strain was 'as if I was looking down a microscope with my eyes fixed on the centre and all round was hazy'. In normal vision, the object in focus is clear and we are unaware of the objects not in attention. It is, however, quite easy to perceive the world in this different way. If we look at an object, while at the same time trying to be aware of what is in the periphery of vision, we will get this eye-strain effect. It may be that no object will be in focus, or more commonly there will be clear central vision with a gradual fading towards the periphery. The eye ceases to be something taken for granted and may, in eye-strain, feel to be 'out on stalks'.

Light, itself, becomes unpleasant in this condition. There is no evidence that this is due to any increased sensitivity to light or retinal fatigue or an accompanying pain in response to light. Photocoagulation, an operative procedure in which a powerful beam of light is focussed on the retina to produce a local burn, is not accompanied by any pain; so there is no reason to suppose that the presence of light could produce pain in eye-strain.

Eye-strain, by definition, is one of the short-term changes in perception that we are considering. This can be seen because the symptoms last only a little while and can be made to go by closing the eyes or lying down in the dark. Indeed, many other remedies can be effective, Aspirin, anti-depressants, fresh air and hatha yoga exercises have, among many other remedies, all been found to be successful in relieving eye-strain symptoms in some patients.

The cause of the eye-strain effect is not as simple as it might seem. There may be a certain correlation between time spent doing some visual task and the eye-strain symptoms, but it is not always so. The nature of the task may be very important. The effect can even be induced by tasks involving excessive noise and other non-visual stimulation. Heaton (1968) stresses the importance of not accepting a unitary precipitating factor. However, the most commonly accepted cause is eye muscle fatigue.

Carmichael and Dearborn (1947) persuaded people to read continuously for six hours by giving monetary rewards. They tested their observers at intervals but could find no obvious change in their visual behaviour. Visual acuity, eye-movement electromyography (electrical recording from muscles), eye-blink rate, fixations per line, were all found to be unaltered throughout the experiment. Though, undoubtedly, excessive use of the eye muscles will cause eye-strain, it cannot be a complete explanation. It is found that in situations open to interpretation by the individual, eye-strain is more likely. In a difficult visual situation forced upon a person, rejection of the situation may lead to eye-strain: a child learning to read may not be able to live up to the aspirations of his parents and eye-strain may result.

The effects of eye-strain differ from the previous effects discussed in this chapter, in that they are global—that is, the total perceived world is involved. The phenomenal appearance of the world changes and may become unreal. This is not the case with all other short-term changes in perception though it can result from drugs. If eye-strain is one of the least investigated causes of altered perception, the effect of drugs is probably the most generally discussed.

Drugs

This is a vast topic, since the number of drugs which can potentially affect visual perception is enormous and they can alter perception in many different ways. Crews *et al.* (1970) provide a list of the drugs which can, if taken in sufficient quantity, cause defective vision. This list contains many commonly prescribed drugs.

The effect of drugs can even be indirect, as when, by means of some drug, the eye is paralysed. In normal vision, if an observer moves his eyes to the right he sees whatever is to the right of him. The world itself remains stationary. Helmholtz, in the last century, found that if the rectus muscle of the eye is paralysed with curare so that the eye cannot move and then a command is made for the eye to move to the right, the world will jump to the right; this suggests that even the passive observer plays an important part in perception. For a fuller account of the implications of this finding see Gregory (1966). Of course, this experiment does not rely on drugs for the effect to be shown; Mach 'bunged up his eyes with putty' and obtained the same result.

Drugs which depress the level of activity of an observer will make him generally less sensitive and less able to detect the presence of light. Major sedatives like the barbiturates, tranquilisers like chlorpromazine and the phenothiazines, and alcohol, all have this effect, though the pupil dilation which accompanies alcohol intake may compensate somewhat for such a decrease in basic sensitivity. The depressant effect of many of these drugs is, of course, common to all sensory functions, though Granger and Ikeda (1968) found that alcohol, at least, has a specific action on the retina. Eysenck, Holland and Trouton (1957a) found that a depressant (sodium amytal) also reduced the duration of the spiral after-effect; after-images, too, seemed reliably to decrease in intensity and duration. Drugs which increase arousal may improve the sensitivity of the observer, but the effects are not always so reproducible as those obtained with depressant drugs.

There are very few drugs which specifically affect colour-vision, if we discount the report of Kravkov (1941) that arousal of the autonomic nervous system by any means (e.g. adrenaline) decreases visual sensitivity to orange-red light and increases it to blue-green light. Chloroquine (taken for malaria) and phenothiazine may, in large doses, cause loss of colour-vision, though this (Siegel and Arden, 1968) is because they affect the retina as a whole. Depending on the site of their action they may affect only the rods, in which case only sensitivity to light as measured, for example, by the rate of dark-adaptation will be affected.

If the material of the eye takes up some chemical this can give the appearance of a coloured filter having been interposed between the observer and the world. Duke-Elder (1954) confirms that this occurs in picric acid poisoning. A similar yellow-filter effect occurs in santonin and sulphonamide poisoning. Digitalis can cause red, blue, brown, white and yellow vision, though, according to Wagener *et al.* (1946), for some reason digitalis causes the individual object and not the whole world to appear coloured.

Siegel and Arden say that there are two drugs which specifically affect colour-vision without seriously affecting other visual functioning. The first is Furaltadone (Altafur), an antibiotic, which caused a permanent colour-loss in part of the retina to a patient given large doses. The second is Troxidone, an anticonvulsant drug used for petit mal epilepsy, which has a temporary effect. In both cases, however, the patients' major visual complaint was not the colour deficit, but an accompanying severe dazzle.

There are other drugs whose effect on visual perception is in some way specific. Steinberg *et al.* (1961) report that nitrous oxide made objects appear to be further away, though another depressant drug, chlorpromazine, did not. A change in the size of objects can also occur. Holmstedt and Lindgrem (1967) report that an apparent increase in the size of objects, especially in alcoholic delirium, is more common than a decrease in size. However, the latter can occur from atropine poisoning and also from other chemicals.

Drugs which can have a profound effect on mental activity may still have very little effect on the basic perceptual processes. By introspection, moderate doses of cannabis may improve visual clarity and acuity. However, careful testing has not been able to verify this in the laboratory. For example, no effect has been found on the brightness threshold for the detection of light, upon depth perception or visual acuity. Theodor and Miller (1972) even report a loss in sensitivity to the offset of a brief light-flash. Effects of marihuana on visual perception can be found, but these are with complex perceptual processes especially concerning the amount of visual imagery. This is an activity that may not be related to the attempt to process the incoming visual information.

Moskowitz *et al.* (1972) asked observers to smoke marihuana, after which they were to fixate a target and report stimuli by pressing a switch.

The stimuli appeared from time to time in the periphery of vision. The more marihuana smoked the fewer stimuli were reported. This could be because the drug caused a narrowing of attention upon the fixation point. It might also be because the observers could not be bothered to press the switch. The latter explanation might be rejected since, when the stimuli were reported, the reaction time was as quick as without the drug. It is important, however, to consider this factor, since the apparant lack of sensitivity could very easily be caused by an unwillingness to respond. The inability to notice peripheral stimuli is, of course, not a specific effect of marihuana; very similar results would probably have been obtained with alcohol.

Sharma and Moskowitz (1972) found that the illusory movement of a stationary light in an otherwise darkened room (the Auto-kinetic Phenomenon—see page 188) increased after smoking marihuana. The Auto-kinetic Phenomenon depends on many factors, relying perhaps initially on unconscious attempts to deal with feedback from the eye muscles (see Gregory, 1966). But because there is only illusory movement, the Auto-kinetic Phenomenon is very much open to suggestion and depends on the suggestibility of the observer. The exact nature of the role of marihuana with respect to this illusion is not known. However, Sharma and Moskowitz advise against night driving under the influence of marihuana !

The drug most often discussed with regard to effect on visual perception and the accompanying hallucinations produced with large doses is, of course, lysergic acid diethylamide (LSD). But any drug that produces a delirium can also cause hallucinations: bromide, caffeine, carbon monoxide, camphor, quinine, and many others are all substances that have been reported to produce hallucinations. Indeed, many drugs if taken in sufficient quantity will affect perception. The striking point about LSD is the minute amounts which cause such pronounced changes.

It is possible to produce drug-induced visual hallucinations in the blind (Krill *et al.*, 1963), though not in those who have been blind from birth. Here, the visual phenomena reported obviously bear no relationship to any external stimulus which is actually present; such hallucinations therefore fall beyond the limits of the classes of perceptual event we are considering. Generally, we are interested in the different manner in which two observers can perceive the outside world, rather than in any fabricated perception, even though no doubt this would vary between individuals. However, it may always be more or less true that the observer's relation to the external world will be a matter of give and take. The person who is perceiving may well affect the actual perception. Looked at from this point of view, hallucinations can be seen to lie at one end· of the continuum of interaction between the observer and the outside world.

In any case, perception under the influence of drugs may take into account, to some extent, the outside world. Also, the effect of drugs is similar to the effect of eye-strain and the other effects already discussed, in that we have a situation in which two observers have the same initial perception and, after the treatment, the perception of the visual scene differs, and then returns after a short time to the pre-treatment situation. LSD may again prove to be a limiting case, in that the effects can be long-lasting or even permanent.

Hallucinations produced by these drugs change the size, colour and form of objects and produce complex geometric patterns which are similar to those in Arabic lattice-work. The latter stages of the drug-induced state where, for example, mysterious animals may appear, will not concern us here, because, as Kluver (1928) reported, they are better experienced with the eyes closed or in a darkened room. Similarly, the hallucinations reported after deprivation of the senses will not be considered at this point. In these situations, it has been reported by some experimenters, although not by others that deprivation from stimulus input, or constant stimulation by the same input, produces hallucinations (for a review see Zubeck, 1964). These hallucinations may be caused by the restructuring of the outside world—an idea which is central to the theme of the last chapter of this book.

We have noted that several drugs can affect colour vision, but perhaps the most dramatic effects are obtained with the hallucinogenic drugs. The vividness of the colours perceived increases, though Cohen (1964) reports that the threshold for colour detection remains unchanged and that visual acuity is diminished. But these affects are trivial compared to the gross perceptual changes that can occur. The shapes of objects may change and the importance of an object to the individual may alter. In this manner, these visual effects are different from others considered in this chapter. For example, the basic stability of the outside world can disappear: 'The walls flapped in the breeze like tapestries—they run like melted wax' (Savage, 1955); or, 'The most inconspicuous object outside one's normal attention suddenly lit up in a host of brilliant colours difficult to describe: objects like cigarette ends, and half-burnt matches in the ashtrays, coloured glass on a distant rubbish heap, ink-blots on the desk, monotonous rows of books, etc. In particular, certain indirectly viewed objects attracted my attention almost irresistibly through their vivid colouring—even the fire shadows in the ceiling and in the walls and the dim shadows which the furniture cast on the floor had a rare and delicate colour which gave the room a fairy-tale magic'. (Serko—quoted by Jaspers (1962).)

The effects can be more specific: 'Looking down at one moment the feet would seem to be far away and small, just exactly as they do when opera glasses are used the wrong way round. Then, the effect would reverse and the legs and body would look very short. The feet appeared to be about fifteen inches below my eyes and it seemed that they had come up rather than I had gone down.' (Asher, 1961.) Asher also reported that colour distortions were still there the next day and that people's faces had an unpleasant green tinge.

Summary

The effects of these drug-induced experiences, when considered against the effects of eye-strain, may seem great, but it is an even greater step to other differences of a short-term nature in perception, such as the tilt after-effect. The heading 'short-term differences in perception' thus covers a multitude of perceptual phenomena. The division by duration that we have made does not mean that all such effects have a single causation. One could not expect that the global changes occurring in drug-induced states would be similar to the quite small, apparently trivial, changes caused by manipulation of a small part of the visual input.

After reading this chapter, one would not be blamed for wondering if the world could ever be the stable place we all know it to be. It has been shown that straight lines can appear curved and curved lines appear straight, left can be right and right can be left, grey can appear virtually any colour, the visual world can appear wonderfully vivid or drained of all colour, and much else besides; and, most importantly, it is the same external visual world that is being perceived all the time while these differences are experienced. In fact, we have probably just skimmed the surface of all the possible factors that could temporarily alter an observer's perception.

We have concerned ourselves in this chapter only with temporary effects. After perhaps quite short periods of time, the two observers who see differently when viewing the same things will come to see them in the same way. Because of this, are we to regard these phenomena as no more than mere perceptual curiosities? They are perhaps not so important as the more long-lasting effects on perception, but if they have sown the seeds of the concept of the essential plasticity of the perceived world, they will have served a useful function. However, in the next chapter we shall be concerned with differences between observers that are permanent, or at least of a very long duration.

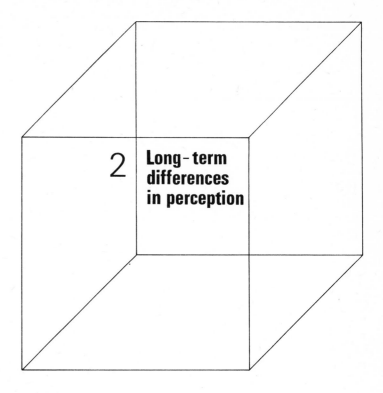

2 | **Long-term differences in perception**

Perceptual differences of organic origin

Figure 22a shows a diagram of the human visual pathways. The optic nerve (causing the 'blind spot' where it leaves the eye) transmits impulses from the retina to the lateral geniculate bodies and thence to the visual cortex, situated at the rear of the brain. Light received by each eye is transmitted to both halves of the visual cortex. This is because there is a bifurcation of the optic nerves at the optic chiasma. When an observer is looking straight ahead, light coming in from the left ends up in the right visual cortex irrespective of whether it is received by the left or the right eye. Light coming in from the right ends up in the left visual cortex.

It is obvious that if there is a disturbance of these pathways there will be an effect on perception. The effect, however, may not be immediately obvious. Figure 22b shows the visual field of the two eyes when various lesions are made. The hatched areas represent areas of blindness. In A, the effect of a lesion made behind the left eye is shown: complete blindness in that eye results. B shows the effect of a lesion which splits the optic chiasma so that there is no transference of impulses to the opposite hemisphere. C shows the effect of a lesion just prior to the lateral geniculate body of the left visual hemisphere, and D the effect of a lesion just prior to the lateral geniculate body of the right visual hemisphere. In practice, damage to one visual cortex often results in a patient having slightly different blind areas in each eye, rather than exactly as indicated here.

Since there is a direct relationship between points on the retina and parts of the visual cortex it might be predicted that there would be specific areas of blindness for specific lesions in the visual cortex. It is, however, not always as simple as that. Teuber (1968) gives procedures for estimating the exact location of such areas of acquired blindness (scotomata). These will depend on the testing situation and the target that is used for testing. The illumination, colour and size of the target and whether it is moving or stationary may all affect the exact area of blindness found. However, scotomata exist which are found so readily that these factors are relatively unimportant. The method of testing usually involves the patient staring fixedly ahead while targets are moved in from the periphery of vision. It would be preferable to use a method which allowed the patient to move his eyes naturally, but such tests are complicated.

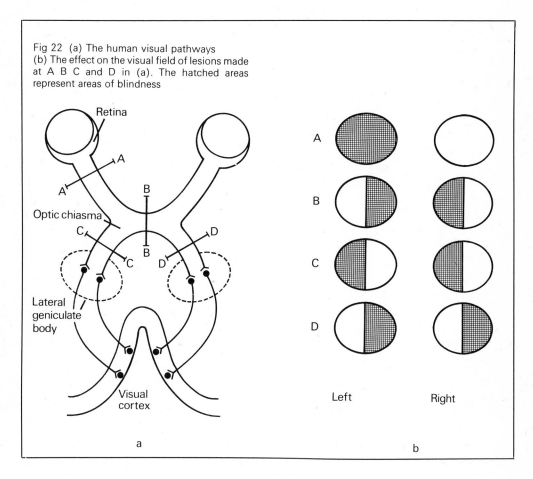

Fig 22 (a) The human visual pathways
(b) The effect on the visual field of lesions made at A B C and D in (a). The hatched areas represent areas of blindness

Very small lesions in the cortex may be impossible to detect. On the other hand, large-scale lesions may cause total blindness. However, Teuber also points out that, paradoxically, total destruction of the visual cortex may leave the patient at least able to detect gross changes of illumination.

Even when there is a definite scotoma, the patient will not perceive it as such and instead is likely to complain that his acuity is diminished and that he has difficulty with detail. He does not report having blind patches, because he himself completes the missing part of the visual field. However, the scotoma can be detected, as the patient will not be able to tell the difference between a continuous line and a line with a gap in it.

In other special situations these areas of blindness may have perceptual consequences. We have seen above (page 28) that Mackay (1957) found that an orthogonal after-effect in the form of a rosette could be induced in a random pattern of dots after looking at Fig. 17. This effect can also be seen as a complementary image using a direct superimposition. If a patient with a scotoma views such a display, he experiences the complementary image only in the area of his normal vision. The dots still appear to be random in the area of the scotoma.

Quite commonly there are narrow regions of blindness projecting from the main area of the scotoma. If these are near the fovea they can be detected when the patient looks at a coloured surface. Teuber, Battersby and Bender (1960) found that when patients stared at a red surface, green was induced in these projections of the scotoma. Moreover, the after-image was red while the after-image for the rest of the visual field was, of course, green.

Perceptual alteration can result from other organic changes: a detached retina will mean a progressive loss of vision; a tumour which presses against the optic nerve can produce a gradual loss of vision, leaving only a small central area of the visual field. A gross case of organic deficit can be caused by a cerebral thrombosis, which often results in the loss of one half of the visual field (see C and D, Fig. 22b). Surprisingly, the effect on perception need not be great. Lesions in the left visual hemisphere can to some extent be compensated for by eye movements. It seems (Luria, 1973) that lesions in the right visual hemisphere leave the patient able to see only the right-hand side of a picture he is looking at, or of a book that he is reading, and moreover, in general, he is unaware that the deficit is in himself rather than in the stimulus.

Organic disturbance does not always cause a blind area only, but often also an area of decreased functioning. This can be noted in changes in dark-adaptation or in the ability to distinguish between a rapidly flickering and a continuous light. Masking effects, too, seem to be easier to produce. Sometimes there is a change in perception rather than an absence of perception. Distortions of space (see below, page 66), similar to those caused when looking through displacing spectacles, can also be caused by lesions in the visual cortex.

Such effects on perception can be enormous but might here be considered unimportant, in that obviously they are predictable as a result of organic damage. Differences in perception that occur from uncorrected short- and longsightedness also fall into this category. However, the effect on the shortsighted (myopic) person of having only nearby objects in focus may have broader implications. Rice (1930) suggests that the shortsighted 'bookworm' has his love of books forced on him by being unable to excel at sports and games because of his restricted field of vision. It is also suggested that myopics tend to be more contemplative, since they inevitably rely less on visual cues and stimulation as a way of analysing the world. Trevor-Roper (1970) provides an interesting, though somewhat speculative, account of the way such defects as myopia have affected well-known figures in history: the Medici family, for example, who, at least partly because of their inherited myopia, concentrated more on scholarly and financial matters than on soldiering. Keats, too, according to Trevor-Roper, is often stated to have been myopic, with a resulting concentration on auditory themes *(Ode to a Nightingale)* or nearby visual objects *(Ode on a Grecian Urn)*.

Visual agnosia

It was suggested by Freud, among others, that in certain circumstances some people were unable to recognise familiar objects. This inability, called 'agnosia', was, in his patients, not related to a disturbance of the visual apparatus. However, reports of the condition have become less common as testing for visual defects has become more accurate. Visual agnosia may arise from lesions to parts of the visual cortex. These lesions do not leave the person blind nor in any way diminish his visual acuity, but he has difficulty in combining parts of an object and recognising them. The term 'visual agnosia' is used for a large number of defects in recognition which do not necessarily have the same cause.

Visual object agnosia can take many forms but, characteristically, the patient cannot identify some objects although he can see and avoid them. Luria (1973) gives this account of a patient trying to decipher a picture of a pair of spectacles:

There is a circle…and another circle…and a stick…a cross-bar…why, it must be a bicycle!

The patient may well be able to identify a drawing of a watch, but if a few lines are placed over the drawing he is no longer able to do so. This failing is especially common if the stimulus is exposed for a brief interval such as half-a-second. Strange objects, or common objects in a strange setting, are not recognised. Sometimes a cartoon-like impression may not be recognised whereas a naturalistic drawing may be. Photographs of an object may not be identified, while there is no difficulty with the actual object. For such patients sometimes only the outlines of objects can be seen, and objects which have a wavy outline and indistinct colour may be hard to distinguish.

It is not always easy to decide how much the defect is due to a deficit somewhere in the visual system and how much to some other cause. Critchley (1964) points out that agnosia often occurs as a result of severe toxic conditions such as carbon monoxide poisoning and thus one might expect the loss of other general factors in addition to specially visual agnosia: for instance, general memory loss would certainly contribute towards the lack of recognition. All agnosias, and this must include dyslexia (word-blindness), are bound to be complicated and multi-dimensional disabilities.

Patients suffering from visual agnosia may perceive the world in a different way. Critchley (1953) gives a description of a patient to whom faces were 'strangely flat: white with very dark eyes . . . like white oval plates . . . all the same. He could see but not interpret facial movements and grimaces . . . Gazing in a mirror he described the delineaments of what he saw, but could not recognise the face as his...'. This report suggests not so much a forgetting process as a reinterpretation of the visual world.

The same is perhaps true of a patient suffering from simultagnosia—the inability to pay attention to more than one aspect of a visual stimulus at a time. Of course, this is more or less true of everyone. The White Queen in *Through the Looking Glass* was adamant about it: 'The Queen said with great decision: "Nobody can do two things at once, you know".' But in simultagnosia this inability takes a more extreme form. For example, a patient cannot put a dot in the centre of a circle, since he cannot attend to both dot and circle at the same time. Williams (1970), discussing a patient she had studied, reported that if he was 'shown a page of drawings, the content of which overlapped (i.e. objects drawn on top of each other), he tended to pick out a single object and deny that he could see any others'.

Without doubt, there are emotional factors which can contribute to the inability to perceive certain aspects of the visual input, but it has been suggested by Kinsbourne and Warrington (1963), and by Birch, Belmont and Karp (1967), that the cause of simultagnosia is a processing difficulty. They suggest that the inability of the patient to copy whole figures and his tendency to get stuck on parts of them are caused by a change in his temporal processing of the visual input. Birch *et al.* found that if two stimuli were presented separated by time intervals of 300–600 milliseconds, both could be identified, but they could not if the time interval was less. This is similar to a deficit observed by Wallace (1956), who showed that older observers were inferior to younger ones in identifying complex visual displays, though there was no difference for simple ones. Luria (1973), referring to earlier work, has suggested that, provided any defect to the occipital (visual) cortex is only partial, simultagnosia can be suppressed by injections of caffeine; this suggests that the processing difficulty may result from a lack of arousal.

There are also differences from the normal in the scanning of patients with visual agnosia. It was observed that a certain patient with visual object agnosia could not fixate objects normally and would easily turn his gaze to another stimulus. This patient would enter a room cautiously, turning his head from side to side. According to Luria, Karpov and Yarbus (1966), faulty scanning can lead to patients making impulsive hypotheses about the content of visual stimuli. However, when brain damage has occurred, it is usually impossible to dissociate processing of visual information from processing in other sense modalities, because the general integrative machinery may also have broken down. It is also possible that the perceptual act which seems so unitary may in fact be divisible. Warrington and James (1967), for example, as others before them, make a distinction between stages of perception: they found that, on a picture-recognition task, patients with lesions localised on the left side of the brain made naming errors, while patients with right side lesions made recognition errors. Ettlinger (1967), too, found patients who were unable to name colours when they were presented to them but could sort the same colours into hues and shades without error.

Figures which require completion rather than identification are harder for patients with right-sided lesions. A peculiar feature of lesions in the right hemisphere is a commonly-reported agnosia for faces. Patients with this disability can recognise only a few very familiar faces, and even close friends may be identified only by their voices. Agnosias occur for the recognition of objects other than faces in cases of right-sided brain damage, but these are not reported as frequently, probably because the inability to recognise faces is the most troublesome. Scanning and interpretation of the input may not be so important a factor in the brain-damaged person as in others, but it is, as we shall see, an area which will provide interesting findings. But before proceeding further we shall try to make a distinction between the causes of the long-term differences in perception.

Distinguishing between organic and functional defects

We have turned our attention in this chapter to situations where two observers viewing a scene make different reports, not because of any prior treatment that one of the observers has undergone, but because of something intrinsic to that person. This individual difference may have been acquired through experience but has now become stable, so that the differences reported are not transitory in nature. Of course, it may be that the individual difference has a genetic basis and was present at birth. The question whether an individual's perception is innate or acquired through experience will concern us more when we discuss the development of perception. This problem of unravelling 'nature' from 'nurture' is complex, since even an inherited deficit manifests itself in relation to the available environment. Even when perceptual abilities can clearly be seen to be based on experience, it is often a difficult task to delineate the exact nature of the experimental determinants.

A distinction can also be drawn between the differences in visual perception which are related to an organic change or deficit and those of psychological causation where no such organic change is known. In the limiting case it is easy to see that organic factors act in a different way: damage to the receptive system will inevitably affect perception, since, in order to perceive, the observer needs the correct visual apparatus as well as the incoming stimulus.

In the last analysis, it may be difficult to distinguish psychological causes of perceptual differences from organic causes, because it may always be possible to relate a psychological change to some physical change. This is not to say that one should, at the outset, look for some physical defect when perceptual differences are shown. But, as we have seen, there are instances when changes in visual processing can be clearly linked to organic change; while these effects can be similar to changes of psychological origin, they can also be distinguished from them.

We have seen from the work on stabilised retinal images (page 21) that it would be possible to create an 'artificial scotoma' by continuous presentation of a black disc. Does this differ from a true scotoma which arises, say, from a retinal deficiency? We have noted that patients with such retinal or cortical defects do not notice the blind areas in their visual field, as the background seems to 'fill in' the scotoma. If we were to arrange for the stabilised disc to be surrounded by a non-stabilised area, would the colour and brightness of the surrounding field fill in the stabilised part? Gerrits and Timmerman (1969) found that such a filling-in process occurred, but that whereas the true scotoma would fill in instantaneously, it took several seconds at least for the stabilised area to fill in. A similar time-lag occurred when the light in the surround was turned off: the patient with a true scotoma saw darkness immediately, but for the stabilised 'artificial scotoma' the filled-in parts faded away slowly.

Teuber (1968) suggests that changes similar to those caused by organic defects can be caused by certain drugs, the only difference being, in this case, the temporary nature of the effect. One volunteer, having taken mescaline, asked, 'What are you doing to the floor?', saying that the left half of the floor had distorted and was sloping away. Two minutes after this, the observer had a demonstrably complete blind half of the visual field, which lasted for several minutes.

Charcot drew attention to the changes in the perceived world of the hysteric. The hysteric's visual field can appear to be tubular with roughly circular, concentric contractions. Similar visual field restrictions occur in organic disease, but in this case the perceived size of an object alters with the distance of the object, which does not happen for the hysteric. Also, in hysterical cases, changes occur in the amount of the visual field that is seen. If an object is moved radially and towards the centre of the visual field, the perceived visual field can appear as a contracting spiral. An expanding spiral field is seen by the hysteric if testing starts in the centre of the visual field. Star-shaped fields have also been reported, and the type of field may change according to the distance at which the hysteric is tested: for example, a spiral field at two feet and a tubular field at four.

In hysterical visual field deficits, areas of blindness are sometimes reported. Since these are hysterical rather than organic in origin, they may change when tested at a later date. In rare cases, complete hysterical blindness may occur, but the behaviour of the hysteric is slightly different from that of the really blind person. If a normal person has his sight tested on the Snellen chart of letters of varying sizes (as used by opticians), his performance will diminish as he goes further away from the chart: the performance will decline with distance from the chart in a uniform way. The hysteric's performance in such a test does not depend so clearly on distance, and he can often be persuaded to read lower and lower on the test chart by a pretence of altering the lenses he is wearing: his visual functioning alters according to his expectation of the task. In the case of the rare, hysterically-induced complete blindness, Grosz and Zimmerman (1965) point out that, though the hysteric's behaviour is distinguishable from that of the organically blind person, the hysteric will adjust his behaviour accordingly when told how the really blind person would act.

Another defect which can have either an organic or a psychological origin is night-blindness. This can be caused by a deficiency of vitamin A or by disease, but in the Western world it is usually psychological in origin. These two types of night-blindness can be differentiated in the case of the dark-adapted observer. In the dark-adapted state (page 9), electrical recording from the retina differs from that of the light-adapted state. In hysterical night-blindness, the electrically recorded response to a flash of light is the same as that of a normal person and, of course, differs from that in a true deficiency.

The visual field of an observer deficient in vitamin A is characterised by a widening of the blind spot (where the optic nerve enters the eye) and a contraction of the peripheral field of vision. Figure 23a represents the normal visual field in the dark. Figure 23b shows the increased area of the visual field in which nothing is seen, as observed in experimentally

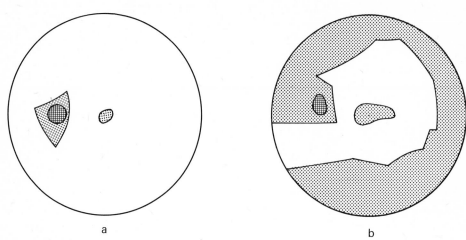

a   b

Fig 23 (a) Visual field of normal eye for a dim self-luminous
target of 3 mm
(b) Visual field experimentally produced by Vitamin A
deficiency for a dim self-luminous target of 3 mm. The
hatched areas are blind spots tested in daylight with a 2 mm
white target. Dotted areas are those blind in the dark (reprinted
from an article by Livingstone, P. C., *The Lancet* Vol. ii, 33, 1944)

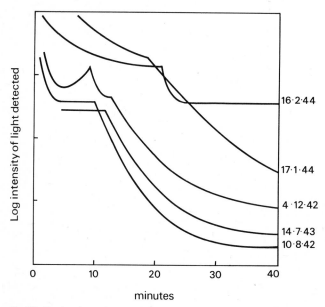

Fig 24 Dark-adaptation curves for induced Vitamin A
deficiency (reprinted from *Vitamin A Requirements of Human
Adults,* Medical Research Council Special Report Series No
264, 1949)

produced vitamin A deficiency. As the deficiency worsens, the night-blindness becomes more severe. Figure 24 shows the curves of dark-adaptation induced in an observer by artificially depriving him of vitamin A. If we compare this result of Hume and Krebs (1949) with that of normal dark-adaptation (see Fig. 4) then the marked change is obvious. Night-blindness produced this way can be cured by treatment with vitamin A preparations, though it may be found that the hysterically night-blind person will also be helped if he believes that he is obtaining the correct treatment.

While it is possible to distinguish between hysterical blindness and organic blindness, it may be impossible to distinguish between the hysterically blind person and the malingerer pretending to be blind. This difference is a question of the conscious awareness of the observer. The hysterical person is unaware that his blindness is not real, but the malingerer is fully aware of this. Consideration of someone pretending to be blind or even pretending to be hysterically blind raises issues beyond the scope of this work.

We have seen that there is no specific pattern of visual defect which can be associated with a psychological rather than an organic cause, but that there are differences which can be observed in certain circumstances. These differences, however, may be of a subtle nature: for example, changes in the apparent size of objects occur both in brain damage and in schizophrenia, the only differentiation being their relative instability in the latter case.

We now turn to consider the differences that occur in specific perceptual phenomena. The first of these is colour-vision.

Differences in colour-vision

Colour-blindness is of amazingly recent discovery. According to Geldard (1972), the first case recorded was that of a Mr Harris of Cumberland who, in the eighteenth century, was perplexed by an enquiry after a lost red stocking. He insisted that the word 'red' in the description of the stocking was quite superfluous. Colour-blindness can be both genetically determined and acquired through some disease or injury, but whatever the cause it is very stable. In fact, it is so stable, and the person having the defect so completely attuned to the world as he perceives it, that it can be very hard to detect.

Before considering the deficits and misperceptions of colour-vision there are some theoretical points which should be discussed. Earlier, we considered the phenomenon of the stabilised retinal image and whether it could be cited as a genuine difference in the way in which two observers perceived the visual world. In normal vision, different receptors are being stimulated while we are looking at a single object. If, because of some experimental intervention, this does not happen, it is perhaps not surprising that different perceptions result. Any object looked at from slightly differing angles will of course give slightly differing perceptions. Now, does the lack of a certain colour receptor or the corresponding cortical cells present us with a similar case? How can we expect observers to have the same perception if they do not have the same physical apparatus? The case of the comparison between a blind and a sighted observer is an extreme illustration of this point.

The instant that the receptors of two individuals are stimulated there must be the possibility of differing perceptions, resulting either from the physical state of the receptors, be it temporary or permanent, or from some cortical differences between the observers. Such cortical differences can be the result of inheritance or injury, or acquired through experience, and it is likely to be impossible to distinguish the cause. Also, to try to distinguish between changes in perception caused by the eye and those caused by the brain is to miss the important point that we are dealing with a single processing system which, though it may be altered at various stages, relies on all its parts. Thus, to decide to ignore changes which can obviously be linked to some receptor deficit or absence would be arbitrary. We shall be considering cases where two observers have differing percepts of a scene, whereas a photo-receptive device (e.g. a camera) recording the transmitted light shows no difference between the two. Of course we are not considering the difference between a photograph of a scene and an observer's percept of it—it may well be that these would differ. If the two observers had the same percept, however strange it was, it would not relate to our enquiry. What we are concerned with here is the case when two photographs of a scene would be the same (one to another) but two perceptions of the same scene would be different (one from another). This is the approach that will be adopted in considering all these long-term differences in perception.

Observers with normal colour-vision are called normal trichromats. Trichromatism refers to the fact that normal observers require three primary colours to produce all the other colours. It is found that by mixing together different proportions of the primary colours (red, blue and green) any other coloured light source can be matched. Colour-blind individuals differ in the amount of each primary colour that is required or in the number of primaries needed.

An anomalous trichromat, like normally-sighted observers, makes use of all three primaries in matching different light sources, but he will use different proportions from the normal. Usually these people are either red-anomalous (protanomalous) or green-anomalous (deuteranomalous). Dichromats are observers who match different light sources by a combination of only two primaries. There are three basic forms of dichromatism:

protanopia (red-blindness), deuteranopia (green-blindness) and tritanopia (yellow–blue defect). Monochromats can match any colour of light source by light of any one colour or even by a white light which, in fact, means they have no colour-vision at all. Plate 6 shows attempts to portray the visual experience of the trichromat, the red–green blind dichromat, the yellow–blue blind dichromat and the monochromat.

Screening for colour-blindness can be done in several ways. The most common is the Ishihara Test. Circles of different hues and sizes are presented to the observer (Plate 5). The circles of similar hue are seen by normal observers as belonging together, so in Plate 5 the normal observer sees the number 74. However, the anomalous trichromat or red–green dichromat may read the number as 21. More precise measures can be obtained by finding the proportion of, say, red and green required to match a yellow in an optical device called an anomaloscope. Here again, protanopes and deuteranopes can be distinguished from the normal and from each other.

An individual with normal colour-vision, when asked to match a white light to a spectral colour, will find this impossible. This is not true of a protanope or a deuteranope. Light of wavelength 490 nanometres[1] (nm) will be seen as a blue by a trichromat, but will be matched to a white by a protanope or a deuteranope. This matching to white is called the 'neutral point'. According to Walls and Matthews (1952), there may be some variation in the neutral point between these two defects. The neutral point is also found to be slightly dependent upon the temperature of the white light used for comparison. Tritanopes also have a neutral point, but this is at a different place (Wright, 1952) and is to be found somewhere in the region a trichromat would see as yellow.

Other differences exist between the normally colour-sighted and the colour-defective. Wavelength discrimination is very much poorer in the colour-blind and brightness of colours is also changed. Helmholtz argued that the red-blind person should see the red end of the spectrum darker than the normally-sighted person, which is indeed the case. Similarly, deuteranopes have less sensitivity to blue-green wavelengths. The totally colour-blind monochromats (who do not possess the necessary receptors) also find bright lights unpleasant and their visual acuity is low.

The colour defects mentioned above are not equally common. The most common are the red–green deficits. It has been found in many European countries that around 8 per cent of males have a certain degree of red–green colour confusion, but only 0·5 per cent of women. This is because the inheritance of certain forms of colour-blindness is mediated by a sex-linked recessive gene. Generally, women carry the disposition to colour-blindness, whereas men will exhibit the defect if given the necessary gene combination.

1. A nanometre is equal to 10^{-9} metres. A nanometre used to be called a millimicron (mμ).

The frequency of colour-defective people varies even within a given country. Vernon and Straker (1943) report that, in the UK, as one travels down a line from Aberdeen to Plymouth there is a progressive increase in the number of colour-defective males. Tests in non-Western cultures have all revealed smaller frequencies than in Western samples. Indeed, Pickford notes a total lack of colour-blindness on an island in the East Indies, which could be attributed to the fact that only non-colour-blind people learned to eat the right berries!

The two defects of tritanopia and monochromatism are very much rarer and nationwide searches have been conducted in the past in order to obtain an adequate sample for research.

A rare but most interesting form of defect is the person who is unilaterally colour-blind, i.e. colour-blind in only one eye. We have up to now considered cases where one person will have a different percept from another when viewing the same scene. Here, with the unilaterally colour-blind person, we have the opportunity to find out what the colour-blind really see by asking him to close one or the other of his eyes. Graham and Hsia (1958) asked a unilaterally colour-blind woman to make judgements about which colours looked the same with her deuteranomalous eye, as compared with her normal eye. This study showed that with her colour-blind eye all colours were matched with either a yellow or a blue.

Besides giving a fascinating insight into the experienced colour-vision of the colour-blind, these studies raise important theoretical issues. Without going into these in depth, one can speculate on the ability of the deuteranope to see yellow. It is often said that the normal trichromat sees yellow as a red–green mixture, but the deuteranope who has a weakened sensitivity to green has no problem with yellow. The explanation of how we see colours is obviously not simple.

Graham, Hsia and Stephen (1963) investigated a patient who was unilaterally tritanopic because of a vascular accident. The major difference between inherited and acquired colour-defects is the possibility of recovery or change in the acquired colour-defect. Graham *et al*. report the following:

The experiment shows that in the normal eye colours have the usual characteristics, orange for 600–17 mμ; red at 640 mμ and 680 mμ. In the other eye, a wavelength of 600 mμ appeared very much desaturated, almost colourless but tinged with a golden hue or a golden pink near 620 mμ, continuing thereafter to give a golden pink and reddish through 680 mμ.

Below the neutral point all blues were matched by one wavelength in the defective eye. Thus the acquired deficit is very similar to a genetic tritanopia. The fact that both defective and normal colour-vision can appear in one person allows us more confidence in the belief that the perceptual world of a colour-defective is different from the normal. This knowledge is always uncertain as we must, of course, rely on the introspective report of the observer, yet it is much easier to accept the differences in the report of a person unilaterally colour-blind than to compare the reports of two different people.

This may also apply to the case of hysterical colour-blindness reported by Pickford (1949). Here, the colour-blindness differed according to the changed personality-state of the patient. The patient in his normal state was a deuteranope. However, accurate testing with an anomaloscope showed him to be completely colour-blind during his illness. It was suggested that the colour-blindness resulted from the fear of being strangled with his mother's coloured scarf, and also from identification with his father who, as a coal miner, could see little or no colour in the semi-darkness underground!

There can be other causes of changes in colour-vision. Lesions, especially at the back of the head, may be associated with some impairment in the identification of colours. In spectral phenomena associated with migraine, common shapes such as stars, triangles and circles occur. Critchley (1965) reports one of his patients (blind from a cataract) as complaining so bitterly of incessant golden rain pouring down before her sightless gaze that she underwent two leucotomies in a vain quest for relief. These hallucinatory phenomena differ from drug-induced states not only in kind, but also in that they are long-lasting, even permanent; but they resemble them in that they may bear little or no relation to any external stimulus.

Some patients report their visual experience to be as if a coloured filter had been placed before their eyes. One such patient, who experienced the effect of a yellow filter, was unable to distinguish the potato, pickle and mustard on his plate. However, according to Critchley, the alert patient can resolve many of such difficulties through his knowledge of the known colour of an object.

One effect on colour-perception due to cerebral disease is that of illusory visual spread. In this the colour of a perceived object can extend far beyond the edges of an object. For example, the design of a dress may appear to spread over the arms and face of the person wearing it. Also, the various colours in the scene may appear at different distances from the patient and he may feel that he could dip his fingers into a series of coloured layers. In such cases the colours usually take on a different character and the patient may be put to great difficulties in trying to describe them.

In general, we have seen a deficit phenomenon with respect to changes in colour-vision: that is to say, there is an inability to see what the normally colour-sighted individual sees. There are, however, as we have seen, examples in which colour anomalies have been of the additive type, in which a patient sees something extra. These can be of the migraine spectral type or the filter type. The latter is of more relevance here, since the colour of an object is affected by the wavelength reflected from that object, and it is perceived as a combination of this and of the filter colour; therefore the external stimulus plays an important role.

People without obvious colour-defects can choose relatively different colours (wavelengths) when asked to match a wavelength to a word name. Requests to different observers to point out the spectrum stimulus that corresponds to a psychologically unique colour, whether it be red, yellow, green or blue, meet with different answers.

TABLE 1.The results of early experiments to find the wavelengths corresponding to pure yellow, green and blue (after Dimmick and Hubbard, 1939).

| | | Wavelength in nanometres | | |
Experimenter	Date	Yellow	Green	Blue
Bezold	1874	578	532	468
Donders	1884	582	535	485
Hess	1888	575	495	471
Rood	1890	581	527	473
Hering	1898	577	505	470
Voeste	1898	577	505	470
von Kries	1907	574	503	
Westphal	1909	574	506	479
Dreher	1911	575	509	477
Ridgway	1912	577	520	473
Goldytsch	1916			468
Bradley	1920	579	514	469
Goldmann	1922	568	504	468
Priest	1926	583	515	475
Bruckner	1927	578	498	471
Schubert	1928	574	500	467
Purdy	1931	571	506	474
Ornstein, Eymers and Vermeulen	1934	578	528	487
Verbeek and Bazen	1935	580	530	
Schouten	1935	576	512	472
Dimmick and Hubbard	1939	582	515	475

Table 1 shows the results of some early experiments in asking observers to perform this task. It can be seen that psychologically pure yellow can mean anything from 571–583 nm. On such a wide range as this, it is very unlikely that yellow would be the first description of all these wavelengths by any single observer. Indeed, Arnheim (1954) quoting Hiler (1946) reports that the colour corresponding to 600 nm has been described variously as orange chrome, golden poppy, spectrum orange, bitter-sweet orange, oriental red, saturn red, cadmium red-orange or red-orange. In all probability, though, these represent nothing more than differences between observers in naming colours rather than any perceptual difference.

The colour perceived in any circumstance will depend on many factors besides the assumed normal colour-vision of the observer. The experimental conditions, the lightness (tone) and the saturation of the stimulus will all affect the name given to any colour. But even under the same conditions of testing, what one observer would call a pure yellow or green will differ from another observer's account. This is one of the reasons why colour-blindness testing does not involve naming colours. It would be pointless, for example, to assess the discrimination of the Zuni Indians in the yellow-orange colour region by asking them to name colours. These people use the same names for all colours in this range. Indeed, there are differences in colour terminology in many other languages, such as those in West Africa which have no clearly defined word for blue.

However, the fact that a language does not have a word for a colour does not necessarily imply that the perception for that colour is deficient. This can only be tested experimentally. Attempts to do this have shown that lack of a colour name affects the memory of a colour rather than its perception. Thus Brown and Lenneberg (1954) found that if a Zuni observer was given a task to match a colour that he had seen only seven seconds previously, there was no deficiency in his ability to do so, any more than there would be if it were in front of him. Lantz and Stefflre (1964) argue that this inability to find a relationship between the ease of coding (to use the terminology of Brown and Lenneberg) and recognition after seven seconds is due to the method of determining codability. Lantz suggests using 'communication accuracy', which is how well someone can identify a colour by the name someone else uses. This did produce an effect of codability even at five seconds. But it is still very doubtful that any such relationship would hold if the colours were actually in front of the observer. Codability may affect the recognition of colours over long periods but this is surely not a perceptual ability. It is not impossible that linguistic codability does affect the way one looks at an object, since language can be used to point out aspects of the stimulus, but this is a different matter from that considered in the experiment of Brown and Lenneberg.

We have said that cultural differences in colour-naming would not lead us to suspect that response differences between cultures are perceptually based, but there is even evidence for a similarity in the perceptual—memorial ability of cultures with different language structures. This comes from an experiment by Heider and Olivier (1972) with the Dani of New Guinea, whose language has a vastly different colour-naming structure from English. It was nevertheless found that the memory-imagery for colours was very similar to that of English-speakers, despite the lack of colour names in Dani.

People with colour-defects will, of course, label colours differently from others. It is tempting, on this basis alone, to say that they are seeing the colours differently. Pickford (1951, 1964) comments on some of these colour appearances. A painter found on testing to be deuteranomolous called sky blue 'lilac' and, when asked to point out the red in his painting, indicated a purple area. While a normal person may have difficulty in talking about a reddish-green, the artist in question, Donald Purdy, found no difficulty in doing so. The colour in question would be seen as brownish to the normal eye. Purdy had a preference for blueish-green and brownish colours and this seems to have been determined by his colour-defect. But he could compensate for his deficiency and use bold colours for the purpose of selling his paintings.

Trevor-Roper (1959, 1970) has discussed the paintings of many artists and suggested from their choice of colours that some had defective vision. Constable, for example, may have been a protanope in view of the autumnal tints which dominate some of his paintings and the blueish-green which is to the fore in others. He also points out that Strebel claimed that Leger was colour-blind, because of the blue and yellow colours which dominate his work, and later proved himself correct by testing Leger. Trevor-Roper also suggests that the natural increase with age of the yellow pigment in the retina causes a lack of blue discrimination and may thus have been the cause of the change in colour-range of the later paintings of Rouault, where the 'claret red gives way to a profusion of yellow-green'.

One of the most remarkable by-products of defective colour-vision was 'Stroudley's Improved Engine Green'. This was an unusual locomotive paint colour adopted on the Highland Railway and on the London, Brighton and South Coast Railway by William Stroudley when he was locomotive superintendent of those companies. It was, in fact, a golden ochre colour, yet it has been suggested that Stroudley actually thought the yellow engines were true green.

Disturbances of shape and space

Disturbances of shape can occur with brain damage, especially to the occipital lobes (the visual cortex). Contours may lack stability, and with prolonged viewing be even more unstable. Thus, unlike the normal person when shown a shape, the longer the patient has to view and organise his percept the more unstable it becomes. In certain circumstances the image can be very long-lasting. Critchley (1951) quotes a rare case of this visual perseveration caused by brain damage: after someone had walked past the foot of a patient's bed from left to right, she had, a moment or two later, the impression that the same person walked past again in the same direction. With brain damage, the stability of stationary objects can also be suspect. Static objects may appear to move, and moving objects to move at the wrong speed.

Objects at times can appear smaller, larger or further away than normal. These deficits can be psychological or physical in origin. If, in a given area of the retina, a smaller number of cones and rods receives the image of an object, that object will appear smaller when viewed with that eye. The opposite occurs if the object stimulates more receptors than normal. These same effects can also result from disorders of accommodation. Normally it is necessary to make an accommodative effort to see objects close at hand. If for some reason this is not necessary, an object can be seen as being further away than it really is, thereby producing an increase in perceived size. The opposite may occur with a paralysis of accommodation.

If there is an optical imbalance of some sort, this can cause distortion in the perceived size, shape and distance of objects in the left or right half of the visual field. This does not occur very commonly but is easy to produce artificially by placing an appropriate prism in front of the eye. Bartley (1972) quotes a case of a journalist who, because of some defect, saw horizontal surfaces as tilted. In fact, he used a book under one side of his typewriter to make it appear level. Bartley stresses that in the clinical situation such visual abnormalities are always accompanied by other non-visual maladjustments such as headache and nausea.

Similar visual defects can also occur with lesions in the occipital cortex. Depending on the lesion involved, only parts of the visual field may be affected. A patient may see one part of a face as 'blown up' and another part as very small. These effects are generally accompanied by other visual changes and are one of the most common results of injury to the posterior parts of the brain. They also occur when associated with lesions in other areas and can arise from psychological conditions. Chapman (1966) reports a patient who was diagnosed as schizophrenic as saying:

I was sitting listening to another person and suddenly the other person became smaller, and then larger, and then he seemed to get smaller again. He did not become a complete miniature. Then today with another person I felt he was getting taller and taller. There is a brightness and clarity of outline of things around me. Last week I was with a girl and suddenly she seemed to get bigger and bigger like a monster coming nearer and nearer.

In a similar vein, Arieti (1962) notes that in schizophrenia patients report that only part of a person, such as a nose or an arm, will be perceived, or, similarly, only part of an object, such as the keyhole in a door. As the schizophrenic condition worsens the fragments seem to get smaller and become difficult to describe.

Heaton (1968) notes similar changes occurring in a woman of 21 suffering from recurrent depression, who said:

When I feel ill people seem big and near to me, at the same time I feel I am outside of myself and not sure what is real. The world seems to be just where I stand and everything is closed in. When I feel better, things seem further away and a more manageable size.

Patients sometimes report the space between objects as being more important than the objects themselves. Heaton (1967) makes a distinction between depth and distance perception. He says that differences between objects are seldom altered in psychological illness, whereas changes in the depth or solidity of the world often occur. This goes along with the impression of a flat, unreal world. The fact that the world appears flat may also explain the reduction in size and distance of objects found by Weckowicz (1957) in schizophrenia.

However, these findings have been disputed. Blumenthal and Meltzoff (1967) suggest that schizophrenics are also more inaccurate in their estimates of the distance apart of two objects. This again may not be related to a perceptual deficit if Stannard *et al.* (1966) are right when they maintain that the poor performance results from using a misplaced guessing strategy. Stannard *et al.* found that if their schizophrenic patients were given feedback on their judgements they became more accurate. Hamilton (1972) has also attempted to resolve the conflicting results by suggesting that estimates for size and distance may be connected to the cognitive strategies of the particular observer.

Consideration of these difficulties of interpretation brings us back to theoretical problems, since we justifiably wish to find some order in these differences in visual perception: it would seem too unreasonable if everybody perceived the world in a completely different way. Therefore in the next section we will discuss attempts to differentiate people by their reactions to visual stimuli.

Classification by reaction to visual stimuli

If one is in agreement with Allport (1937) when he says that perceptual processes are 'too trivial to tap the developed volitional functions of personality' then the endeavour to classify people according to their reactions to visual stimuli must be misplaced. However, many investigators have felt that attempts to specify differences in perception by relating them to some larger factor must be worthwhile. Indeed, this is an area full, one might even say littered, with findings.

Eysenck, Granger and Brengelmann (1957) undertook to find out how normal, neurotic and psychotic observers performed in a wide variety of perceptual tasks. If there was any consistent pattern in the results from these different groups, then on those tasks where there were significant

differences they were generally in the direction of the neurotic and psychotic observers not performing as well as the normal. Normal observers
had better night vision (as measured by the rate of dark adaptation), better
visual acuity and longer visual after-images. Normal observers also saw
the Muller-Lyer Illusion more readily and adapted more easily to the distortion produced by displacing spectacles.

A study of Herrington and Claridge (1965), however, suggests that
psychotics have longer spiral after-effects than normals. This may be due
to the generally longer reaction times of psychotic patients which would
make them take longer to report that the after-effect had ceased. Holland
(1965) gives a detailed account of the use of the spiral after-effect as a
clinical tool. Inability to see the after-effect would normally be taken to
indicate brain damage, but one should bear in mind the finding of
Efstathiou and Morant (1966) that fixation of the centre of the spiral is
very important in establishing the illusion. If observers were instructed to
fixate the periphery of the spiral then a group of normal observers could be
made to return scores which would usually indicate brain damage. Also,
Morant and Efstathiou (1966) ask why the waterfall illusion fails to discriminate between the normal and the brain-damaged observer unless it is
because there is no difficulty in fixating with the waterfall illusion.

There are other findings which, if not contradictory, seem hard to relate.
For example, Zahn et al. (1963) report that schizophrenics do not habi-
tuate easily to visual stimuli, but Hakerem et al. (1964) report that schizophrenics take a comparatively short time to reach maximum pupillary
contraction when exposed to a light flash.

It may be that there is some pattern into which all such findings can be
fitted, or that some such pattern will be worked out, but at the moment it
does not seem likely. Indeed, there are methodological reasons for doubting the worth of some of the findings that have been reported. Firstly,
most research in this area has not distinguished the perceptual sensitivity
of an observer apart from the way he approaches the perceptual task. How,
for example, in a visual threshold task, does one distinguish a cautious
observer reluctant to commit himself from one who has a poor visual
sensitivity and cannot see the target? In the past this has not been easy to
do, though the introduction of a signal-detection procedure which
distinguishes perceptual sensitivity from response factors would allow this
necessary distinction to be made (see Frith, 1973). Secondly, the categorisation of the psychotic patient as, say, schizophrenic, may leave room
for much doubt. There may, however, be more success with divisions of
the non-psychotic personality.

The categorisation of individuals into different personality types is a
common obsession amongst psychologists. The validity of the classification has, however, often been doubted. Confirmation of the classification
has sometimes been attempted by dividing groups of observers according

to their reactions to illusions and other perceptual phenomena. This has not always been crucial to the theory but, as with Eysenck, has been used for further verification of ideas based on other research. Eysenck divides people into the more outward going (extravert) and more withdrawn (introvert). It is suggested that the extraversion–introversion dimension is associated with cortical inhibition or satiation and that cortical satiation will increase more quickly and to a greater extent with extraverts. Introverts would therefore, in general, have a higher cortical arousal (Eysenck 1963), and might be able to make a finer discrimination than extraverts. It was found by McLaughlin and Eysenck (1966) that this was the case for visual masking. When the interstimulus interval was decreased it was extraverts who first reported the disappearance of the earlier stimulus.

It is possible that the difference between extraverts and introverts might also be noted in their reaction to the figural after-effect (page 17). The figural after-effect was considered by Köhler and Wallach (1944) to be caused by some kind of satiation process. Eysenck has suggested that this after-effect should be greater in extraverts, but research has not always supported this view. Clinical applications of the figural after-effect also seem to be diminishing and Eysenck (1967) points out the difficulties with the figural after-effect even from his theoretical standpoint.

Eysenck (1967) has also hypothesised that extraverts would have a shorter spiral after-effect than introverts. One interesting study which verified this is due to Claridge and Herrington (1963). The duration of the spiral after-effect was measured not by the direct verbal response but by brain-wave, i.e. electro-encephalographic (EEG) recordings. While paying attention to an object, the alpha rhythm (8–13 cycles/sec) of the brain declines. Alpha rhythm is abundant with the eyes closed. If the observer is asked to close his eyes when the spiral stops rotating, the time taken before the alpha rhythm returns can be used as a measure of the spiral after-effect. A correlation was found between this measure and the verbal report of the duration of the after-effect.

It should be borne in mind that though the EEG measure seems to be more objective, at some point the confirmation of its worth comes from the subjective report. A group of obsessional (introverted) patients had much greater spiral after-effects as measured by the EEG than did a group of psychopath (extraverted) patients. In fact, there was no overlap between the scores of the two groups. The subjective report differentiated between other groups of introverts and extraverts though the EEG measures, while showing the same tendencies, did not reach statistical significance.

However, the relationship between extraversion and the spiral after-effect has not always been found and there have been contradictory studies. Levy and Lang (1966) say that the spiral after-effect is due to a complex interaction between extraversion, neuroticism and impulsiveness.

Claridge (1967), too, suggests that the spiral after-effect may be connected to both extraversion and neuroticism, believing, unlike Eysenck, that these dimensions are not independent. Introversion—extraversion is linked by Eysenck to the neurotic criterion groups of dysthymics (anxiety, reactive depression and obsessional patients) and to hysterico-psychopathic disorders. Claridge argues that, while dysthymics have longer spiral after-effects than hysterics, this finding cannot reliably be extrapolated to normal observers rated on the introversion—extraversion dimension. Therefore, even though the movement after-effects have produced interesting individual differences it is still necessary to be cautious in their use for the purpose of classification.

Another and different usage of visual phenomena in differentiating between personalities comes from the Swedish investigators Andersson, Nilsson, Ruuth and Smith (1972). They regard the after-images and after-effects described in Chapter 1 as being of a special kind. To them, these visual after-effects are neither of the outside world nor entirely from within, but represent a border territory in which the personality can be uncovered. Their approach to the study of after-effects is not to give one trial or to take the average of a set of readings but to consider the change in the after-effect which occurs with repeated trials.

The work of Holland (1965) would suggest that with repeated trials there is a reduction in the duration of the spiral after-effect. Andersson *et al.* strongly deny that this is always the case and say that the change which takes place demonstrates the adaptive strategy applied by the observer to the situation. This departure of studying the observer's responses over some time and looking for changes is one that is certainly worth repeating in other contexts. They found that, at the end of a series of after-images formed from looking at a red object, anxiety-prone observers saw larger and/or darker after-images than at the beginning of the series. Anxiety-prone observers also had longer-lasting spiral after-effects. Depressives, on the other hand, tended to have after-effects of decreased duration. It is difficult to believe, though, that all of Holland's observers were as severely depressed as those in the studies reported by Andersson *et al.*

Compulsives saw after-images as greener than did others. Though the after-image produced from fixating red is green, if it is desaturated it can often be described as a blue-green. The fact that the experiment was carried out in dim blue illumination may also account for the large number of blue after-images reported. And compulsives, perhaps because they took the task seriously, were more willing to extricate the after-image from the surrounding illumination—but not because they wanted to 'avoid anxiety-laden (black) images by suppressing the blue color component'.

In fact, this alternative explanation for their findings relates to a basic concept in the approach of Andersson *et al.* which regards the adaptation by the observer as a strategy in which reality forces from outside the person are in conflict with subjective forces, the changes which take place in a series of visual after-effects being a by-product of this struggle. It is therefore suggested that these changes can be used to monitor cognitive development, mental illness and personality change—indeed, even to predict the likelihood of being involved in a car accident. They did in fact find that individuals with short after-effects were prone to traffic accidents. But we have seen that extraverts generally experience shorter after-effects and, since there is some sort of correlation between extraversion and being involved in traffic accidents, the theory of Andersson *et al.* may not be necessary to explain these findings.

It is, of course, consistency in the observer's way of processing the visual world that is being looked for when perceptual phenomena are investigated with reference to a personality dimension. It is not very interesting to know that extraverts are bad at one task and good at a comparable one. Because of this, the dichotomy of introversion—extraversion has been applied to many perceptual tasks, and to investigating basic detection abilities such as the ease of detection of a flash of light in difficult conditions. A real-life parallel to the latter might be the detecting of an aeroplane 'blip' on a radar screen which involves a tedious search and the possibility of other distractions. Extraverts and introverts are seen to differ in their performance on this task, and this has been related to their level of arousal. Perhaps extraverts get bored with the task and their performance declines as the period of watching continues. Certainly, background noise while an extravert is watching out for signals seems to help his performance.

It has been demonstrated that if anxiety-provoking words are shown briefly to observers, neurotic introverts see them most quickly. This result suggests the likelihood of individuals being differentially primed to receive incoming stimulation. This is an important finding in that introverts are considered chronically aroused and that their priming is ever-present. This is different from the day-to-day, situation-to-situation changes which may produce selective attention in the input of every observer.

Thouless (1932), and Tolman and Brunswik (1935), found that when different people were asked to judge the size or shape of an object they did this in different ways. They found two main approaches. The first of these they called the 'synthetic' attitude, which pays attention to the actual object and therefore achieves a higher accuracy in the judgement. Accuracy in this situation means, for example, that a person 6 ft high is judged still to appear 6 ft high at whatever distance he is from the observer. The second judgemental approach was called the 'analytic' attitude, which allows perception to be corrected by thought processes. This way of looking at an object takes account of the fact that the size of the image on the retina changes with the distance of the object. Why paying attention to the retinal size of an object when asked to judge its size should be called 'analytic' is a little mysterious: it is linked, no doubt, with making a judgement of how something really is received by the eye as opposed to how it 'looks'. Certainly it will lead to a more inaccurate response. Weber (1939) and Singer (1952) found that extraverted people more easily adopted the 'synthetic' attitude and gave more accurate judgements. This was especially the case if the size or shape judgement concerned an object such as a face rather than a more meaningless object such as a square. However, it is quite easy to make any observer take up the 'analytic' viewpoint if the instructions are biased in that way. Indeed, it is likely that these judgemental differences arise from the way different people interpret instructions.

Cognitive structure and the reaction to visual stimuli

The division of people into two basic types occurs over and over again in personality theory. Klein (1970) provides a review of some of these dichotomies. The dichotomies that he would wish to consider are those which arise from differences in cognitive structure. They represent differences between individuals not merely in the manner in which they handle and process perceptual information, but in the methods they adopt to interpret the world. These theories are based on a comprehensive theory of cognitive control which is too detailed to be discussed here except insofar as it relates to perception. The first of these dichotomies that will be considered is that of 'levellers' versus 'sharpeners'.

Levellers are those people who are unresponsive to change and whose personality description is given as 'self-inwardness'. They retreat from objects, avoid situations requiring active manipulation, exaggerate their needs for nurture and denigrate themselves. Sharpeners, on the other hand, generally find competition pleasant and are ambitious even aggressive in pushing themselves forward. This has been described by Klein as 'self-outwardness'.

What perceptual tasks differentiate levellers and sharpeners? In fact, very few: it seems that if given a picture puzzle which contains a hidden figure (Fig. 25) levellers find it comparatively hard to find. However, this inability to find a hidden figure also correlates with other personality variables. It is also one of the cornerstones of field-dependence theory, which will be discussed later. The relationship between field-dependence and self-inwardness is not clear.

The tonal contrast within a figure is one of its crucial properties that determine which aspects are given most attention. It can therefore cause the black part of a figure to look even blacker. Since sharpeners are said to accentuate differences, it might be predicted that this effect will be stronger for them as compared to the levellers, who tend to diminish differences. This prediction has been confirmed.

Another division based on cognitive structure is that between people tolerant and intolerant of unrealistic experiences. This has been related to the phenomenon of apparent movement (page 34). The factors which control apparent movement are many; Korte's Laws were discussed in the previous chapter. Whether or not any motion is seen depends on the brightness of the stimuli, the distance between the stimuli and so on. What was not mentioned previously was the nature of the stimuli, as only simple light sources were considered. If the two light sources illuminate similar objects, such as the same person running, it is relatively easy to see movement. However, if the two light sources show incompatible objects, e.g. a cat and a dog, then there are definite individual differences in the ease with which apparent movement is seen. This can be recorded as a tolerance or intolerance of an unrealistic experience, since normally a cat will not change into a dog. This personality dimension is related to performance in other tasks, both perceptual and non-perceptual. Basically, those individuals who resist the apparent motion are those who find any change from the *status quo* unpleasant. Because of their reactions in the Rorschach Ink-Blot Test (Plate 2) they have been labelled 'form-bound'. The other type of observer who sees apparent motion readily, even if the objects moving are incompatible, is labelled 'form-labile'.

Attempts to divide people according to their ways of perceiving have often been too ambitious. A correlation has been found between some perceptual phenomenon and some often ill-defined personality concept, and too much has been made of it. For example, it has been suggested that a person who is intolerant of an unrealistic experience may also be intolerant of ambiguous situations in general. Frenkel-Brunswik (1949) put forward this theory after finding that there was a class of person who resisted the reversals of the Necker Cube (page 146). However, she expressed the view that caution should be displayed in assuming the generality of the construct. Since that time, intolerance of ambiguity has become associated with the concept of the authoritarian personality and has been held to be a determining factor in a host of interpersonal and political situations. But Kenny and Ginsberg (1958) could not find any evidence for this generalised trait when they investigated a collection of these supposed interrelated variables. In fact, only seven of the sixty-six correlations between measures of tolerance to ambiguity were found to be significant, and two of these in the opposite direction to that predicted from the construct.

It is not enough to find some isolated correlation. Klein sums this up well when he says: 'In itself the correlation offers no information about the *perceptual* principles that account for variations in [perception]... One might as well correlate moonbeams with cobwebs.' To make sense, any findings must be incorporated into a larger framework, and this has been found difficult to do.

It is also worthwhile to consider the nature of the dichotomies which have been proposed. Extraverts and introverts represent only the two extremes of a continuum: there are not just two types of people, but a range of personalities with the extremely withdrawn at one end and extremely outward-going at the other. Dichotomies such as that of levellers and sharpeners, according to Klein, need not necessarily even lie on a continuum. Also, the dichotomies proposed by different workers do not seem to be completely distinct; however, it cannot be the function of this work to unravel them. As another warning on any proposed relationship between personality and perception, it might be mentioned that the stability which seems necessarily inherent in these classifications may in fact not be so. We have mentioned that observers can take up either the 'analytic' or the 'synthetic' mode of perceiving. Perhaps also people can be introverted or extraverted according to the situation.

All incoming stimulation is received by the observer who tries to make 'sense' of the environment. It is possible in certain circumstances for an observer to receive information from different sense modalities which are in some way contradictory. When the conflict is between the knowledge of the world through vision and through another sense, an important personality characteristic seems to be defined by whether or not vision dominates.

A field-dependent person is dominated by the framework in which objects are placed. Dixon and Dixon (1966) relate an experience which illustrates a situation where conflicting cues arose. They found themselves

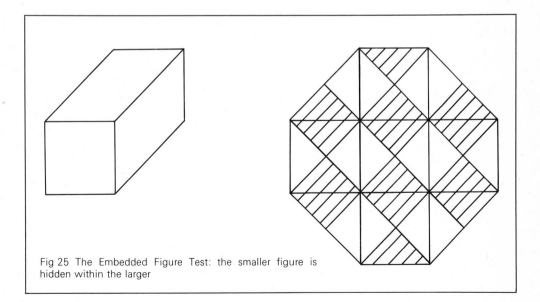

Fig 25 The Embedded Figure Test: the smaller figure is hidden within the larger

in the cabin of a deep-keeled yacht which, having grounded, began to list and fill with water. The phenomenal vertical was taken from alignment with the cabin walls rather than from gravity as shown by a hanging coat: the water, which stretched from floor level on one side of the cabin to deck level on the other, appeared to be slanting upwards even though the observers knew that it must in fact be horizontal. They found that vision dominated and moving about was difficult. A similar feeling can be obtained in the 'crazy house' at Battersea Funfair in London.

Differences have also been found between observers in the ease with which hidden figures are found (Fig. 25). When people are tested in this task, some take very much longer than others to find the small figure within the larger. This finding has been related to the personality variable of field-dependence. Witkin *et al.* (1954) found that the people who did well in this hidden-figure task also did better on two other perceptual tasks. In the first of these, called the Rod-and-Frame Test, the observer sits in a darkened room where all he can see is a luminous square frame surrounding a luminous rod. The frame, which can be tilted at any angle by the experimenter, is kept stationary while the rod is moved. The observer's task is to report when the rod is vertical. This can be done using the objective vertical as defined by the direction of gravity. It can also be done with reference to the field of vision and thus aligned to the sides of the square frame.

In the second task, called the Tilting-Room—Tilting-Chair Test, the observer sits in a small room on a specially designed movable chair. The room can be tilted into any position and the chair can be tilted in the same or the opposite direction. Sometimes the observer has to straighten the room to the vertical, sometimes the chair. The starting points of the chair and room are varied and do not necessarily correspond to the true gravitational vertical.

In these tests the observers who are quicker at finding the embedded figure (Fig. 25) are those who set the rod at the true vertical, ignoring the frame, and also those who set the chair at the true vertical, ignoring the room-tilt. This way of responding is termed 'field-independence', as opposed to that of the other type of person who exhibits 'field-dependence'. These seem to be very constant traits, since re-testing after three years produces a very high correlation with the original scores. But not all experimenters have found that the Embedded Figure Test correlates very well with the Rod-and-Frame Test. This is especially the case for other than Western cultures, as we shall see.

Field-independence is considered to be related to the outlook of the individual in analysing the world and is found to increase with age, especially between the ages of 10 and 13. The field-independent person is one who relies on his own internal feelings and convictions. He is active, socially independent and able to analyse his perceptual performance. On the other hand, the field-dependent person is affected greatly by social pressures. He is relatively passive, low in self-esteem and self-reliance and anxious about his aggressive and sexual impulses. The field-dependent person, according to Shrauger and Altrocchi (1964), characterises other people according to the external physical features, whereas the field-independent person makes judgements about other people according to their internal psychological make-up.

These personality differences were assessed from personality-testing devices, the validity of which has been questioned, but if significant correlations arise between the results of these tests and perceptual variables it is important to look for some explanation. It should be remembered, however, that field-dependence/independence is another continuum and that the world is not sharply divided into two camps. Indeed, Witkin reports that, in particular, field-independent people are able to adopt either the 'synthetic' or the 'analytic' approach to a judgemental task, whereas field-dependent people are generally able only to adopt the 'synthetic' attitude. This attitude of analysis by field-independent people is mirrored by their checking behaviour in the Embedded Figure Test: Boersma et al. (1969) found that the eye movements of field-independent people differed from those of the field-dependent. The former were searching more systematically for the hidden shape, looking from the figure they had to find to the complex figure, and back again.

One of the interesting findings from research by Witkin is that of a sex difference in the results of these perceptual tasks. In general, women were more often field-dependent than men. This was presumed to be related to the female's greater desire for social approval. This difference showed itself most clearly after puberty, when girls became less field-independent than they had been at an earlier age. It was found that field-independent boys were more popular amongst their contemporaries, whereas the reverse was true for field-independent girls. There would seem to be definite social pressures existing for the modification of the way in which we deal with the visual world. However, there is the possibility that boys are more familiar with geometric figures and this would help them in the Embedded Figure Test. Also, Sandström (1951) reported that women were less successful in pointing at a luminous spot in a darkened room, which suggests a more general perceptual disability than field-dependence.

We have seen that the isolation of personality differences through people's reactions to perceptual phenomena is not a simple matter. As a further warning it might be pointed out that the inability to find the target figure in an Embedded Figure Test has also been related to brain damage and schizophrenia. Teuber and Weinstein (1956) found that brain-damaged servicemen did significantly worse at this task than did a matched group of non-brain-damaged controls. Indeed, Embedded Figure Tests are sensitive to an enormous variety of brain lesions. Similarly Werner and

Strauss (1941) report that brain-damaged children found the background of such figures more distracting than did normal children. In this task, however, the children were asked to report what they saw rather than to find an object, and there is a distinct possibility of differences in interpretation of this task compared to the other. This may have affected what aspects of the figures were attended to. Interpretation of the instructions may also be the explanation of the result of Weckowicz (1960), who found that schizophrenic patients were much less successful than other psychiatric patients when asked to find figures embedded in others, while their perception of the isolated figures themselves was not impaired. In general, attentional processes are an important part of the differentiation between individuals in their reactions to visual stimuli, and these will therefore be considered in greater detail.

Attentional processes

The arousal state of the observer may affect his ability to recognise simple stimuli. This can differ according to the personality of the observer. Frith (1967) showed that increasing arousal made extraverts more sensitive in their judgement of whether a light was on steadily or rapidly flickering on and off. Increasing arousal did not have this effect with introverts. This was because, as we have already noted, introverts are deemed to have a normally high level of cortical arousal and any further increase makes them, if anything, over-aroused. This explanation of the finding exposes one of the difficulties with experimental work in this area, as it is complicated by the fact that poor performance can be caused by either a high or a low arousal level—one can be too nervous or half asleep and get the same result.

Schizophrenia can be looked on as a breakdown in the mechanisms controlling arousal which results in a state of chronic over-arousal. Neale and Cromwell (1969) have noted that schizophrenic patients prefer simple shapes, and attribute this to the patient's being in a state of over-arousal and therefore avoiding complex stimuli. Venables and Wing (1962) have made a clear distinction between paranoid and non-paranoid schizophrenic patients. It is only the non-paranoid who is in this highly-aroused state. We should therefore expect that the non-paranoid schizophrenic would need a shorter inter-stimulus interval between two flashes of light, before saying he saw only one, than does the paranoid schizophrenic. This is the case, and a further conclusion must be that if arousal is increased then sensitivity should not be improved for the non-paranoid patient. This is the same argument as was used above concerning introverts. Hieatt and Tong (1969) did not reliably find this relationship with increasing arousal on a visual task. It was found, however, for an auditory task. One of the difficulties that may account for this is that we do not have a 'pure'

measure of cortical arousal but have to rely on various incidental physiological indicators.

The discussion of physiological indications of arousal is not our primary
interest, since some degree of arousal is simply a prerequisite before
attention or, more interestingly, selective attention can operate. It is the
differences in selective attention that differentiate one observer from
another in a given situation that concern us. To some extent these can be
investigated on a physiological level by the study of the evoked potentials
from the cortex. It is found that presentation of a stimulus evokes, in the
first place, an electrical response in the appropriate part of the cortex: a light
evokes a response in the visual cortex. These evoked potentials differ
according to the ongoing activity of the observer. When the observer is
given a set of instructions about stimuli which are to be presented it is found
that the strength of the evoked potential to these stimuli increases compared with the response without such instructions (for a review of this work
see Tecce (1970)). Thus, the act of paying attention can have a measure-
able consequence on a physiological level, but complex attentional
processes are better studied in other ways.

A common word presented for a very short time will be found to be
recognised more quickly than an uncommon word. This difference
applies to everybody. Postman, Bruner and McGinnies (1948) suggested,
however, that individuals may have preferential recognition for certain
word areas that concern them. They categorised their observers on the
basis of the responses to the Allport-Vernon Scale of Values. According
to his responses to this questionnaire, an individual was assigned relative
scores on each of six value areas, these being theoretical, aesthetic,
economic, social, political and religious. It was suggested that someone
who scored highly in a given value area would be more sensitive to words
related to that area than to words in an area less highly valued by him.
Thus, an observer scoring highly in the religious area and lowly in the
economic area would have a lower recognition threshold for a word such
as 'sacred' than for a word such as 'income'. These expectations were
confirmed. A similar result was reported by McClelland and Liberman
(1949) for achievement and non-achievement motivated people. It was
also reported that, on a temporary basis, when observers were hungry or
thirsty, words related to food or drink were perceived more quickly.

This area of investigation is full of methodological pitfalls which make it
difficult to reach solid conclusions concerning the processes involved in
the supposed change in perception. Opponents of the notion of this
motivated perception try to find non-perceptual explanations to account
for experiments which purport to show that perception can be altered by
a motivational state.

One experiment to which it is difficult to give any alternative explanation
is that of Lambert, Solomon and Watson (1949). These investigators

studied children's judgement of the size of poker chips. This was done by equating an adjustable spot of light on a screen with the size of the poker chip. Two groups of children were found who could do this task equally well. One of the groups was then made to attach greater importance to the poker chips, by teaching the children to turn a crank eighteen times to produce a poker chip which could then be inserted into a slot to give some sweets. After a ten-day learning period it was found that the children who had gone through this association procedure over-estimated the size of the chip compared with the other group. On the eleventh day of the experiment, the children who had been rewarded found that the poker chips, when inserted into the slot, no longer produced any sweets. This new contingency was appreciated by the children, since now, when they were tested, there was no difference between the two groups in the judgement of the size of the poker chips. The perceptual judgement seemed to be directly related to the motivational state: as the motivation altered, so did the perception.

No doubt it is possible to find alternative explanations even for this experiment. Certainly, many people find themselves unable to accept this type of result. Perception, it is felt, is not at the mercy of our motives and generally seems to be very stable. Some workers in this field have tended to suggest that the internal state is a much more important determinant of perception than is the external stimulus, and there has been a natural reaction against this view.

Klein (1970), who believes in motived perception, does at least suggest that 'peripherally active motives have more impact on *pre*-perceptual events...and on various *reactions* to the percept than on perception itself'. The notion of peripheral motives raises the question of whether there is an unconscious process of selection and defence against the world, rather in the way Freud suggested. This controversy of unconscious perception does not concern us here and it is not possible to do justice to all viewpoints in this work. The reader is referred to Klein (1970), Dixon (1971) and Kline (1972) for further material on issues in this area which are still very much alive and in dispute.

There are reasons why many experimenters have been unwilling to accept the possibility of motivated perception. One of these is that it would appear to follow that the observer can 'see in order not to see', and this way of expressing the results obviously creates logical problems. 'Seeing in order not to see' is basically a semantic confusion regarding the word 'see', but it implies that there is a mechanism which selects the input after it has already been received. But if it has already been received, how can it be selected? This is not an insoluble problem if looked at from a different angle—that is, from the viewpoint of differences in the observers' attentional processes.

We are not all equally responsive to all stimuli. A sleeper will awake to his own name being called more readily than to someone else's; he seems in a sense to be attuned to that specific stimulus. In a similar way it may well be that specific visual stimuli are given priority. And, as we have seen, there may be permanent differences relating to the personality of the observer.

Since the publication of Broadbent's Filter Theory in 1958, many researchers in the field of perception have returned to the problem of attention and considered the mechanisms whereby we attend to only part of the total amount of stimulation we receive. As we cannot deal with all the messages that continually impinge upon our receptors, some selection mechanism must be postulated. It is a short step from this deduction to suppose that individuals differ with regard to their selection mechanism. Treisman (1969) has suggested a model for selective attention that could be used to explain why some people see something more readily or, indeed, less readily than other people. In her theory, all messages are first analysed in terms of their physical characteristics. One of these, for example, may be colour, as von Wright (1968) has shown to be possible. The input is then differentially 'attenuated' according to the task that the observer has set himself.

In the next processing stage, all the signals, including those that have been 'attenuated', are put into a pattern recogniser. This consists of 'dictionary units' with different and variable response thresholds. Output from these units varies with the strength of the incoming signals and with the state of readiness (threshold) of the dictionary unit. Now, words that are emotionally important to us can suffer one of two fates. If we want to be ready to jump when seeing them—such as our name on a list— then the dictionary unit corresponding to our name will be primed and have a low threshold. If, on the other hand, we want to repress a word, such as an obscene word or something which reminds us of an unpleasant experience, we can have the associated dictionary unit permanently depressed—i.e. it will have a high threshold. Of course, the stronger the signal, the harder it is to repress the word. There has been a great deal of speculation about this; others (Deutsch and Deutsch, 1963) have speculated on slightly different lines. Though a full explanation of motivated perception based on selective attention still remains to be worked out, it is certainly possible in theory.

The part of the visual field in focus at any given time is very small. Therefore, if in some way the observer's attention is drawn to a part of a display then, of course, his inspection pattern will differ from someone who looks at the display 'normally'. This selection or narrowing of attention occurs when an observer is concentrating on one task: it is well known that it then becomes harder for him to do another. Hockey (1970), for instance, found that observers performing a tracking task involving central vision did not readily notice lights going on in the periphery of vision if the central task became more difficult. The observers, in fact, did even better at the central task, but it was at the expense of the secondary.

Again, because of the fact that the part of the visual field in focus at any given time is only very small, it is necessary to make numerous eye movements when any complex or large scene is being viewed. These eye movements differ from individual to individual. Where the frontal lobes are damaged, the eye movements of such patients when they look at complex pictures are chaotic, when compared with the normal. Also, the fixation pattern is relatively unaltered whatever the patient is looking for in the picture. Eye movement patterns also differ between people with normal vision. An experienced painter looking at an abstract painting will inspect it in a different way from a non-painter. Similarly, a doctor will inspect an X-ray film in a manner different from that of a patient. Abercrombie (1960) gives an excellent account of how these changes can take place in the training of medical students, showing that the way of inspecting an object may be related to what the observer expects to see or to his knowledge of what to look for.

In the sense that has been mentioned before, individual differences in scanning could be considered as not being pertinent to individual differences in perception. This is because we should expect different percepts with different inputs. However, we shall see that they tell us much more than this.

Thomas (1968) reports experiments in which the eye movements of psychiatric patients were recorded when they looked at life-size photographs of themselves or of other people. The pattern of attention differed between patient and non-patient. The non-patient paid most attention to the face, whether the photograph was of himself or of another person. The patient tended to avoid looking at the faces. Also, the duration of the fixation varied greatly in the patient group, sometimes being very short and sometimes very long.

Attentional differences can be isolated in other ways. Hess (1965) reports that one night while he was lying in bed looking at a selection of 'strikingly beautiful' animal photographs, his wife commented on the size of his pupils. She suggested to him that this must be due to the bad light in the bedroom, but Hess thought this unlikely. He felt that interest in something might be reflected by a desire to see more of it and therefore cause a dilation of the pupils. Next morning he tested this hypothesis on his laboratory assistant. He included in a pile of landscape photographs a picture of a scantily-clad woman. Then Hess mixed up the pile of photographs so that he did not know which was which, and watched the pupils of his laboratory assistant as he viewed them. Hess found that it was easy from this observation alone to detect which of the photographs was the 'pin-up'. He also found that there was plenty of anecdotal evidence to link pupil dilation with interest. Magicians doing card tricks have been said to identify the card a person is thinking about by watching his pupils enlarge as he views the alternative cards. Chinese jade dealers were also reported to be aware of this phenomenon. They would watch the prospective buyer's eyes to find out for which piece he would pay a high price.

All this suggests that pupil size can be used to detect interest. Hess found that, prior to the Johnson–Goldwater contest for the US Presidency, about a third of his sample of university students and employees had a greater pupil dilation to Goldwater, even though all professed to be in favour of Johnson. This could be evidence for some love–hate relationship, though Hess suggests that in the liberal atmosphere of the university they could not reveal their true feelings. Hess would say that pupil dilation gives a truer indication of the interest of an observer than does verbal response. But it does not tell us why a person is interested. An interest in somebody does not necessarily imply liking that person.

It was also observed that pupils would constrict if confronted by something visually distressing, such as a crippled child. This was also found to be the case with abstract paintings, even in those people who, according to Hess, professed to like them. If a picture was extremely disturbing, for example, one of piles of corpses in a concentration camp, then there was an initial brief dilation followed by a constriction upon subsequent showings of the picture.

Fig 26 The different responses to the same pictures by female (black bars) and male (grey bars) observers (reprinted from 'Attitude and pupil size', Hess, E. H., *Scientific American*, April 1965)

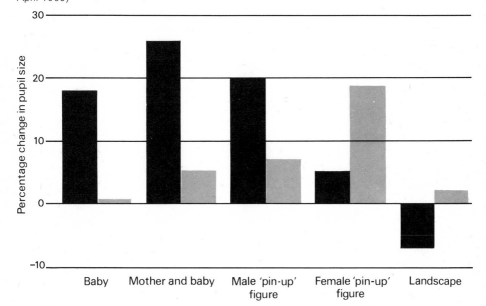

As we have said, individual interest may be reflected in pupil size. Hess showed that men and women differed with respect to what interested them. Figure 26 shows the change in pupil size for men and women as they were shown pictures of a baby, mother and baby, a male pin-up, a female pin-up and a landscape. The last showed little difference between the sexes, but for the others the differences were fairly predictable. The baby, mother and baby and male pin-up were all of more interest to women, and the female pin-up of more interest to men. Sex differences also affect the scanning pattern of an observer. It was found that the eyes of young men moved twice as quickly in examining pictures of young women as they did when looking at ink-blots. Hess (1965) found that the inspection pattern of Kroll's picture *Morning on the Cape* was different for male and female observers. The upper picture of Fig. 27 refers to a male observer and the lower to a female observer. The numbers represent the order of fixation and the symbols indicate attention. The oval symbols indicate normal attention, round symbols denote less attention than normal, while square symbols denote increased attention. Though these scanning patterns are those of individuals, they do reflect the general patterns of sex differences in looking at pictures not obviously sexual in content.

Gardner *et al.* (1959) considered that each individual has a basic cognitive style which can affect the way in which the visual input is processed. Individuals have different degrees of 'scanning control', which is the first stage of the scanning procedure and determines the 'extensiveness' of the search. A second stage of the scanning process, called 'field articulation', relates to selective attention to certain aspects of the visual field.

The tendency to deploy one's attention over a wide field, or to concentrate it rather narrowly on a small area, Klein (1954) refers to as being due to either constricted control or flexible control. People classified as having a cognitive style which was 'constricted' scan narrowly, whereas 'flexible' people would scan over a wide area. It is suggested that under conditions of stress wide scanners tend to increase their scanning behaviour, whereas narrow scanners tend to decrease their scanning behaviour.

A group of each of these types of people was made thirsty, by making them eat an unusual combination of foods. They ate a meal of 'spaghetti with a hot spicey sauce, heavily garlicked and salted; peanut butter on salted crackers; dried very salty herrings; and anchovies; topped off by a dessert of salted peanuts and dried chickpeas'. Requests for water were politely denied. Following the meal, they were shown a picture in the centre of which was a strawberry ice-cream soda. This was surrounded by various letters and numbers. The picture was flashed for one-tenth of a second, which is long enough to recognise some of the objects but not long enough to allow scanning movements. This was repeated twenty-five

Fig 27 The analysis of a picture by (above) a male and (below) a female observer. (Leon Kroll's *Morning on the Cape* is reprinted by courtesy of the Museum of Art, Carnegie Institute, Pittsburgh, USA)

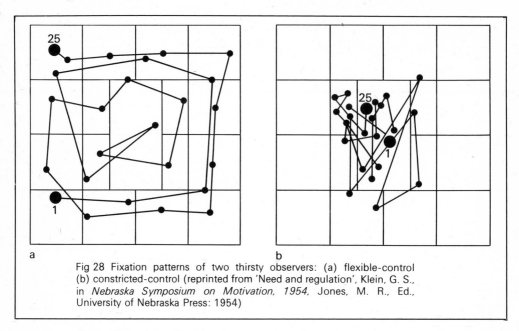

Fig 28 Fixation patterns of two thirsty observers: (a) flexible-control
(b) constricted-control (reprinted from 'Need and regulation', Klein, G. S.,
in *Nebraska Symposium on Motivation, 1954*, Jones, M. R., Ed.,
University of Nebraska Press: 1954)

times. The observers were requested to identify as many items as possible.
The part of the picture fixated was assessed roughly by the positions of the
objects identified. Figure 28 shows the pattern of fixation for a flexible-
control and a constricted-control observer. By following the line from one
large dot (1) to the other (25) it is possible to trace the course of the
fixation points for both observers. The tendency for the constricted-
control observer to fixate on the ice-cream is very marked. The flexible-
control observer was able to make use of the information in the periphery
of vision. In fact, the lack of fixation on the ice-cream soda by the flexible
group seems a little surprising. As Gardner *et al.* (1959) would wish to
generalise from such findings to other processing behaviour one must
bear in mind that the behaviour described above occurs under conditions
of need, and it does not necessarily follow that these attentional differences
will be shown if the need disappears.

It was found by Gardner and Long (1962) that narrow scanners over-
estimated the size of objects. Also the Horizontal–Vertical Illusion (Fig. 31)
was greater for narrow scanners. These differences in scanning behaviour
seemed to be fairly consistent, since they found high correlations with the
original scores when re-testing the same observers. All these findings are
very interesting, but such scanning differences have yet to be related to
other variables.

Even if we cannot relate styles in scanning behaviour to other personality
variables, there would still seem to be some reason to study the way people
look at objects. When observers are asked to assess which of two squares

is the larger, the total number of fixations used varies from person to person and remains fairly constant on re-testing a fortnight later. Buchsbaum *et al.* (1972) refer to this as a difference in 'scanning tempo'. However, they also make the point that such differences could be considered just individual eye-movement strategies for a size-estimation task. It would require tests on many more tasks for an individual style of scanning to be isolated.

Some such factor may have been isolated in the work of Luborsky *et al.* (1965). They investigated two groups of people who were diagnosed as different according to the defence mechanism adopted: repression or isolation. The defence of isolation was found to be associated with venturing the look all around a pictorial scene, including the background. Repressors fixated mostly on the central figure of a picture they were asked to inspect. One could speculate on the relationship of this dichotomy to others we have dealt with, such as that of levellers versus sharpeners. Luborsky *et al.* argue that the desire to take in information can be seen to be connected to the desire to accentuate differences between stimuli.

Attentional difference or disturbances have also been noted in senility, brain damage, schizophrenia and perhaps also in sub-normality. Are these scanning differences crucial to these disorders? Meldman (1970) considers that all psychiatric disorders can be classified as diseases of attention. Thus a neurotic condition could consist of hyper-attention, and in hypochondria or schizophrenia this could cause a focusing of the patient's attention onto a particular organ of the body. Meldman's work also rests to some extent on the finding that different groups of psychiatric patients view the Necker Cube (page 146) in different ways. As we shall see, there are clearly two ways of perceiving this two-dimensional drawing if we are to create a three-dimensional figure. Meldman (1965) says that anxiety and phobic states are associated with high rates of alternating perceptions (reversals) of the figure. Patients with these symptoms had more than 28 reversals in a two-minute period, while neurotic depressives had a very low reversal rate, in the order of 17 or less in a two-minute period.

In patients diagnosed as schizophrenic, further changes in these attentional processes have been reported. McGhie (1969) gives as an example the following:

I notice so much more about things and find myself looking at them for a long time. Not only the colour of things fascinates me but all sorts of little things like markings on the surface pick up my attention too.

It is possible that changes in the way the incoming information is processed may affect the way the visual world is perceived. McGhie goes so far as to say that 'perception would revert to the passive and involuntary assimilative process of early childhood'. This passive reception on the part of a schizophrenic differs greatly from the behaviour of the manic patient who, while he is as easily distracted, is only so because of a constant scanning of the environment for new stimulation.

It has been suggested that the schizophrenic patient has a lack of 'perceptual selectivity'. This relates to the field articulation of Gardner *et al.* (1959) and refers to the differences found in attending to complex perceptual fields. Chronic schizophrenics have been found to exhibit small amounts of scanning and poor field articulation. Silverman (1964), who has investigated attentional processes in schizophrenia, regards these deficits as part of the active process which prevents the ego being endangered. Silverman also distinguishes between types of schizophrenia: he says that paranoid schizophrenics differ markedly from the non-paranoid type described above. Differences between these two groups were also noted by Venables (see above) in that non-paranoid patients had a lower fusion threshold for paired light-flashes. This was suggested to indicate a state of cortical over-arousal. The paranoid patient is over-active in scanning his environment, though the extensive scanning becomes less as the illness becomes chronic. This may be due to problems involved in knowing what to select and reject, causing excessive scanning: a solution to this problem being found in the acute stage by only observing a few stimuli.

A word of caution concerning these studies is raised by McKinnon and Singer (1969) who point out that the medication many of the patients take can cause a reduction of the number of eye movements made. This is an important point, but it does not explain the fixation of unusual objects, as the medications would not affect what is fixated. Caution at the conceptual level is advised by Wachtel (1967) concerning the different ways in which the terms 'broad' and 'narrow' attention can be used. Research in this area also raises the general point that one should be careful not to confuse unitary disease names with unitary ways of dealing with the visual world. With such an undefined and global term as schizophrenia, one must be extremely careful not to be led to believe that there is a constant set of responses associated with the label.

Another attentional explanation has been put forward by Shakow (1966) to account for reactions of schizophrenics compared with those of non-patients: 'It is as if, in the scanning process which takes place before the response to a stimulus is made, the schizophrenic is unable to select out the material relevant for an optional response'. The differences between groups of schizophrenics is illustrated in the example, given by Shakow (1962), of the behaviour of different patients as they go through a wood:

If he is of the paranoid persuasion he sticks even more closely than the normal person to the path through the forest, examining each tree along the path, and sometimes even each tree's leaves with meticulous care... He is attracted...by any and all trees, and even the undergrowth and floor of the forest in a superficial flitting way.

These attentional differences do not directly reflect the unreality which is paramount in the perception of the schizophrenic. It has been suggested by certain psychiatrists that much of the work mentioned here misses the essential change in the perception of the schizophrenic. A transaction is said to exist between the self and the world, which, if the self is integrated (Laing, 1959) is seen as real and meaningful. On the other hand, if these transactions are delegated to an inner self which is in fact not the true self, the world is experienced as unreal. Thus things may appear strange and other people may not look the same as before. It may even appear to the schizophrenic that a curtain is between himself and the world. Such patients often complain to opticians that things are looking different from normal and they search for an explanation in terms of changed eyesight.

We have seen that these attentional differences are an important part of the way individuals react to the visual world. They may even help us to explain some of the cross-cultural differences in perception that we shall next consider.

Cross-cultural differences in perception

In some circumstances scanning patterns can differ markedly. This can also be seen between cultures. European figurative painting is generally composed with the observer at the focus of the scene. Chinese painting, on the other hand (Tyrwhill, 1960), places the observer at an angle and makes parallel lines open slightly as they recede, thus emphasising his central but also moving position. Chinese scroll paintings force the eyes in different directions as compared with a European painting. In fact, Tyrwhill stresses the necessity of looking at Eastern art in a different way. An Indian temple for example, should not be viewed from a fixed point like a painting but rather in a 'panoramic' way, moving the field of vision through an angle of 60–90 degrees. Moslem art, too, requires different ways of looking, with a concentration upon intricate detail.

These differences which people exhibit when looking at pictures are probably acquired through experience, just as our grandfathers had to learn to interpret the moving pictures of the cinema. This still applies in cultures to which the cinema is still new: audiences have been unable to understand where people disappear to when they walk off the edge of the screen.

The ease with which we discriminate between, say, the letters on this page, should not make us forget the often painful learning process that was necessary to promote this skill. Similar learning processes must go on with the Nuer of the Sudan who make minute discriminations between their cattle. The same also applies, no doubt, to Malinowski's (1923) report of the Trobriand Islanders' ability to select physiognomic likenesses—it being vitally important to them to know if one is like the relatives of one's father or one's mother.

Pictures need to be interpreted because they are a two-dimensional representation of what we normally see in three dimensions. This is illustrated by Deregowski (1972) who quotes from Robert Laws, a Scottish missionary, active in what is now Malawi at the end of the nineteenth century. Laws reported:

'Take a picture in black and white and the natives cannot see it. You may tell the natives, "This is a picture of an ox and a dog", and the people would look at it and look at you and that look says that they consider you are a liar. Perhaps you say again, "Yes, this is a picture of an ox and a dog". Well, perhaps they would tell you what they think this time. If there are a few boys about, you say, "This is really a picture of an ox. Look at the horn of the ox, and there is his tail!" and the boy will say: "Oh yes, and there is the dog's nose and eyes and ears".'

Recent experimentation has confirmed these anecdotal reports that pictures may be interpreted in different ways by people of different cultures. However, it is important not to overstate the case, since there is evidence that in some such circumstances pictures will be interpreted normally. Deregowski, Muldrow and Muldrow (1972) stress that this is the case if the picture clearly depicts material familiar to the observer. Generally speaking, we all have to learn what a picture means. Impressionist painting looked nothing more than meaningless areas of colour to most people at the turn of the century. Nowadays, many if not most observers can see organised shapes in these pictures. Without knowing how to look at a picture, it can be hard to see what it represents.

Deregowski, Muldrow and Muldrow suggest that, if looking at a picture is an unfamiliar act, the observer will try out hypotheses until he arrives at a solution. This is exemplified by a protocol taken from their work in which a large picture was shown by the experimenter *E* to a man *S* from a remote Ethiopian tribe.

E: (points to the picture) What do you see?
S: I'm looking closely. That is a tail. This is a foot. That is a leg joint. Those are horns.
E: What is the whole thing?
S: Wait. Slowly I am still looking. Let me look at it and I will tell you. In my country this is a water-buck.

This difficulty in interpretation applies not only today but was also experienced in the past. The art historian Gombrich (1960) quotes Boccaccio as saying that Giotto's paintings offer the viewer clear representations which can only be taken for reality. However, a painting such as Giotto's *Madonna and Child Enthroned with Saints and Angels* is for us now a little confusing. It was the convention of the time to denote the importance of a person by size. To our eyes, size differences denote distance difference. Therefore, the saints in the picture are behind the

Madonna according some distance 'cues' and are at the same distance, or even in front, according to others.

It is with the understanding of depth in a picture that most difficulty arises. Hudson (1967) has investigated the perception of depth in a picture by various cultures such as the Bantu in South Africa. One picture he showed his observers depicted the return of a black worker to his village. It showed him in front of a thatched round hut typical of the tribe. When describing the picture, some of the observers referred to a 'winged being, a devil, an angel, the temptation of Eve in Paradise'. Now, it so happens that the artist had drawn the picture so that the thatch of the hut could be perceived as feathers or wings coming from the figure's back and above his shoulders. This possible interpretation was not noticed by the experimenter or the artist. Similar difficulties were encountered in other pictures administered by Hudson (1960), and he interpreted them as being due to the observers' inability to recreate a three-dimensional reality out of a two-dimensional picture.

Hudson showed his observers the picture shown in Fig. 29. The hunter's spear can be seen to be aligned on either the elephant or the antelope. The task was to name the animal the hunter was aiming at. The results showed that white children at the beginning of primary school had a certain difficulty in perceiving in depth. More than a quarter said that the hunter was aiming at the elephant. However, by the end of primary school most white children gave answers which showed their ability to interpret

Fig 29 (Reprinted from 'Pictorial depth-perception
in sub-cultural groups in Africa',
Hudson, W., *Journal of Social Psychology*, 52,
1960)

the picture in three dimensions. It was found that the performance of even black graduate teachers was very poor, in fact not significantly different from that of black schoolchildren who, on the whole, did not interpret the picture in three dimensions. It was not simply the case that the black graduates were of a very low academic standard, since they had attended multi-racial universities and had sat examinations common to black and white students. These findings suggest a very profound difference in the interpretation of depth in pictures, but it should be pointed out that contrary findings were reported by Kilbride and Robbins (1968), who found that educated Baganda had no difficulty in interpreting a picture in three dimensions.

The interpretation of a picture is based on a way of looking at this kind of material. We have seen that not knowing how to look at a picture can produce very odd responses. Tomkins and Miner (1959) found that illiterate Bantu gave responses to a picture which were similar to those of white neurotics, but this was not because of any repression of the content of the picture but rather because they organised the picture (for probably very different reasons) to see in the same way. The fact that white labourers from an isolated and culturally restrictive rural community also saw pictures as flat probably means that habitual exposure to pictures is important if the interpretation is to be three-dimensional. The environment of these white labourers and also of the Bantu is in fact particularly lacking in pictures. A sample of Indian children tested at the same time was found to be equally ready to interpret a picture on a two-dimensional basis. In this case, the reason may be the nature of pictorial representation in Oriental art to which these children would have access.

Though it seems that experience with pictures is an important factor in interpreting them, it should be pointed out that a developmental study carried out by Hochberg and Brooks (1962) could not confirm this. They brought up their child for 19 months with as little picture material as possible, but at the first showing of a picture the child could recognise the objects in it. This is, of course, not conclusive evidence as only one child was involved, from whom it was not possible completely to exclude two-dimensional representations of objects.

Some Bantu graduates were, in fact, able to see Fig. 29 as an ambiguous figure which could be seen in two ways, either flat or in depth. This ambiguous aspect of perception is very interesting and will be returned to in a subsequent chapter. It also should be mentioned that there seemed to be an inability on the part of Bantu children to represent a natural event in three dimensions. An elephant drawn with all four legs spread out, as if it had been flattened from above, was seen by them to be a live elephant. Indeed one of the children commented that it must be a very ferocious animal because it was jumping wildly about. White children saw this picture as an elephant's skin.

Evelyn Waugh, in *Black Mischief,* satirises the attempt of a ruler to promote birth control by means of a poster campaign, the meaning of which was totally misconstrued. The posters were of the before/after variety: 'before', a man was shown living in poverty surrounded by children; after using contraceptives he was shown with fewer children in more comfortable surroundings. However, the 'before' picture was seen as the·more desirable. In the story everything worked out all right, as the contraceptives were interpreted as producing the children in the 'before' picture.

It would seem from the misinterpretation of posters in present-day Africa that Waugh may have been nearer the mark than he perhaps imagined. It has been found that animals represented on posters are often seen as different species. A cobra with hood extended was seen as a fish, and calves were seen as hyenas, dogs or even lions. The two halves of posters of the before/after variety were not seen as being connected. This was because the facial and other characteristics of the people were different in the second picture.

Another poster, showing the danger of throwing tools, was perceived by black workers as meaning that they should pay attention to their jobs. This was because the poster was seen two-dimensionally and the thrown hammer appeared to be lying on a window-sill; so the workers portrayed looking at the hammer were interpreted as gazing into space. When posters require interpretation over and above the perception, the confusion produced is even worse. This is the case with symbolic or allegorical posters: the skull and crossbones may be explicit to Western eyes but it is naïve to think that this should be so for other cultures.

However, a study by Deregowski and Serpell (1971) shows that three-dimensional models are seen in the same way by Zambians as by a European control group, as could be noted from their performance in a matching task. This concordance did not apply to photographs of the same objects, which were sorted by Zambian children in a different way from the three-dimensional objects. This reinforces the point that it is only the interpretation of photographs that is lacking, and that this is something that has to be acquired.

The basic types of eye movement made in reading are similar in languages as different as Arabic, Chinese, English and Hindu. However, in mature English readers there is a learned tendency to scan from left to right. This does not occur in Arabic where the normal scan is from right to left. Chinese and Japanese readers normally scan up and down. Tinker (1958) found that English written vertically in the Chinese manner was some 50 per cent slower to read than the normal left-to-right presentation. However, with practice this difference decreased.

It has been hypothesised that, as the scan is naturally from left to right in English, there will be a tendency to fixate on the right. It was found by

Mishkin and Forgays (1952) that for English readers words presented very quickly are better recognised in the right visual field. Orbach (1967) and Ghent–Braine (1968) studied Israelis to see if the opposite was true, since Hebrew reads from right to left: it was found to be so, but only for adult readers, again suggesting a learned pattern.

Visual illusions such as the Muller-Lyer would be of little or no interest to us here unless they were perceived differently by different cultures—it is not enough that they are seen wrongly by everybody. There is a certain degree of difference within cultures, but it has been suggested that between cultures large differences exist in the extent to which illusions are seen. Rivers, at the turn of the century, reported that both the Todas of Southern India and the inhabitants of the Torres Strait (Papuans) were less susceptible to the Horizontal–Vertical Illusion (Fig. 31). More rigorously, data have been collected by Segall, Campbell and Herskovitz (1963, 1966) concerning the differences in perceiving geometric illusions between more than fifteen cultures.

Segall, Campbell and Herskovitz were aware of the difficulties in cross-cultural research, in particular the ever-present and crucial problem of communication, especially when the experiment is conducted through an interpreter. Because of this doubt about the validity of the response, it was thought essential to consider only observers who were consistent in their response pattern. In this analysis, therefore, all non-consistent observers were discarded from the data. Of course, consistency of response does not necessarily imply understanding of the questions asked. In the Muller-Lyer Illusion it is quite easy to misinterpret what has to be made equal with what: if the overall length of the two parts of the figure is considered, then obviously one is larger than the other.

Segall et al. hoped to avoid possible misunderstanding by colouring the crucial vertical lines of the illusion red and the rest of the figures black. In an adjustable version of the illusion it is therefore possible to make the question clearer by asking the observer to equate the red sections for length. Despite all these precautions, it was still found that Caucasians saw the Muller-Lyer Illusion significantly more than all other cultures tested. With an American sample, a 20 per cent discrepancy was necessary for the two lines to be considered equal, as drawn in Fig. 30. On the other hand, the Horizontal–Vertical Illusion was seen to roughly the same extent by many groups, but was experienced to a greater extent by certain West and East African observers.

Rivers suggested that since these two illusions operate in different manners for Westerners and non-Westerners, they had a different causation. The Horizontal–Vertical Illusion, he thought, was based upon physiological differences, and the Muller-Lyer upon psychological. Segall et al. consider that a learning (experiential) explanation could better explain both of these illusions. It is suggested that it is possible to interpret these

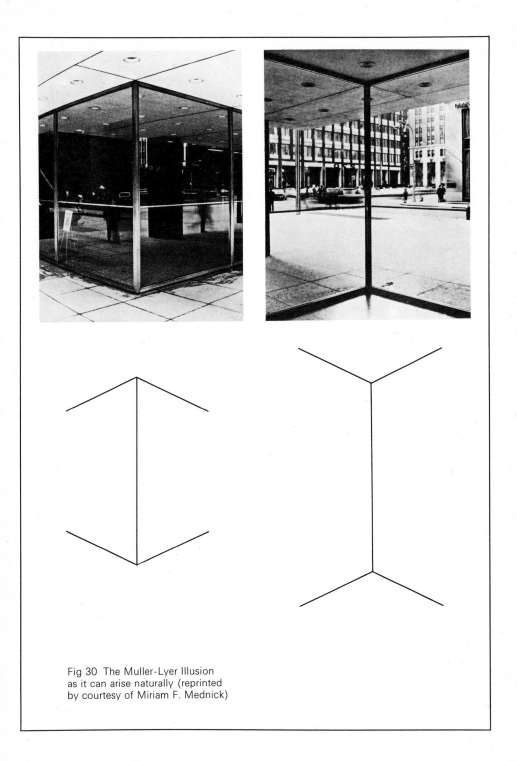

Fig 30 The Muller-Lyer Illusion
as it can arise naturally (reprinted
by courtesy of Miriam F. Mednick)

figures as being in depth. We have seen that different cultures may display differences in the perception of depth in pictures. It is also reported that forest-dwelling pygmies brought out to the open plains saw a distant rhinocerous as a curious species of ant, interpreting a large distant object as a small nearby one.

The theory relating visual illusions to depth perception is not new, but Gregory (1966) has developed it further. If parts of a two-dimensional line-drawing could trigger off some mechanism, however inappropriate, for estimating distance, this might give rise to differences in perceived size between the parts of the figure, since, if lines are perceived to be at different distances from the observer, the only way they can present the same length to the retina is if they are in fact of different lengths. As our misperception of the figure is immediate, this triggering must be due to some unconscious process—certainly we do not go through geometric equations in order to perceive the difference in length between the lines.

How then are these depth cues inferred? It is suggested that they are the result of Western man's carpentered environment: that is to say, we live in and are surrounded by rectangular rooms and furniture of primarily right-angled construction. The lines of the Muller-Lyer Illusion can be seen clearly in the corners of a room and the edge of the box-construction in Fig. 30. The highly-carpentered urbanised Western environment presents such configurations continuously to our eyes. It is argued that when we see the simple line-drawings of the Muller-Lyer Illusion we refer back to our environment. As this would only apply to a person brought up in an urban surrounding, susceptibility to the illusion should therefore arise predominantly in Western man. Similarly, distance may be perceived in the Horizontal–Vertical Illusion, and this should be more evident in people living in flat open country than in the forest.

While differences in the extent of illusion have been found between cultures, these are not always consistent with the directions suggested by this experiential hypothesis. Jahoda (1966) tested this hypothesis with illiterates from various tribes in Ghana, who were tested in their villages. Because of the wide differences in terrain found in Ghana it was possible to find two peoples quite distinct from each other, living in flat terrain, and compare these with forest-dwellers. The results did not fit at all with the theory for the Horizontal–Vertical Illusion, though they did for the Muller-Lyer. Procedural differences may account for the discrepancies with the results of Segall *et al.*, and Jahoda points out the difficulties of experimentation in the cross-cultural setting. Interestingly enough, while many men of the villages tested by Jahoda had worked in different areas as seasonal labourers, there was no difference in the extent of the illusion between them and the women of the village who had rarely gone more than a few miles away.

Another difficulty for the experiential hypothesis is that there are two

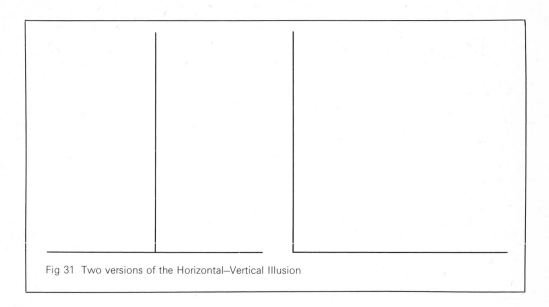

Fig 31 Two versions of the Horizontal–Vertical Illusion

basic versions of the Horizontal–Vertical Illusion (Fig. 31) which give markedly different amounts of illusion: the intersection of the horizontal line has a much greater effect. If they are both caused by an interpretative process—that is, the figure is 'seen' as being a road or river going into the distance—then one would not predict any difference in the extent of the illusion between the two versions. However, since there is a difference, there must be different explanations for the two forms of the Horizontal–Vertical Illusion, or some secondary factor must be called into play with one of them. Such factors would not be hard to find: for example, the intersection of the horizontal line may make it more difficult to estimate length.

The contradictory results of tests of the 'carpentered world' hypothesis might well make one look for alternative explanations. Some experimenters have suggested that Rivers may be right after all in suggesting a physiological basis for some of these illusions. We have already said that we would expect a different perception if we possessed a receptor system which was altered, as it is in the case of certain people who have unusual colour-vision. Rivers suggested that since the retina of the Papuan is more strongly pigmented (yellowed) than that of Western man, this would result in a relative insensitivity to blue and green. This is not very different from an idea put forward recently by Pollack, who found that contour detectability was related to density of eye pigmentation, in that it decreased with age as pigmentation increased. As it is also known that the Muller-Lyer Illusion decreases with age and that there is some tentative evidence for contour contrast affecting the illusion, then retinal pigmentation may after all be an important factor.

While generally only rural Africans have been found to exhibit no illusion for the Muller-Lyer, if Pollack is correct this should apply to all dark-skinned peoples. Pollack and Silvar (1967) tested this with a black-and-white version of the Muller-Lyer upon groups of Negro and Caucasian children in the United States. They still found that Caucasian children exhibited more illusion. Similarly, in another study it was found that Egyptian observers were intermediary between Negro and Caucasian observers in the extent of the illusory effect they experienced. This could again be related to the retinal pigmentation, since the Egyptian group would be intermediary between the other two. Such findings have made Berry (1971) re-analyse his data on the Muller-Lyer Illusion as seen by Scots, Eskimo, Australian Aborigines and people from New Guinea. He found a closer relationship to skin colour (hence retinal pigmentation) than to the carpentered nature of the observers' environment.

More support for this explanation comes from the predicted insensitivity to blue. It is worth noting, by the way, that the experiment of Pollack and Silvar was conducted under dim blue illumination. It might be expected that increasing retinal pigmentation would cause less illusion for a blue figure of the Muller-Lyer than, say, a red figure. Jahoda (1971) tested this hypothesis with students from Malawi and Scotland, and indeed it was only with the Malawian students that the colour of the figure made any difference, there being less illusion for the blue version.

However, the theory is not supported by all available evidence. Using coloured versions of the Muller-Lyer, Ebert and Pollack (1972) were able to find a correlation only between yellow figures and the amount of retinal pigmentation. Moreover, Bayer and Pressey (1972) were unable to find a correlation between pigmentation and extent of the Muller-Lyer Illusion, even with black-and-white figures. However, they used only Caucasian undergraduates as their observers in this experiment. The observers were divided by an ophthalmologist into groups according to the extent of their retinal pigmentation. No differences could be found in the experience of the figures, even between the extreme groups with the greatest variation in retinal pigmentation. It could, of course, be argued that, in using only Caucasian observers, it was not possible to obtain enough difference in retinal pigmentation to prove the point. This may be the case; but Bayer and Pressey point out that to perform the experiment across cultures or socio-economic groups confounds other factors, such as the amount of carpentered environment. One might expect, however, that in the area of Chicago used by Pollack the carpentered environment would be the same for both Negro and Caucasian children; and, contrary to the result of Pollack and Silvar, Stewart (1973) could not find any difference between these two groups in their susceptibility to the Muller-Lyer Illusion when she tested children from the same area.

It is possible that a physiological explanation is correct even if the seemingly unlikely one of Pollack is not. It may be possible that a carpentered environment early in life changes the receptive cells of the brain. This may seem unlikely, but Blakemore and Cooper (1970) have shown that restricting the visual experience of a kitten to certain orientations hinders the development of the necessary cortical cells for other orientations. One does not like to extrapolate from cats to man, but there would be some justification in this instance. Astigmatism, which is a naturally-occurring optical defect arising from a non-spherical part of the refracting surface of the eye, causes clearest vision along one axis of that eye and most blurred vision along the axis at right angles to the clearest. This may go uncorrected for many years in childhood. It has been shown by Mitchell *et al.* (1973) that corrected sight in adults still bears the scars of this visual deprivation, and acuity along the line of the naturally-occurring poorest vision is worse than for other directions. In observers with normal vision, acuity is generally found to be best for horizontal and vertical lines. Campbell and Maffei (1971) have suggested that there are more cells responsive to these directions than to any other orientation. The experiments which form the basis for this suggestion were made with Western observers, and it could be argued that it was the carpentered environment of Western culture which was the cause of the selective development of the visual cortex. The necessary experimentation on non-Western observers to test this hypothesis has not been carried out.

However, tentative evidence supporting the notion of early experience affecting differences in acuity comes from a study of Annis and Frost (1973). They compared Cree Indians from a remote part of Quebec with Euro-Canadians, with respect to the ability to see lines at different angles. The rationale for expecting a difference was that, even though he would have seen plenty of horizontals and verticals, a Cree Indian child brought up in among wigwams might well have been exposed to more diagonal lines than would the urban Euro-Canadian child. And indeed it was found that the normally-occurring better acuity for horizontal and vertical lines was not found in Cree Indians. Their acuity for lines of different orientation did not differ statistically, though the trend was in the direction of the Euro-Canadian results. Unfortunately, it was not possible to test both groups of observers under exactly the same conditions. This may explain the fact that the Crees appeared to have an all-round poorer acuity than the Euro-Canadians, which is unlikely in a hunting people.

It is difficult to come to definite conclusions about the causes of the differentiation between races with respect to these visual phenomena. Most reports do suggest that there are differences, but perhaps it should be remembered that it is hard to prove that there is *no* difference between two groups of observers. Scientific journals have been loth to publish reports of absence of difference—there are so many possible reasons why this sort of result could be obtained. Finally, one should bear in mind the communication difficulties and experimental problems involved in cross-cultural research.

Racial differences have been observed to operate in other perceptual tasks. There are many reports of the difficulties of people of Africa and Asian societies in judging the sizes and shapes of objects. Generally, it has been suggested that differences arise because people of these cultures are more influenced by the real nature of an object. Beveridge (1935, 1939), in his studies in West Africa, found that students there were less dominated by the stimulus reaching the eye compared with Europeans doing the same task. A circular disc was presented to the observer, who viewed it from an angle which produced an elliptical image on the retina. West Africans judged the disc to be more nearly circular than did Europeans. However, Beveridge did not find his African observers had a similar dominance for the real nature of the brightness of an object when it was placed in shadow: the results were not clear-cut, but if anything they were in the direction of taking less account than the Europeans of the true brightness of the object.

In an experiment to investigate the perception of shape, Thouless (1933) found that Indian students also gave responses based on the real shape of an object, just as Beveridge subsequently found for West African students (above). Thouless went further to conclude that the nature of Indian art was determined by this perceptual difference. This is exactly the reverse of the argument that was used previously to explain the differences in interpreting photographs and pictures encountered by Indian observers, when it was suggested that it was because of their experience with this art form that they had such difficulty in seeing pictures in depth. Thouless implied that there is some basic perceptual difference which therefore causes the difference in the art of Indians and Africans compared with Western societies. But we have seen, when relating performance in perceptual tasks to personality, how easy it is to make any observer take any attitude when assessing the shape or size of an object. Whether an observer takes up either the 'synthetic' or 'analytic' attitude, described earlier, can easily depend on the interpretation of the instructions given by the experimenter.

Witkin et al. (1962), discussing the field-dependent individual suggests that the mothers of field-dependent people tend to be dominating, emotional and anxious, while the fathers are generally passive. Dawson (1967) was able to test this hypothesis cross-culturally, comparing the Temne and Mende tribes of Sierra Leone. The Temne mother is extremely dominating and discipline in the home is very strict; the Mende mother is not so dominating, and individual initiative is encouraged much more than with the Temne. It could therefore be predicted that the Temne male would be more field-dependent than the Mende male. Dawson found evidence in support of this contention.

Wober (1967) wants to make a distinction between the Embedded Figure Test (Fig. 25) and the Tilted Room Test. The latter relies more on proprioception and is done as well by Africans as Europeans—a result reported by Beveridge in 1939. Beveridge rotated his observers up to 25 degrees from the horizontal while they were inside a dimly-lit cupboard. He required his Ghanaian observers to adjust a stick to be parallel to the ground outside. They were slightly better at this than a group of European observers. Okonji (1969), too, reports that the correlation between the Rod-and-Frame Test and the Embedded Figure Test is not as high with Nigerian observers as it is with Europeans and Americans.

According to Wober, it is in the processing of visual rather than proprioceptive information that the major cross-cultural difference lies. In the past it has been pointed out that uneducated African people find difficulty in identifying visual objects if they are rotated or upside down. This may be true, but all people find difficulty with such tasks and the difference may be quantitative rather than qualitative. There is also the factor of orientation preferences brought into play by the uneducated African, which were found by Serpell (1971) to be important in matching tasks. In all, it is a big step to conclude from observations such as those of Wober that African culture promotes a different way of perceiving the world. It has also been suggested that the African relies more on hearing and the body senses than on vision in dealing with the world. Such a difference is, of course, possible, but there remains the strong possibility that the wrong type of visual stimuli have been used in testing. Serpell (1972) presents some preliminary evidence that, if a familiar but nevertheless complex visual task is used, English and Zambian children will do equally well.

The sex difference in processing the visual stimuli in the Embedded Figure Test has been found throughout the world. Witkin (1966) reports sex differences in the direction of greater field-dependence in women in the United States, England Holland, France, Italy, Hong Kong and Sierra Leone. Okonji showed much the same in Nigeria, though the effect was diminished at university level, with no difference between men and women on the Embedded Figure Test but with more male field-independence as measured by the Rod-and-Frame Test.

Dawson also reports that in Sierra Leone kwashiorkor, the tropical disease resulting from protein deficiency, produces an endocrine dysfunction that causes secondary feminine characteristics. Those men that had this disease were found to adopt a more field-dependent attitude to these tests. But Lloyd (1972) argues that children with this disease get a different social environment, so one cannot necessarily link field-dependence with some hormonal factor.

This correlation between sex and field-dependence has not been found by Berry (1966) or McArthur (1967) with Eskimo. Eskimo women did as well as men on this task. The fact that 'Eskimo women...are in no way treated as dependent in the society' was interpreted by Berry as being an important causal factor in their more analytical search behaviour in this task, as measured by their ability to find the embedded figure. This finding suggests a learned rather than genetic basis for this sex difference.

If these and other cross-cultural differences are based upon learning and experience, it would follow that any individual who had encountered different experiences would have different perceptions. With this in mind, the next chapter will deal with differences in perception based on development.

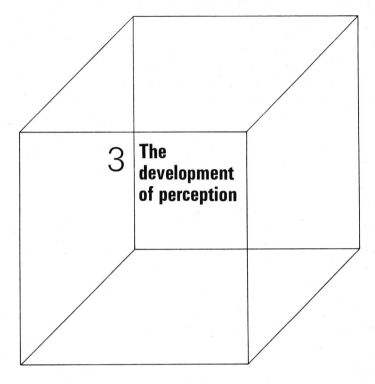

3 | The development of perception

The nature–nurture issue

No-one can doubt that adults can, as a result of their experiences, come to react differently to perceptual situations. An account of some of these varieties of perceptual learning can be found in Epstein (1967). Several of these studies have already been mentioned and were begun as investigations into the question of the learned nature of perception; among these were the studies of the transformation of the visual world by wearing distorting spectacles. A similar and, in the long run, equally unproductive approach to the question of whether or not perception is initially based on learning, consists of experimental or naturalistic investigation into the deprivation of the senses.

Von Senden (1960) collected reports of the rare cases of individuals born blind because of cataracts, who later recovered their sight. Adults who were perfectly able to recognise objects by touch proved incapable, after cataract removal, of recognising the most familiar objects by sight. The perception of a square, circle or triangle was very poor: the most intelligent and best-motivated patient had to seek out corners painstakingly to distinguish between these simple shapes. In such cases there is, in fact, practically zero capacity to learn to identify these figures when presented visually. The person in this situation is able to detect visually the presence of an object but seems to be able to do little more—Von Senden records the following with respect to such a patient being shown a watch:

'Is it a round thing or a square one?'—(no answer).

'Do you know what a square is?'—He positions his hands so that they form a pair of surfaces which make contact almost at right angles, whereby producing an angle which is part of a cube.

'And a circle?'—He again bends his hand round with the fingers pointing towards the wrist and thereby produces an almost complete ring. After this fashion he therefore has some knowledge of circularity. In looking at the watch, at which his gaze is obviously directed, he remains incapable of saying whether it is round or cornered. However much I insist on an answer, none is forthcoming. I put the watch away again, without saying anything to him, and without letting him feel it. On the following morning the same question; the same inability to answer. So I then let him feel the watch. No sooner has he taken it in his hand, than he immediately says, 'That's mine, it's a watch'.

One of the major troubles with such investigations, if one is trying to answer the nature—nurture question, is that the observer has had all his perceptual development up to that point without sight. He will inevitably rely on modalities other than sight, even if he has the opportunity to use his newly-acquired vision. This is confirmed by another report by Von Senden:

I now made her write some letters on the board. She did this, though without making use of her vision, but merely as the blind do, in that she followed with the chalk the movements whereby the index finger of the left hand was likewise tracing out the form of the letter on the board beforehand.

Even though these letters were perfectly legible to normal readers, the patient in this experiment could not read them herself.

Such reports show the difficulty with this type of study where the aim is to determine whether some perceptual ability is learned or innate, since any lack of progress may be due to the patient relying on his previously-used sense modalities. The difficulty in adapting to this change of modalities can, in fact, be so extreme that depression commonly results, and sometimes even suicide.

Studies in which children are given an enriched visual environment to see if this affects their perceptual development seem to be very few indeed. Practically, of course, this is difficult to organise and separate from other factors: an enriched visual environment would usually accompany an enriched home background. However, such research on the perceptual development of animals suggests that there should be an improvement, and therefore this approach seems worthy of further study (see page 122).

Research into cross-cultural development would seem a natural approach for determining the effects of experience, since a great variety of natural experiences are available. However, the crucial early years in perceptual development have been only marginally investigated cross-culturally. In general, the question of whether perceptual learning occurs in certain perceptual attributes is disputed. For a comprehensive account of this area of the work the reader is referred to *Principles of Perceptual Learning and Development* by Eleanor Gibson (1969). The nature–nurture issue will not be ignored, but we shall concentrate here on the differences that exist between a child and an adult in perceiving the same scene, irrespective of whether the difference is maturational or experiential in origin. Developmental differences have been investigated using a great variety of perceptual tasks. The first essential is to itemise the changes in these tasks. Visual acuity, colour and space perception have been chosen as representative.

Changes in visual acuity

The work of Fantz (1961) has shown that the visual discrimination of young children is greater than was previously thought. Fantz placed very young babies in a special chamber (the experimenter viewed the child through a tiny hole). On the roof of the chamber were two objects. When one of these was seen reflected from the pupil of the infant, a timer was started, which was turned off when the eyes turned away or were closed. Since individual babies might lie on one side or the other with greater frequency, the position of the objects to be viewed had to be alternated to control for a position bias. If, during an experimental session, the baby looked at one object more than the other, this showed that he must be able to tell the difference between the objects. Of course, this simple result does not tell one why the baby preferred to look at one rather than the other; nor can we conclude (though it is very tempting to do so) that an absence of preference necessarily means an inability to discriminate.

Since Fantz knew that babies preferred to look at patterned rather than plain surfaces, he provided the alternatives of looking at a striped pattern or a uniform grey square which overall reflected the same amount of light. It was found that the width of the stripes could be decreased, and a preference still be shown, as the baby grew older. Infants under a month old were able to distinguish $\frac{1}{8}$-inch stripes from a uniform grey at ten inches' distance. By the age of six months, the baby in this situation could distinguish stripes $\frac{1}{64}$ inch wide. Thus, if we had infant observers, one of six months and the other of one month, their attentional preferences for striped patterns would differ. It may be possible that with even more sophisticated techniques the visual sensitivity of babies would be found to be finer still, though a six-month-old baby is not far off adult performance. An adult can distinguish stripes $\frac{1}{300}$ inch wide at a 10-inch distance, a level which is achieved at the age of ten years.

A six-month-old baby can to some extent be seen to be approaching adult performance. But it may be possible that, with even more sophisticated techniques, the visual sensitivity of babies will be found to be even finer than now thought. Some indication of this comes from Atkinson *et al.* (1974), who replaced the stationary striped pattern with one that flashed on and off or drifted across the field of view. Such a stimulus would obviously attract the baby's attention more readily, and it was found that preference for the striped pattern was now still evident with stripes narrower than the critical width established by Fantz's experiment.

Colour-vision

Experimental research on the development of colour-vision has produced many conflicting results. This is not surprising, since early workers took little account of the dimensions of colour. Any colour can be defined by three factors. The first of these is hue, which is associated with the wavelength of light. The second is lightness or tone, which corresponds to the lightness–darkness dimension. This second factor is exemplified by the grey appearance of colour reproduced in a black-and-white photograph; it is often called 'brightness', although 'brightness' commonly means 'vividness'. The third factor is saturation, and refers to the purity of the colour. A colour becomes less pure if more white is added. The experience of a colour will also differ depending on whether it is reflected from a surface or acts as a light source. That is to say, a red on the printed page differs in quality from the same red used as a filter in front of a light.

Saturation has often been ignored when testing children for their colour perception. An early study by Gilbert (1894), which estimated children's ability to judge the saturation of pieces of red cloth, found that even children of six years were unable to use saturation as a means of discrimination between colours. Cook (1931), using the standard source of colours (the Munsell colour system) instead of the rough-and-ready attempt of Gilbert, found, however, that six-year-old children could use the dimensions of saturation to a high degree of accuracy.

In everyday terms we do not consciously analyse colours by these three dimensions. Mundle (1971), seeing in the Munsell colour book (which arranges colours according to their lightness and saturation) a page labelled 'red', failed to understand how colours ranging through near black, near white, pink and scarlet could all be categorised as the same red. He reiterated the comment of William James (1890) who said that 'to introspection, our feeling of pink is surely not a portion of our feeling of scarlet'. But without such a factorial analysis it is impossible to tell which aspect of the colour an observer is responding to; this may well account for some of the contradictory results. This is certainly the case in adult colour-vision, according to Siegel and Arden (1968), with respect to the supposed red–green defect arising from excessive intake of alcohol and tobacco, which is in fact due to loss of brightness sensitivity. Warren (1969), however, would maintain that this factorial analysis is the cause of the confusion.

Preyer (1888) tested his own son, using ovals of the primary colours, and found that the question, 'what colour is this?' was answered correctly for yellow when the child was 112 weeks old. Preyer reported that blue was the last colour to be correctly named. However, his report suggested that other children did not necessarily follow the same developmental progression, and Baldwin (1955) gave the example of a nine-month-old child who preferred blue to all other colours.

Staples (1932) attempted to dissociate the hue from the lightness of a colour. She used 250 children and tested them from sixty-nine days of age to twenty-four months. They were given the chance to respond to red, yellow, green, blue and grey paper squares of equal lightness. She reported that by the end of the third month there was a differentiation between the various colours based upon hue alone, and that these first four basic colours could be distinguished when the child was around one year old. She found that the greatest response was to red, then yellow, followed by blue and lastly green.

Spears (1964, 1966) performed in essence the same experiment, though using a different response measure, on sixty infants aged four months. However, Spears found a preference for blue, followed by red, yellow and grey, but only the preference for blue over grey was statistically significantly different, which is directly opposed to the result of Staples. Moreover, other studies investigating infants' colour-vision could not find any colour preference whatsoever. This might have been predicted from the studies in which electroretinogram (e.r.g.), an electrical recording from the retina, has been investigated. A study by Barnet, Lodge and Armington (1965) found the e.r.g. for new-born babies for a coloured light source to be exactly the same as that for adults.

Fagan (1974) has adopted the testing procedure of Fantz described above to study the development of colour-vision. The infant is given the alternative of looking at a pattern resembling a chequerboard made up of squares of two different colours or of looking at a large square of one of the colours. Fagan found that the patterned stimulus was the one that was preferred. This is the result that would be predicted, as will be seen later. However, there was also a difference according to the two colours that made up the pattern. If the colours were very different, for example, red and green, this pattern was looked at more than a pattern of red and orange; and again, a red and orange pattern was preferred to one made up of two shades of red. So there is clear evidence that children of 4–6 months can tell the difference between colours, though Fagan found no marked preference for any particular colour.

It may well be that the differences observed in earlier studies were due to uncontrolled factors of some sort. Certainly, lightness is an important factor in drawing the attention of the child, though no more so than colour (Segers, 1936; Fantz, 1961). The ability to fixate a light is present in new-born children; Champreys (1881) noted that his son took great pleasure in looking at a candle at various times before he was nine months old. Reaction to lightness is similar in the child and in the adult. Trincker and Trincker (1955) found the dark-adaptation curve (Fig. 4) of a one-month-old child to be like that of the adult. All this suggests that, in the field of visual sensitivity, the young infant has a greater capacity for visual discrimination than is generally thought. The study of the development of colour-vision shows that it is of the greatest importance to use the most sophisticated techniques in child development experiments, so that the child has the greatest opportunity to show his ability.

Space perception

Wicklegren (1967) reported that in the first few days of life any perception of distance must arise from one eye only, because it had been observed that convergence of the two eyes (used as a cue for distance) was not operative at this stage. However, binocular convergence for objects at different distances could be seen to improve rapidly during the second month. Experiments using the apparatus of Fantz showed a preference for looking at solid objects. This preference is manifest at one month and does not require binocular vision. This suggests that the appreciation of texture and shading may well be effective in the perception of solid objects and therefore of depth.

Experimentation with the pre-verbal child is, of course, fraught with complications inherent in trying to get the child to show his perception in some secondary fashion. With respect to depth-perception, Walk and Gibson (1961) and Walk (1966) have used a device called a 'visual cliff'. Using this apparatus, the child is placed on a board between two plates of glass, beneath which the distance of the floor appears to be different on each side. Reflections from the surface of the glass are avoided so that the child can only use the visual depth cues as a guide. The child can choose whether to crawl off the board to a level apparently the same as that of the board or to one which is apparently some way beneath. Ninety per cent of children from the age of six-and-a-half months to fifteen months, when first tested on this task, avoid the 'deep' side most of the time, even if their mother tries to coax them across. As a test for the development of depth-perception this is not without fault as human babies do not crawl until they are about six months old. They can perceive depth when first tested, but they have obviously already had a great deal of previous visual experience. To investigate the possible learned factors in depth-perception, other methods would be required.

Bower (1964), therefore, used a head-turning response which could be encouraged by reinforcement from the mother. Head-turning was first encouraged as a response to a twelve-inch cube presented at a distance of three feet. Bower then observed the baby's response to the same cube placed at nine feet. He also investigated the response to a change of size of the cube: a thirty-six-inch cube was placed at either three feet or nine feet from the baby. It was found that children aged seventy to eighty-five days were able to detect the change of size or distance. This could be measured by the number of head-turning responses made during a thirty-second period. Taking the average scores, there were most (58) head-turnings to the original twelve-inch cube at nine feet, next most (54) to the thirty-six-inch cube at three feet, and least (22) to the thirty-six-inch cube at nine feet. The original stimulus at the original distance elicited 98 head-turnings during this period.

These are very interesting results, but in a way they do not make sense. It could be argued that if the child has the appreciation that it is the same cube moved from three feet to nine feet then he must, by definition, have an awareness of the distance. On this view the appreciation of the true size of an object is not possible unless the distance away from the observer of the object is known.

Bower (1965) found that his results could be repeated with younger children (forty to sixty days old). In this study he further suggested (following-up work done on the 'visual cliff') that the important cue for distance-perception is motion parallax. This is the cue to distance that can be noted when travelling in a train and looking at the passing countryside: objects at different distances seem to go past the eye at different speeds. Bower suggests that motion-carried information is more basic than static pictorial information. This opinion is reinforced by the finding that the children made little response to a colour slide of the cube used in the experiment described above. This does appear to conflict with the apparent ease with which pictures were recognised in the study of Hochberg and Brooks (1962). However, there is a considerable difference in age between the children used by Bower and the child in the Hochberg and Brooks study.

Bower's results, like those on the development of colour-perception, suggest that certain of the cues for distance-perception are available at a very early age. But for Bower they suggest more than this. He regards the development of perception as a development of the ability to process information: infants can register any single attribute of the visual world but do not have the cognitive ability to combine several attributes. Bower suggests that any visual deficit is more a matter of the baby's being over-whelmed by the visual world than of his finding it a meaningless 'buzz'.

These results cannot be taken to mean that no improvement occurs as the child grows older. Indeed, estimation of size and distance does improve with age. Smith and Smith (1966) tell us that five-year-old children are as good as adults at judging distances unless some reduction in viewing conditions prevails. Under any reduced viewing conditions there will be a poor judgement on the part of young children, but this will still improve with age.

Harway (1963) found the same to be true when he asked children to mark off one-foot unit distances away from them across a field. They were given a standard foot rule at their feet for reference, and were then asked to indicate points on the field representing distances of two feet through to twenty feet, in one-foot intervals. Some were unsuccessful, especially the youngest age group tested (five to six years), some of whom had reached the end of the seventy-five-foot field before giving their nineteenth judgement. Performance was rather poor in the five to ten-year-olds, but the twelve-year-olds were as accurate as adults.

However, we should be rather careful here to consider whether in fact it was the perception of the young children that differed from that of the adults. This task and similar tasks (Zeigler and Leibowitz, 1957) require the child to exercise his cognitive judgements as well as his perceptual abilities. It may well be this cognitive judgement which is being measured. If this is not the case, then we must assume that a distance of twenty feet for an adult looks like a seventy-foot distance for the young child. This is a possible though unlikely interpretation. In fact, Wohlwill (1963) found that young children were better at estimating distance than older children when asked to judge the half-way point to a marker in an open field. Wohlwill suggests that the older children had overlearned the cues necessary to estimate distances, and paid exaggerated attention to them. A similar result was obtained by Wohlwill (1965) using photographs of the fields.

Visual illusions

We have already noted that the perception of visual illusions may involve depth-perception. This is by no means proven to be the case. An examination of the development of visual illusions with age and experience should, however, be important for the proof of any such connection. There is a definite connection between the perception of geometric optical illusions and age. Binet (1895) found that the Muller-Lyer Illusion decreases with age. The experiential hypothesis which bases the Muller-Lyer Illusion upon learned depth-cues has great difficulty with this finding. As Segall and Campbell (1963) wrote, 'Our line of reasoning demands that somewhere during the life-span there must be an increase of susceptibility with age'. Evidence for this increase does not seem to be available.

There remains the possibility of an increase in illusory effect with the pre-verbal child since, naturally, most developmental studies have been with school-age children. But, at the very least, a second explanation besides that of learned depth-cues would be required to explain the subsequent decrease in susceptibility.

Piaget sees development as moving from an initially 'pure' perception to involve more cognitive activity. This causes changes in the way a child looks at a figure and the ensuing perception. This is because centration (the fixation of attention) on any part of a figure is said to provide an over-estimate of that part of the figure compared to the rest. As young children have a tendency to view a figure with relatively few fixations, they will not be able to eliminate any distortion. Piaget calls these fixation errors 'Type I' and, since they are eliminated with age, they are normally associated developmentally with a decrease in illusion. Support for the relationship between eye movements and extent of illusion comes from the work of Piaget and Vinh-Bang (1961a). In this systematic study there was found to be a clear connection between the number of fixations and the over-estimation of a part of the figure. As the more adult way of viewing was adopted, without any biased fixation, the illusion decreased.

As adults are able to scan a figure more quickly than children, it might be expected that, if an illusion was shown for a very brief period of time, there would be differences between children and adults in their perception of it. The Oppel-Kundt Illusion is that an unfilled space looks smaller than a filled space (see Fig. 32). It is found that if the time of showing is increased, the extent of the illusion increases up to a fifth of a second and decreases after half-a-second. Piaget and Vinh-Bang (1961b) report that the adult maximum is at a fifth of a second, while the child's is at half-a-second.

It should be pointed out that there is contradictory evidence regarding the effects of fixation and the extent of an illusion. Illusions still exist when there are no eye movements at all, e.g. when they are presented as stabilised retinal images (page 6). Piaget (1961) has himself provided an example where the Oppel-Kundt Illusion operated irrespective of which part of the figure was fixated. Piaget argues that one cannot always equate fixation

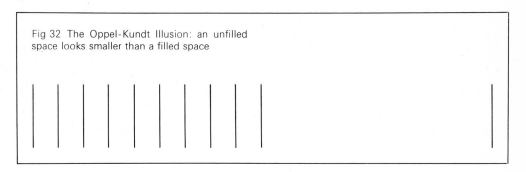

Fig 32 The Oppel-Kundt Illusion: an unfilled space looks smaller than a filled space

with centration. This is certainly true of an after-image, where one can pay attention to various parts of the figure while, of course, there is no change in fixation. The trouble, from an experimental viewpoint, with this argument is that any result proves the hypothesis which Piaget is testing. This is so because one does not have any objective way of telling what is being attended to except by fixation. Centration must have some measurable attribute if it is to involve experimentation.

Pollack (1963) also claims that one gets the same decrease in the illusion with age if the illusion is presented for only a very brief interval. If eye movements are an important factor, this does not seem likely. Pollack, as we have seen, believes that change in physiological factors such as retinal pigmentation account for illusions such as the Muller-Lyer, and produces evidence that these changes occur with age. However, as was noted previously (page 97), the causal relationship between eye pigmentation and decrease of illusion relies on the finding of contour detectability also decreasing with age. Weintraub et al. (1973) tested the prediction that, in general, the extent of illusion would decrease as the contour contrast decreased. They could find no evidence of this happening. One must therefore suggest that up to now no really satisfactory explanation of the decrease in the Muller-Lyer Illusion with age has been proposed.

There is a type of illusion which, far from decreasing with age, appears to increase. These illusions are based on a temporal or distance factor and rely to a greater extent on some cognitive judgement by the observer. Piaget calls this a 'Type 2' error and says it arises because the process of decentration in its turn produces its own errors. They are due to changes in fixation and scanning rather than the time spent fixating, as is the case with Type 1 errors. Illusions producing Type 2 errors often involve making a comparison and therefore it is not surprising that Spitz and Blackman (1958, 1959) found that there was a greater correlation between intelligence and Type 2 illusions than Type 1 illusions.

Pollack (1969) is in much greater agreement with Piaget with respect to Type 2 errors. Pollack (1964) argued, following Piaget and Lambercier (1944), that it should be possible to convert a Type 1 illusion into a Type 2 illusion. The Muller-Lyer decreases with repeated presentations and is generally reported to decrease with age. Pollack argued that if the arrowheads of the Muller-Lyer were presented before the lines, a different type of judgement would be called for. Considering the length of the straight line with the outward going fins as a measure of the illusion, Pollack says that the magnitude of the illusion decreases with age under normal simultaneous presentation. However, if the parts are presented successively, then the illusion increases in extent and acts in the opposite direction (see Fig. 33). Similar reversals have been found for other illusions by Ikeda and Obonai (1955) and Adam, Gibb and Freeman (1966).

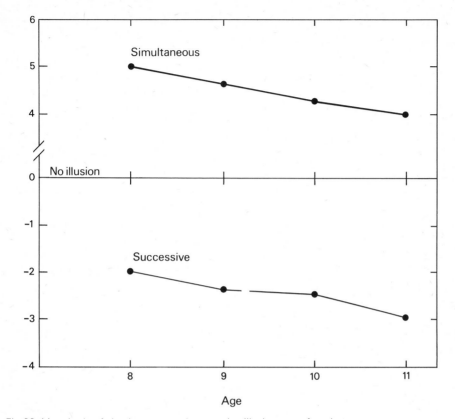

Fig 33 Magnitude of simultaneous and successive illusions as a function of age-level (reprinted from 'Simultaneous and successive presentation of elements of the Muller-Lyer figure and chronological age', Pollack, R. H., *Perceptual and Motor Skills* 19, 1964)

Pollack (1966) also showed a curvilinear relationship between age and the inter-stimulus interval to give optimal apparent movement. Here, there is a decrease from around 80 milliseconds at seventy months to around 50 milliseconds at 105 months. This was deemed to represent some underlying physiological change. By the age of 128 months the inter-stimulus interval had increased to around 60 milliseconds for optimal apparent movement. This increase, according to Pollack, shows the process which allows the child to make greater use of the trace of the first stimulus to mediate apparent movement.

The Type 2 phenomenon is represented by the over-estimation of size and distance typically found in adults (Wohlwill, 1963). A great majority of illusions fit into this category, represented by an increase in illusion extent if a cognitive task or comparison is required and a decrease if no cognitive activity is involved. Pick and Pick (1970) present a table showing

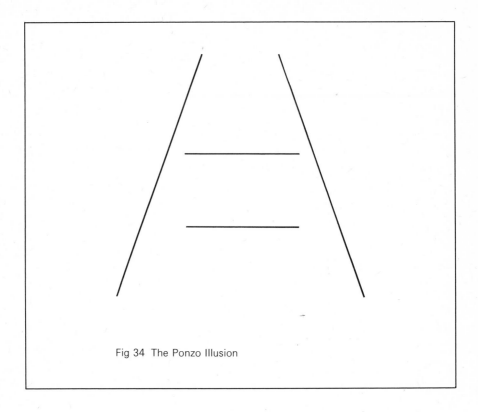

Fig 34 The Ponzo Illusion

the effects of age on the extent of various illusions. While most follow the pattern suggested by the Type 1 and Type 2 errors, there are exceptions, such as the finding of Leibowitz and Judisch (1967) that the Ponzo Illusion (Fig. 34) increases with age. This would be understandable if it were based on learned depth-cues, but in that case the Muller-Lyer Illusion should show a similar result.

The field-dependence tasks mentioned in the last chapter are part of a very wide programme of research suggesting that individual differences on cognitive tasks can affect perceptual behaviour. Wapner and Werner (1957) found that young children behaved differently from adults when asked to judge the outside world in relation to their body tilt. Adults adjust the vertical in the opposite direction to that of the body tilt, while young children tended to assimilate to the muscle activity. Witkin *et al.* (1954) also report consistent developmental trends in the Embedded Figure Test, the Rod-and-Frame Test and the Tilting-Room-Tilting-Chair Test. From eight to seventeen years of age there is a decrease in the reliance upon the outside visual field. This is measured by the increase in speed with which the hidden figure is found and the adjustments nearer the true vertical for the rod or the chair are made.

Because field-independence suggests a more analytic way of analysing the world, one would also predict that as field-independence increases with age, the extent of visual illusions should decrease. We have seen that for most of the geometric optical illusions this is indeed the case. However, it should be pointed out that, in most illusions, Jahoda and Stacey (1970) could not confirm, for adult observers, this relationship between field-dependence and susceptibility to the illusion.

Eidetic imagery

When we considered earlier the phenomenon of perceptual masking it was pointed out that the internal representation of a stimulus is of finite duration. Sperling (1960) has shown this to be generally a matter of milliseconds rather than seconds. Yet there are some people who are reported to be able to see something vividly, as if it were really there, even hours after the object or scene has changed. This eidetic imagery is clearly distinguished from an imagined percept because the 'eidetiker' sees the object as being really 'out there'. When this phenomenon was described by Urbantschitsch (1907) it was ascribed predominantly to children.

Haber (1969) reports his attempts to find children who possessed this ability. While early studies seemed to suggest that half of all children were eidetikers, Haber found that it was nowhere near such a common phenomenon. This was probably because Haber and his associates adopted rigorous standards for the classification of eidetic imagery. A screening procedure produced about twenty children from an initial five hundred.

The child sat before a neutral grey card placed on an easel. He was first tested for after-images by asking him to fixate red, blue, black and yellow squares. This encouraged him to report everything, even if it was not physically present after the stimulus has been removed. The child was then given a picture to look at for thirty seconds, and was told to scan it but not fixate as he had done for the colours. When the picture was taken away he was asked what he saw.

Haber was interested in responses where the child saw pictures in the original colours and not in after-image colours. While nearly all the children reported seeing something after the picture had been removed, these reports were mostly of fleeting and indistinct images or of the after-image (complementary colours) type. The apparent size of an after-image varies with the distance of the surface onto which it is projected; this does not happen with an eidetic image. It was found that when a child reported an eidetic image, the movements of his eyes corresponded with his report. Haber also attempted to distinguish between the memory of the picture and the perception of it as if it were still there.

Between 5 and 10 per cent of the children reported images that lasted longer than half a minute. These children were investigated further. The eidetic image was generally specific to the place of the original picture; if they tried to move the image off the easel on which the original picture had been placed, the image 'fell off the edge'. However, one girl could move the image elsewhere, and she could also bring it back after it had faded. One of the surprising things about eidetic imagery is its survival in spite of the intervention of conflicting stimulation.

The children were not able to be completely specific as to how they kept the image but many said that they must not name the parts of the picture while looking at it, otherwise they could not produce an image. This may account for the finding that the eidetiker's actual memory of the picture was not very much better than that of the non-eidetiker. In a way this is surprising, especially when we consider the following answers of a boy who had just been looking at a picture from *Alice in Wonderland* showing Alice looking at the Cheshire cat:

Experimenter: Do you see something there?
Subject: I see the tree, grey tree with three limbs. I see the cat with stripes around its tail.
Experimenter: Can you count the stripes?
Subject: Yes...(pause)...there's about sixteen.
Experimenter: You're counting what? Black, white or both?
Subject: Both.

Now, if the child had still such a vivid image that he could count the stripes one would expect him to have a much better memory of the picture than an ordinary observer. But it may be that in some ways a non-visual memory is more efficient and therefore compensates.

Haber reports his disappointment at the small amount of printed material that could be held in eidetic imagery. Also, since the children were generally unable to retain two complex pictures at once, it was hard to test the specificity of the images in some same-different tests. It is interesting that a few children were able to get the Necker Cube (Fig. 46) to reverse when it was an eidetic image.

In all, the results were a little discouraging compared with the detailed eidetic imagery reported in the early part of this century. Yet one recent innovation is more striking than all the others. The children were first shown the picture at the left of Fig. 35. This was then removed and the middle picture exposed. Four of the eidetic children reported seeing the face as in the picture on the right of Fig. 35. These children were those who performed better in other tests of eidetic imagery. Their reaction was one of surprise when they found that the pictures fitted together to form a face. While adults sometimes report a face when asked to describe the picture on the left, Haber says that children do not. Thus we have an eidetic image

Fig 35 (Reprinted by courtesy of R. N. Haber)

so strong that it can combine with the non-overlapping middle picture to form another picture, just as if it were still really there.

In a sense, an eidetic image can in fact be said to be still 'really there'. Eidetikers have long been known to be able to project a beard onto anybody's face in order to 'see' what it would look like. One such person, a twenty-three-year-old woman whom Stromeyer (1970) calls 'Elizabeth', reported that she could always do this and could even put the leaves back onto the trees after they had fallen. There have been many examples of impressive photographic memory in the past—Stratton (1917) reported that Jewish memory experts could tell the position of each word on each page of the Babylonian Talmud—but the eidetic memory of Elizabeth puts these in the shade. It might be argued that it is possible to fake the test of Haber described above, because it can be seen what the composite picture is supposed to be from the very first stimulus. Other eidetic feats may be nothing more than an excellent non-visual memory. However, Stromeyer and Psotka (1970), using the technique of Julesz (1964), showed a foolproof way of testing for eidetic imagery. If the reader looks through the stereo viewer at the anaglyphs (Plate 1), with one eye shut, he will see a random array of dots. If he now opens that eye and shuts the other, he will see a further random set of dots. It is only with both eyes open that a three-dimensional picture is seen. Stromeyer gave Elizabeth one of these dot pictures to look at with her right eye for one minute. It contained ten thousand dots. After ten seconds' rest she looked at another ten-thousand-dot picture with her left eye. Without hesitation, Elizabeth reported that she saw the letter 'T' coming towards her. She said that it was identical to the normally-fused picture that would be obtained from stereo vision.

Not surprisingly, this remarkable ability was investigated further. The results were even more staggering. If she was given another random pattern to look at with her right eye for a period of three minutes, broken up by some minutes' rest, she was able to hold the image for twenty-four hours. This was proved, for the next day, given another random dot pattern to the left eye, she saw a square floating above the surface. She could accurately adjust pointers to indicate the borders and depth of the square. Elizabeth had not seen the stereograms before and it is hardly likely that she could have memorised in any other way the position of each dot. She could, indeed, obtain an eidetic image of a million-dot display. This seems an unfakeable test of eidetic imagery, since to perceive the picture in depth it is necessary to have one of the pictures seen through each eye.

Though these pictures are just collections of dots it was found that if they were colour-labelled by being viewed through coloured filters then it was possible for Elizabeth to hold eidetic images for four of them. These images could be recalled at will, but once they appeared they only lasted a few seconds. This must strike us as even more remarkable, since it is hard enough to imagine being able to remember even one of these multi-dot pictures.

We have already mentioned an experiment by Stromeyer (1971) producing a multitude of colours by a combination of the McCollough after-effect and the Land phenomenon. The production of colours by means of a red and green light source (the Land effect) was used by Stromeyer to test Elizabeth's powers of eidetic imagery. Nine grey squares, some light and some dark, were projected in red light onto a screen. Elizabeth gazed at them until she had formed an eidetic image. The next day a different set of grey squares was projected in green light onto a screen at the same place. She reported a gamut of colours—red, blue, purple, reddish-brown, grey, yellow and green. Most importantly, immediately after this eidetic test Elizabeth saw the two sets of squares superimposed simultaneously, and she reported almost exactly the same colours: another proof that the eidetic image was acting as if it was still there.

Similarly, an eidetic image of a spiral could be used to produce the spiral after-effect. Elizabeth first formed an eidetic image of a stationary black-and-white spiral. Then she looked at a rotating spiral (which appeared to contract) for two minutes. Immediately afterwards she shifted her gaze to a black velvet surface and called up her eidetic image of the stationary spiral. It appeared to expand just as if it were a real image.

This woman may in fact be a rather special case, since her powers of eidetic imagery seem to be extraordinary, far outstripping those of anybody else recorded. It is not surprising that many people's first reaction to these results has been disbelief. This individual case has been dealt with here because it has often been suggested that eidetic imagery is more commonly found in children: if we consider the powers of this woman, there would not seem to be a necessary decrease of eidetic imagery with age.

The decline with age has been suggested to be caused by a change in the way visual information is stored. Since we live in a predominantly verbal culture, perhaps it is less efficient to store pictures and we might then expect eidetic imagery to decline with age and schooling.

Other cultures have been investigated to see if eidetic imagery is more common than in Western society. Doob (1966) tells us how he was told that the photographic memory of students at a West African university was so good that they could reproduce texts from their assigned works down to the hyphenated words at the ends of the lines. It has been suggested that the peoples using the non-written languages of Africa might have greater powers of eidetic imagery, though it is hard to see why, as one would expect an even heavier reliance on verbal memory. Doob's report, which incidentally contains a very honest account of the difficulties of cross cultural research, concludes that the prevalence of eidetic imagery in Africa is 'not sensationally high but undoubtedly much higher than that normally reported for Westerners'.

Considering the large variability—no Somali tested had a large amount of eidetic imagery—the hypothesis of the removal of eidetic imagery by an acculturation process is certainly not proven. However, the work of Doob (1964) with the Ibo is suggestive, in that the negative correlation with age occurred only in the urban Ibo and not among the largely illiterate rural group. We may have to wait until an indigenous investigator performs these tests before we can be really sure that other factors operating subtly at the time of testing are not promoting the results so far obtained.

Development of attentional processes

The development of attentional processes is basic to a large part of the perceptual development already considered. As we have seen, very early in the child's life he is attracted by specific objects. Quantifiable physiological changes occur at the time of this orienting reaction and these have been extensively studied, especially in the Soviet Union. The orienting reaction is considered the basic unit of attention. The responses are specific to a particular simulus, continued presentation of which will cause the responses to diminish. This is akin to the adaptation or habituation phenomenon to which we have already referred (page 8).

Voluntary selective attention is a more complex matter. It was noted previously that attentional processes could be studied by investigating the evoked potentials of the cortex. The evoked potentials increase in strength if the observer is given prior instructions, but this is not the case

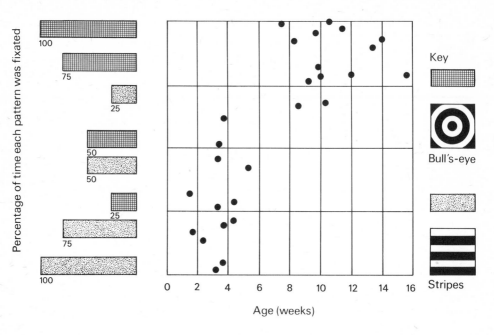

Fig 36 The increase with age in attentional preference for a bull's-eye rather than stripes (reprinted from 'The origin of form perception', Fantz, R. L., *Scientific American*, May 1971)

with the pre-school child. Indeed Farber and Fried (see Luria, 1973) have shown that the full consequences of the instruction, as measured by evoked potentials throughout the cortex, only occur for the first time between the ages of twelve and fifteen years.

While such physiological investigations are very interesting, they have been secondary to other approaches. It has been found that children have distinct preferences for certain stimuli over others. On a simple level, Hershenson (1964) showed that a new-born child prefers to look at a medium rather than a dim or a bright light. Preferences have also been shown for one shape over another. The apparatus of Fantz, described above, can also be used to determine this preference for certain shapes. Fantz (1958) found originally that young children, even at a few weeks old, preferred to look at complex figures rather than very simple ones. This may explain the child's preference, mentioned earlier, for solid objects over flat ones, since solid objects, even as a two-dimensional projection on the retina, are more complex. However, it was also noted that there seemed to be a given complexity level which attracted most attention at a given age. The babies were provided with the alternative stimuli of a bull's-eye or horizontal stripes as shown in Fig. 36. This figure shows the

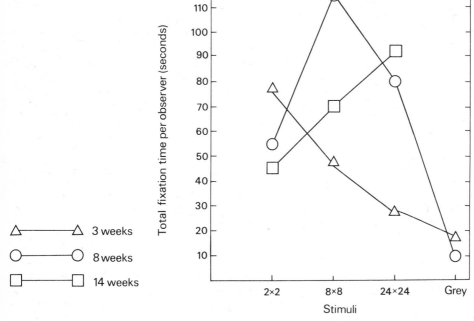

Fig 37 The relationship between level of complexity and attention for different age-groups (reprinted from 'Age differences in infants' attention to patterns of different complexities', Brennan, W. H., *et al.*, *Science* Vol. 151, 21 January 1966. © by the American Association for the Advancement of Science)

percentage of time spent looking at the bull's-eye or the horizontal stripes. Each dot represents a single infant's first test session. It can be seen that by the time the child is eight weeks old there is a change in preference from the tripes to the bull's-eye.

Fantz suggests that the complexity level of the bull's-eye is too great for the processing system of the younger child. Moreover, since each dot in the figure represents the child's first experience with the two stimuli, Fantz suggests that this process is maturational rather than learned. However, it need not be a maturational process on this argument alone, as the previous visual experience of the child may be contributing in a more indirect way to his ability to process the complex figures as he grows older.

Brennen, Ames and Moore (1966) also found, in babies tested from birth to six months, a change in attention according to the increasing complexity of the stimuli. These workers stressed the fact that attention is directed towards objects of medium complexity for the stage of development of the child—a view reinforced by Kagan (1972).

Figure 37 shows the time infants spent looking at a stimulus in the experiment of Brennen *et al.* They chose infants of three ages, namely three, eight and fourteen weeks old. The stimuli were chequerboard

squares and were presented four times for thirty seconds each. The level
of complexity was increased by increasing the number of squares from
2×2 to 8×8 and 24×24. A uniform grey stimulus was also presented as
a control. It can be seen that a three-week-old infant looked most at the
simplest stimulus, an eight-week-old at the medium level and a fourteen-
week-old at the most complex.

However, Horowitz (1969) doubts the generality of these results as
applied to any individual child. Since infants develop rapidly and at
widely different rates the age-range at least may be doubted. This doubt
was confirmed in the inability to repeat the three- and eight-week-old
fixation patterns. The fourteen-week-old pattern was more reliably
obtained; sometimes even at a much earlier age. However, if it appeared
earlier, there was no guarantee that it would still be there the next week.

Individual differences were also found by Hershenson (1964) in his
studies of stimulus preference. Do such results reflect individual attention
differences at a young age, or are there other explanations? All the
obvious controls for position preference were observed, so that poor
experimental methodology is not the explanation of the individual
difference. It is possible that the differences in visual environment of each
child may be the important factor. This is certainly shown in a study by
White and Castle (1964). They investigated the scanning behaviour of
infants brought up in hospital and normally given little personal attention.
One group of such infants was taken up and rocked by a nurse for twenty
minutes a day for thirty days. Records of the infants' visual behaviour from
the thirty-seventh day to the tenth week showed that these infants spent,
especially at first, more time looking round at the environment than did
the infants who had not had this handling. Removal to a more complex
environment at the age of three-and-a-half months produced an even
more marked increase in visual attention.

Using this technique of enriching the visual environment, tentative
attempts have been made to speed up the fixation patterns reported by
Brennan *et al.* (page 121). This can be done by giving the child an opportunity to observe chequerboard squares slightly more complicated than
those preferred at his age (Fig. 37). So far these attempts have not met
with a great deal of success. As there is considerable variation in the rate
of development of any one child, such exposure may result in over-
stimulation, which can be as disruptive to development as deprivation.
Moreover, where any early gain has been established by this means,
it seems to have disappeared by the time the child is nine months old.

Related to the problem of visual complexity is that of visual novelty.
Fantz (1964) presented pairs of patterns to infants; one of the patterns
varied while the other remained the same. Infants over two months ceased
to look at the repeated pattern, but there was no decline in fixation to the
repeated pattern by infants younger than that age. Caron and Caron

(1968) showed older children (fourteen to sixteen weeks) a series of stimuli made up of several different patterns and one repeated pattern. Again, the time spent looking at the repeated pattern declined more rapidly, but complexity was important. When the repeated pattern was a red-and-white chequerboard of four squares the decline was more rapid than when it contained 144 squares. A similar result was obtained with much younger children by Friedman (1972).

The cessation of visual interest shown by the experiment of Caron and Caron was accompanied by restlessness and vocal protest. However, can we be certain that a difference in attention means a difference in perception? Stimulus preference is only an indirect method of telling us in what way a non-attended figure differs perceptually from an attended figure. One can easily promote a stimulus preference by rewarding attention to one object, but, especially in the older child, could it be said that the perception was altered simply because there was a stimulus preference?

It has been argued (Miller, 1948) that labelling a stimulus can affect its perception. This has not always been supported by experimental evidence, though it is not a very different explanation from that William James put forward to explain the learned discrimination of the tea-taster or wine expert. He reported that flour-graders knew by touch alone whether wheat had been grown in Iowa or Tennessee. James illustrated his argument by using as an example a person who initially cannot distinguish between burgundy and claret, but then learns to do so. He suggested that the two wines, being drunk on different occasions, have different associations connected with their tastes. By these associations becoming attached to the taste of the wine in some mysterious way, they 'stretch these (tastes) further apart'.

Katz (1963) argued in very similar vein. Seven- and nine-year-old children were taught verbal labels for a set of four nonsense shapes. One group learned different labels for all four shapes. A second group learned a common label for each of two pairs of the shapes. The children had two of the shapes presented very briefly and were tested on a same–different task. The second group made more mistakes. However, it is quite possible that labelling affects the performance of the child in other ways. It could be argued that the scanning behaviour is affected by labelling. The label then might perhaps direct attention to a common feature between the shapes. If the common feature were located, for instance, at the bottoms of two pictures, the child would only look in that place, thus more mistakes might arise.

Robinson (1955), using a finger-print discrimination task, found that sheer practice on a same–different task was just as effective as labelling. The difference in perception can be explained by attentional differences in the observers' scanning patterns. This is a view put forward by Gibson (1969), who is in fact saying that different things are seen because different stimuli go into the system. However, as she says, 'there is always an interaction between potential stimulation and the exploratory activity, the searching and orienting responses of the perceiving organism'.

This is interesting with respect to a finding of Vurpillot (1968). She presented drawings of houses, some of which had differences in the windows, to children (five to nine years old), who were asked to say whether pictures of two houses were the same or different. The poor performance of the younger children could be related to their poor scanning strategies. Young children spent less time scanning the houses than did older ones, and it was possible that they therefore did not see the differences, so could not make a correct response. Any same–different task is more than a simple perceptual test, and memory and other abilities are involved. These abilities increase with age, but the developmental trends noted may well have much to do with the fact that the child has to learn to look: children of intermediate age were, if anything, taking longer to scan, thus reflecting this ongoing learning process.

Learning to pay attention has been noted with simpler tasks in younger infants, as, for example, has been observed by Ames and Silfan (1965), who found that babies of six months were less likely to hold their fixations on a single part of a stimulus than babies of seven weeks. Gibson (1969) quotes Ames and Silfan as saying, 'it appears to us that while the older infant may be capturing stimuli with his visual behaviour, the young infant is being captured by the stimuli'. This suggests an active change in the way of looking on the part of the older child.

What may be crucial to differences in patterns of looking is the rate at which the child can take in information. It is important to note that mentally retarded children spend as much time as normal children, if not longer, looking at the stimuli in the apparatus of Fantz described earlier. What they do not do is differentiate between the stimuli (Miranda and Fantz, 1973). Children with Down's Syndrome (mongolism), a chromosome abnormality, were found to spend equal amounts of time looking at the bull's-eye or stripes of Fig. 36 at the age when normal children would have a definite preference for the bull's-eye. There may be some small difference in the retarded children's acuity as compared to normal but this would be insufficient to explain the lack of differentiation.

Bond (1972) argues that it is only as the child matures that he can take in more information and that this will be reflected in the child's preferences for simple or complex objects and also in the fixation strategies adopted. Salapatek (1969) showed that four- to six-week-old children tended to look at much less of a simple figure, such as a triangle, than did eight- to ten-week-old children. There was, again, a relationship between complexity and attention, since without anything to look at the child would often become fretful or fall asleep. It was only the older children who directed their attention away from the contours of a figure to look towards

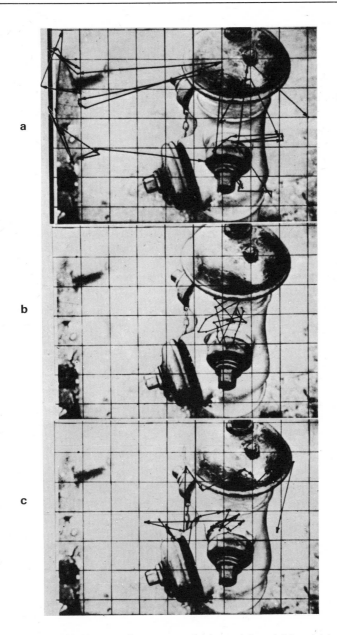

Fig 38 The scanning patterns of (a) an adult and (b) and (c)
two children (reprinted from 'How adults and children
search and recognise pictures'. Mackworth, N. H. and
Bruner, J. S., *Human Development*, 13, 1970)

the centre of the figure. It might therefore be suggested that facial recognition is operative from this age onwards.

It has also been shown that children and adults differ in the way they search a picture for an object. Mackworth and Bruner (1970) investigated the difference between a six-year-old and an adult in tackling this task. One example they considered was where a child and adult were shown a clear picture (in this case, of a fire hydrant). If the picture was clearly in focus, children and adults spent about the same time looking at the picture and both concentrated their gaze upon certain areas. With children, however, the place favoured was very idiosyncratic, whereas the adults generally all favoured the same spot to look at. An effective search of a picture requires more than a concentration of gaze upon highly informative areas: it needs also a wide coverage of the display being looked at. If the picture is clearly in focus, children seem to be deficient in this second skill.

This can be seen clearly if we look at the track lengths of the children and adults as they scanned the picture (Fig. 38). Track length is measured by the distance covered by the eye in moving over the picture. The picture of the fire hydrant measured 8 × 10 inches and was placed at 28 inches from the eye. Figure 38a shows the long eye-track of an adult (66 inches). It can be seen that the adult tried to link up the parts of the picture. Figure 38b shows a child who, typically, was involved with the detail in the centre of the hydrant, having a short eye-track of only 14 inches, and (c) shows another child tracing out the contour of the main shape, moving along the edges in short steps (eye-track length 27 inches) but not in the wide-looking way of the adult.

Children seem to be more cautious with their eye movements. This is borne out by the distinction made by Mackworth and Bruner between steps and leaps. A 'step' involves a movement from one object to the next, using central vision all the time (moving, in their display, less than three inches across the picture). A 'leap', on the other hand, involves a movement so long (in this case, over three inches) that the successive areas looked at are quite distinct. It was found that children made 24 per cent of all their eye movements in steps of half-an-inch or less. Such very short steps only constituted 11 per cent of the adults' searching pattern. The difficulty for children arises, presumably, from their inability to take in as much information as the adult. Initially, the adult 'feels his way around' the picture, to find out the theme, before 'leaping' from side to side. The child does not adopt this scanning pattern. Adults search for the informative areas of a display, whereas a child is dominated by outline of shapes or any area of high brightness contrast. Children tend to end their eye movement leaps on the edges of large patches of colour.

Confirmation of this finding comes from Tronick and Clanton (1971), who found differences in looking behaviour at fourteen to fifteen weeks as compared with four to five weeks of age. At the earlier age there were long periods (up to thirty seconds) where no change of gaze occurred when the child was viewing some brightly-coloured cubes. Tronick and Clanton found that as the child grew older more of the environment was looked at and the sweep of the eye movements was larger.

This is also borne out by the well-known observation that small visual steps are characteristic of the child when reading. The child-like pattern of looking, of course, returns to an adult when confronted with a difficult word. The developmental difference with respect to steps and leaps when searching a picture relies on the picture being clearly visible. Under conditions of poor illumination or blurring, this difference will diminish or even disappear. This is because the task becomes too complex even for the adult to take in so much information.

Great stress is laid here upon the eye movement strategies that differentiate children from adults. The reason for this is that they may give us some insight into the problem of how the visual processing of a child differs from that of the adult. However, it is important here to consider carefully the methodology of the experimenters, since the problem arises, common to artificial laboratory situations, as to whether the eye movements recorded are representative of those occurring naturally. The reason for doubting that they are concerns the method by which direction of gaze is isolated.

To determine which aspect of a picture a child is viewing, it is necessary to know both head and eye position. Usually these are not monitored separately, but the head position is held constant: this is often done by restraining the head in some way by a device such as a bite which the child holds onto with his teeth, thereby of necessity keeping his head still. This is a most unnatural way of looking at a picture and one might well suggest that the eye movements of the child would be unrepresentative. This may well be the case, but it does not necessarily mean that the results

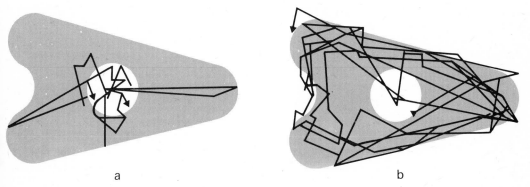

a   b

Fig 39 The difference in scanning patterns when examining an unfamiliar shape between children (a) three years old and (b) six years old (reprinted from 'The formation and development of perceptual activity', Zinchenko, V. P. *et al., Soviet Psychology and Psychiatry* Vol. II, No. 1, 1963)

of such eye-movement studies should be discarded: one does not want to throw the babies' eye movements out with the bath water.

The results presented here are, in fact, taken at face value. If in future they are discarded, it will be because these restraints which have been placed upon the child are found to be such as to make him perform very unusual eye movements. At the present time this is not thought likely.

Zinchenko, Van Chzhi-Tsin and Tarakonov (1963) studied the way a child familiarises himself with an object. Figure 39 shows the scanning patterns of a three-year-old child as compared with those of a six-year-old. These investigators (see Pick, 1964) found that shape identification of three-year-olds was very poor and suggested that this might be connected with the fact that the children were concentrating their gaze on the middle of the object and that their eye movements bore no clear relationship to the object's actual shape. We have noted that Piaget holds that differential eye movements are associated with differential extents of visual illusion. Of course, there is a 'chicken and egg' problem here (which comes first: the eye movements or the poor shape discrimination?)— but it is interesting to find that this observable behaviour is associated with differential perception.

In general, what is important in this area is to isolate the differences in strategies adopted by children when looking at an object, and to see how they develop. Bruner (1969) reports an experiment in which the ability to integrate stimuli in the periphery of vision was seen to develop. Children were observed between the ages of ten days and three months. The stimuli consisted of two highly-decorated balls a little distance apart. One ball descended from top to bottom of a window to the left of a child, being visible for six seconds. Three-and-a-half seconds later, through a window to his right, the other ball could be seen ascending, again taking six seconds. This cycle was then repeated. At the earlier stages, the child looked generally in the direction of the windows as opposed to other areas of the room. A little later in his development, there was a phase when he looked fixedly at each ball while it was visible and then transferred his gaze to the other window when it disappeared. Around sixty days of age, the child showed a most interesting form of visual behaviour in that he from time to time looked away from the ball that was on view and glanced at the other window, before rapidly returning to view the visible ball. Here we see the beginnings of the searching pattern which is characteristic of adult viewing.

As we have already pointed out, differences in perception may not be surprising if we have different inputs to the visual system. But even if the child and the adult look at the same place, this does not necessarily imply that they perceive exactly the same.

Zinchenko *et al.* noted, like Mackworth and Bruner, that in perception there is an initial familiarisation of the scene which is followed by an investigation of the most important areas. This second stage involves a detailed recognition process which will depend on the observer's past experience. There is a problem of how familiarisation is possible prior to recognition, but the answer may be in the attentional units described earlier (page 81). Certainly, older children (Pick *et al.*, 1972) benefit much more than younger ones from information about what is to be presented in a selective attention task. It is revealing, whatever the resolution of this problem, that Zinchenko *et al.* noted developmental differences for these two stages. Between the ages of three and six, the familiarisation stage was much more marked in the older children. Initially, the six-year-olds produced a greater number of eye movements, but once the picture was familiar it produced fewer eye movements in these older children.

The six-year-old child seems comparable with the adult in ability to process visual information in a picture. This should not be taken to mean that the perceptual development is complete at six, since reading fixation times continue to decrease into adulthood: but reading is a more complex task, obviously involving many more cognitive functions.

Differences in scanning behaviour may have other consequences. For example, Ghent (1961) hypothesises that it is differential scanning behaviour that causes a child's inability to recognise objects when they are rotated. Young children, she suggests, always scan from the top to the bottom of a page. However, she found (Ghent 1963) that older children also scan from the top to the bottom. This may, of course, be connected with the schooling process. Confusions which commonly occur between left and right (b and d; p and q) may have little to do with the child's inability to see the differences between them, but rather be a result of some processing difficulty which one might call memory.

Over and Over (1967) found a fair ability to distinguish between orientation in other tasks. Children were given a standard line in a set orientation and many others in different orientations; when asked to find the line oriented in the same direction as the standard they could do this perceptual task very well. Left–right confusions may, therefore, involve more complex processes besides the direct perceptual activity.

In both the child and the adult, perception of an event can be altered by a change in importance of the features of the stimulus that are being attended to. The point to stress is that there is a characteristic difference in the organisational ability which takes account of these features—Potter (1966) discusses this with reference to a child's ability to recognise a blurred picture. Children up to the age of four typically form a hypothesis about a blurred picture and, even if the hypothesis is wrong, repeat it until the clarity of the picture increases so much that the hypothesis must be changed. The following protocol reproduced from Potter (1966) shows this. Thirteen pictures of a cow, ranging in focus from a blur to clear, were shown to a four-year-old. The numbers refer to the stage of focus, *E* and *S* to the experimenter and subject respectively:

1. (*E:* What do you think this picture could be about?)
   S: Some ice cream.
   (*E:* Uhmm. Keep watching the picture and don't look at me.)
2. *S:* (mumbles) Some chocolate ice cream, with white ice-cream.
3. Somebody sleeping in a bed.
4. Somebody a little clearer sleeping in a bed.
5. Even a person clearer than the other one, sleeping in a bed.
   (*E:* Uhmm. Keep looking.)
6. And now—there's somebody even clearer—sleeping on a bed.
   (Repeats this again in 7 and 8.)
9. And, er, even another person sleeping on the bed.
   (*E:* Uhmm. Anything else?)
10. (*E:* What do you see now?)
    A small picture.
    (*E:* What's in the picture?)
    S: (sighs) A bull.
11–13. (Continues to repeat cow. At 13, *E* asks:
    And what else?)
    S: I don't know what the white thing is—is it the bed? It might be sheets.

Note the following about this report: firstly, the child makes assumptions straight away; secondly, once a structure has been forced on to the picture it is especially hard for the child to relinquish it; thirdly, even when the recognition is complete, the child still has the ability to see the previous arrangement. This last finding suggests that the visual stimulus can be interpreted in many ways. The potential ambiguity of the visual stimulus with respect to the act of perception will occupy us in the next chapter.

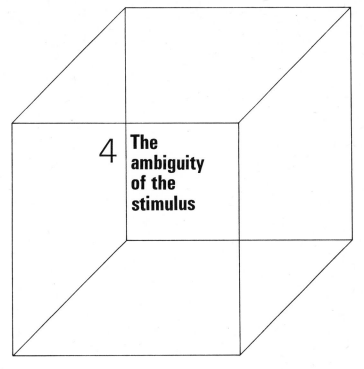

4 | **The ambiguity of the stimulus**

Hamlet: Do you see yonder cloud that's almost in shape of a camel?
Polonius: By the Mass, and 'tis like a camel indeed.
Hamlet: Methinks it is like a weasel.
Polonius: It is backed like a weasel.
Hamlet: Or like a whale?
Polonius: Very like a whale.

Hamlet (Act III, Scene II)

The transactionalist approach

What has been said so far might well make the reader wonder if any two people ever have the same percept when viewing the same scene, although, intuitively, most of us suspect that we do see in the same way most of the time. The ease with which it is possible (at least in certain circumstances) to make two observers view the same scene differently has led various theorists to offer explanations of the perceptual process based on some uncertainty or instability which is an inherent part of perceiving. It is possible to believe that the world as viewed by us is necessarily ambiguous and therefore always capable of reinterpretation, and we shall now consider perceptual ambiguity with reference to a school of perceptual theory known as 'transactionalism'.

To the transactionalist, more than to many theorists, perception is part of a whole interpretive process involving all cognitive functions. Perceptual activity involves an interaction with the outside world and will therefore reflect the way in which the visual world is organised. Transactionalists, as their literature shows, are not concerned with hallucinatory phenomena or trance states. At the beginning of this study it was stated that, as a starting point, we would take as given a real outside world: this, according to transactionalists, would be at worst wrong and at best a misplaced emphasis. It implies that there is such a thing as a true, verifiable percept because it appears that such a percept can be isolated. Transactionalists reject this notion of perception as an untrue abstraction. In essence, the transactionalist approach is not far from a phenomenological standpoint, viewing perceptual activity in the light of an individual's conscious activity, but also being based on his whole experience. The latter means that there is not the same stress on the conscious nature of perception as is found in most phenomenological approaches. Ittelson (1962) summarises the transactionalist approach: 'Neither a perception nor an object as perceived exists independent of the total life situation of which both perception and object are a part. It is meaningless to speak of either existing apart from the situation from which it is encountered.

The term 'transaction' is used because, in the interaction between perceiver and perceived, both are affected and neither can be taken in isolation. Ittelson, writing before the present awareness of the 'experimenter effect' (i.e. that the results of an experiment depend to some extent upon the person obtaining them), shows that this 'experimenter effect' is inherent in the notion of a transaction. He also stresses that transactionalists should beware of setting up a new 'deity' with the transaction as the basic unit: all perception is an interaction and indivisible. Thus Ittelson warns that the approach which he would avoid 'is analogous to the narrow, archaic view of Newtonian physics in which the belief was held that the observer stood outside of the system which he was observing, and was independent of the fact of observation. The psychologist, therefore, is a participant who affects and is affected by the transaction he is observing.'

Because each individual enters into the transaction in a different way, it is suggested by transactionalists that there are as many experiences as there are observers. What they do not make entirely clear, and what is important to define, is the nature of the different ways in which an observer can enter into the transaction. To phrase it in this way, as 'the participant entering into the transaction', seems to suggest that there may be some central system controlling perceptual activity and unaffected by it; but this is not what transactionalists intended. However, in a process in which everything can affect everything else, it is difficult to find a starting point.

Transactionalists believe that 'the world as we experience it is the product of perception, not the cause of it'. There can be no objection to this statement, but it does not necessarily contradict the view that there is a real outside world with verifiable, concrete properties. Transactionalists are here talking about the experienced world which is a result of our way of looking at the world. If our way of looking changes, then our experienced perception will change. The essence of the change in perceptual experience is based upon a probabilistic relationship with events in the world. In this respect, transactionalism has much in common with other theories of perception like the probabilistic functionalism of Brunswik (1955). These probabilities are built into a set of assumptions about the world which act unconsciously, just as in the nineteenth century Helmholtz said our calculation of the relationship between size and distance was unconscious. The assumptions determine our interpretation of the world through some predilection which Ittelson has called 'a weighting process'. These weightings depend on a probability based on what has had value in the past and are therefore deemed to have 'ecological validity' (to use Brunswik's terminology). However, the transactionalist viewpoint differs from pro-probabilistic functionalism in that sheer number of occurrences is not the only issue: assumptions about the world can be made in some circumstances from a single traumatic event, and what we see is not necessarily dependent on the likelihood of its having previously occurred.

Transactionalists do not envisage a static system but hold that it is possible for our perceptions to change. The transaction is considered to be modifiable and transactionalists have been concerned to conduct experiments to show this happening. Such change might occur in two different ways: within our already existing framework of assumptions it is possible that we might alter the weightings and thus change our perception, or we might completely change our assumptions by some unspecified perceptual learning process. Transactionalists believe that the experimental consequences of our assumptions are being validated all the time. Thus Ittelson says, 'Every action can be thought of as an experimental test of a hypothesis which is appropriately modified or confirmed as the result of our test through action'.

Transactionalists have concentrated on experiments in which observers are placed in situations where conflict arises between assumptions. These generally require placing the observer in an ambiguous situation, i.e. one in which observers may fail to agree as to the nature of the stimulus. Indices of ambiguity have been compiled (e.g. by Flament, 1959) which cover all situations from those which are completely unambiguous to those of complete ambiguity. A completely unambiguous situation is one in which all observers make the same response: a completely ambiguous situation is one in which all responses are equally probable, so that if there are four alternative responses, each occurs for 25 per cent of the time or for

25 per cent of observers. If one of the alternative responses is favoured then the situation becomes less ambiguous. That a situation is unambiguous does not mean that perception is veridical, as we have already pointed out with respect to illusions; but an ambiguous situation must be of interest here since it follows by definition that different interpretations are possible. These need not be perceptual interpretations but could, as Flament suggests, be response-determined. In his view, the ambiguity of the stimulus is effective in altering the response uncertainty. Time and again we shall be confronted with this possibility that what the ambiguous stimulus does is not to change perception but to allow response biases to operate. Since that which is perceived can only be communicated verbally, supposed changes in perception may be nothing more than verbal changes. It is worthwhile bearing this caveat in mind because, in general, only perceptual interpretations will be considered.

Distance judgements

An ambiguous situation much favoured by transactionalists concerns the relationship between size and distance. If one considers the retinal image alone, size and distance are never completely defined. In Fig. 40 we see many possible lines of different lengths and orientations, all of which give rise to the same retinal representation. If this retinal image is taken as our starting point (though there is no a priori reason for taking this static view) then we must place our observer in a potentially ambiguous situation.

One such demonstration of this size–distance relationship is the Thereness–Thatness Task devised by Ames. The apparatus contains two visual fields, each of which is viewed monocularly. The task of the observer is to judge the distance of an object in one field compared with another in the comparison field. It has been found that if an object is seen as being

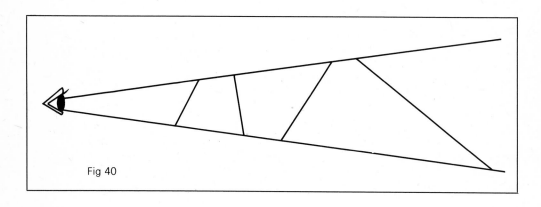

Fig 40

of a standard size, such as a playing-card or cigarette packet, then it appears to be at a distance commensurate with that assumption. If the object is not of an immediately definable size (as, for instance, a piece of paper), the distance estimates of a given individual are still consistent, even though between individuals there may be large differences.

This suggests that we all have our assumptions about the size of such objects, based, perhaps, on our own experiences. Hastorf (1950) proved this conclusively by experiments in which his observers had to estimate the distance away from them of a white card: when it was described as a calling card it was seen at a much nearer distance than when it was described as an envelope. There is nothing very remarkable about this because, in the reduced conditions under which Hastorf conducted his experiments, either view is equally valid. However, Slack (1956) did show that the size we normally associate with objects can be used to distort distance judgements even under normal viewing conditions. Also, Gogel and Newton (1969) report that these size discrepancies can be accomplished with binocular vision.

The fact that a given change in retinal image can be produced by a small distance change from a nearby object, or a large distance change from a far object, was used by Wallach and Frey (1972) to trick the observer into thinking an object had moved a long way when in fact it had not. This was achieved by making the observer receive a sequence of image sizes consistent with that of a diamond of constant size moving back and forth between a distance of 400 and 33 centimetres from the observer's eye. In fact, the object moved between 80 and 25 centimetres. To keep the object in focus, unconscious adjustments of the eyes would be made to the veridical distance. The observer had to make judgements, before and after this deception, upon the depth and size of pyramids situated at 33 and 66 centimetres from his eyes. Comparing the 'before' and 'after' scores, quite a substantial percentage increase in the estimate of the distance of the pyramids was found. Since the only distance cues available were convergence and accommodation of the eyes (the apparatus comprised luminous models in a darkened room), these cues must have been affected by the judgement of the moving object. The ambiguity in the situation had therefore incorrectly weighted the observer's subsequent assumptions about size and depth.

The rotating trapezoid

The rotating trapezoid devised and analysed by Ames (1951) has provoked a great deal of interest and research. It is an extremely compelling illusion. The window frame shown in Fig. 41 is rotated fairly slowly in front of the observer; when it reaches a certain point in its rotation it appears to reverse its direction, and then continues to oscillate back and forth. This is an

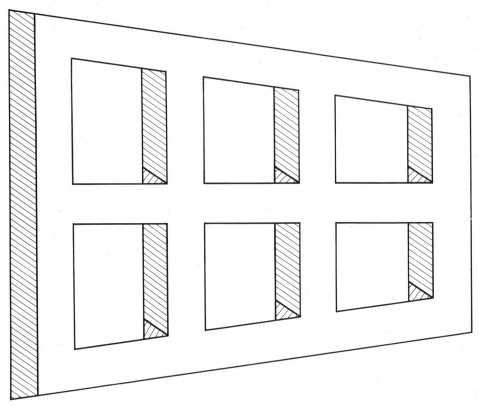

Fig 41 Ames's rotating trapezoid

illusion since it is in fact continuously rotating in the same direction. The window frame is seen as rectangular even though it is not perfectly so, and this is important to Ames's explanation since at some point there will be a conflict between this assumption and the stimulus that is actually received. At a certain orientation of the trapezoidal shape, this conflict will have to be resolved and one of the following alternatives must dominate: we see either a rectangular frame moving back and forth or a trapezoidal frame rotating. Because, on a probabilistic basis, a window frame is likely to be rectangular, Ames holds that we take this as the correct way of seeing and perceive the oscillating rather than the rotating motion.

The explanation given by Ames is held to be substantiated by a cross-cultural experiment by Allport and Pettigrew (1957). They took this illusion to the Zulus who are reported as having a 'circular' culture which does not emphasise rectangular forms—for instance, huts and windows are always circular. It was found that rural Zulus experienced less illusion than those who were urbanised (exposed to a Western type of environment). The results could be taken as going against the contention that experience is the only causal factor, since all observers could be made to see the illusion under some conditions. Slack (1959), however, cites the fact that the urbanised Zulus saw the illusion more readily as being further proof of the experiential hypothesis: why should some conditions of viewing be more favourable for producing the illusion, unless it is under such conditions that the conflict between assumed rectangularity and real trapezoidal shape come to the fore for those people that have experienced a great deal of rectangularity? This experiential explanation has held favour with some theorists (Gregory, 1966) but it is usually a difficult task to assess experience in the cross-cultural setting.

That the illusion has another contributory cause beside a probabilistic one is shown by experiments conducted by another transactionalist, Kilpatrick. If a rod is attached to the window frame it behaves in a curious manner. The rod continues to rotate while the trapezoidal window is appearing to oscillate, i.e. the rod must cut through the window, which is highly unlikely, especially as the window frame is never harmed. However, Kilpatrick found that his observers could be made to perceive the motion of the rod in different ways if they were led to believe different facts about its nature: if the observer thought it was a steel rod, then in a mysterious way it cut through the frame; if it was thought to be made of rubber it was seen to be flexible and appeared to bend round the frame. These two per-cepts, of course, occurred although the rod placed through the trapezoidal window remained unchanged; thus the assumption determined the perception.

This explanation based on the observers' assumptions about the rectan-gularity of objects has been disputed. Pastore (1952) points out that almost any irregular object will give rise to this illusion if rotated and that there is nothing special about window frames: reversals are seen with a plain trapezoid—the window frames are not essential. Indeed, for other objects, the illusion can be traced back at least to the nineteenth century. Kenyon (1898) observed it when watching a fan rotate and Boring (1942) reports that Sinsteden in 1860 noticed that a windmill seen silhouetted against the sky kept reversing its motion so that he could not tell whether he was seeing the windmill from the back or the front.

It would seem that if such reversals are to be explained then the assump-tions made by the observer must be made to include a more general situa-tion than that of the Ames rotating trapezoid. It would seem likely (Murch, 1970) that wrong assumptions *are* made about the rotating objects, but these concern distances of parts of the objects from the observer. Having made these wrong assumptions, the incoming information con-tinues to be interpreted in a manner consistent with the assumptions.

The fact that the world has an ambiguous element to it was forced upon the art historian Gombrich (1965) when he saw this illusion:

I had just attended a demonstration of that intriguing visual teaser, Adelbert Ames's 'revolving trapezoid', in essence a flat, fore-shortened window frame that turns on its axis but looks stubbornly as if it swayed to and fro. As I walked cross-country, I happened to see a broken farm gate propped up in an inaccessible pond. It reminded me of the trapezoid and I suddenly realised that I could not tell its real shape, or position either. There was a moment of slight anxiety as I woke up to the fact that the same applied to distant trees and countless other configurations in my surroundings.

The Ames room

Another demonstration devised by Ames is his famous distorting room. The room is so built that from a special vantage-point it looks exactly like an ordinary room, but in fact one of the far corners is very much nearer than the other. If two people are placed at the two far corners of the room they do not appear to be the same size: the one standing at the corner nearer to the observer appears a giant, while the one standing at the far corner appears a dwarf. Why should this be? The explanation put forward is again in terms of our assumptions of rectangularity: because here this assumption is incorrect, these people must become appropriately distorted. Since it appears to the observer that the person in the far corner is the same distance away as the person in the near corner, they must of necessity be of very different sizes. This must be so in order to make sense of the visual input received.

There are other factors which may contribute to the observer's organising his perception to distort the room. When we discussed the personality variable of field-dependence we noted the very strong tendency to assume that the framework of any scene is vertical. There is a similar assumption that the framework is right-angled. If these assumptions are incorrect, the observer may be very mistaken about the size of an object.

It is possible to reorganise our initial perception of the Ames Room. It is surprising, however, that if the two people observed change places this in itself is not enough to cause such a reorganisation: the person who was once a giant now becomes a dwarf. If our perception were determined by the probability of an occurrence, this would not be likely to happen. In fact, one would be hard pressed to know which was the more infrequently encountered, non-rectangular rooms or giants and dwarfs. Reorganisation of the room is possible by some active participation on the part of the observer (Kilpatrick, 1954), though passive inspection can be effective in some circumstances. It is simply necessary that the assumptions made in perceiving are put into conflict with the incoming stimulation. Kilpatrick found that throwing balls towards the back of the room and tracing the back wall with a stick were both effective. If one imagines a ball being thrown at the back wall it is obvious that some reorganisation must occur at the point where the ball should meet the wall but does not:

the ball cannot keep going towards the wall without the wall being pushed further back (at least, so one would think, but the rod continues time after time to go through the frame of the rotating trapezoid). However, Kilpatrick found that reorganisation did occur and, moreover, the new way of looking at this Ames Room affected the observer's assumptions about differently-shaped distorted rooms. Therefore the assumptive nature of the perceptual process is again validated.

It is interesting at this point to note Ittelson's contention that the 'starting point for perceptual studies must always be perceiving as it is encountered in concrete real life situations'. One striking aspect of the transactionalists' experiments is just how unlike real life are most of their experimental situations. Ambiguity may be a factor in all perception, but never so ostentatiously. One is not allowed to get good distance judgements of the objects in their Thereness–Thatness Task, since viewing is with one eye in reduced illumination with one's head perfectly still. How representative of a real life situation is that? The Ames Room is so constructed that from one point, and one point only, it is like a normal rectangular room. If one were allowed to move one's head, the true sizes of the people would be obvious.

It is often said that experimentation must begin by investigating a small part of the environment and that the great temples of knowledge will arise from these small building bricks. But this would seem to be against the essence of the transactionalists' approach, so it is odd that such 'unrepresentative' demonstrations form the background of their research. This having been said, a great deal of stimulating and worthwhile work has resulted. The virtue of the transactionalist approach, like other important theories of perception, is that it has at its roots the notion of the active perceiver.

Personality differences in the transactionalist demonstrations

The world of the transactionalist is full of potentially valid interpretations. Ittelson et al. (1961) report an experiment by Kaufer in which the judged distance of an object was related to the individual's way of looking at the world. This was done by taking a sample of patients whose major personality characteristic was diagnosed as that of emotionally either 'moving away from' or 'moving towards' other people. It was hypothesised that the two groups would make different judgements as to the distance of the objects. It was predicted that the 'moving towards' group would perceive objects as being nearer to them than the other group. This was found to be the case.

Beloff and Beloff (1961) found that if the object in question was a person's face, the perceived distance depended on the observer's attitude towards the face. They used several photographs of liked and disliked faces, including one which was considered admirable by one group of observers but as representing someone highly objectionable to another group. The task was to set the photographs at the same distance as a neutral standard. It was found that photographs considered favourably were judged to be nearer than those held to be objectionable. For some not immediately apparent reason, women were more susceptible to this effect.

Even if in general these viewing conditions are not representative of the norm, these are important findings. It has been shown, for example, that how important we consider someone determines how large we perceive him as being. Dannenmaier and Thumin (1964) asked forty-six nursing students to estimate the heights of the Assistant Director of their school, their instructor and two fellow-students. It was found that there was a relationship between perceived status and estimated height. Those in authority were judged to be taller than they really were, and those low in status to be shorter. One word of caution concerning this experiment relates to the fact that the judgements were made from memory: there is therefore a distinct possibility that some learned relationship between authority and size affected the memory of the heights and there was in fact no difference in perception.

The fact that a motivational weighting can affect how we view the world is also suggested by an experiment using the Ames Room. If an Ames Room is made large enough for people to walk about in, then, typically, when a person walks across the back of the room he appears either to shrink or swell dramatically, depending on the direction of his motion. This is surprising, since people are generally perceived to be the same size as they walk away from us, at least until they move into the far distance. Does this size change occur when someone we know walks across the Ames Room? Wittreich (1959), reporting an experiment of Cantril, says that this distortion would not occur if the person in the distorting room is the spouse of the observer. One woman, whose nickname gave rise to this being called the 'Honi' phenomenon, refused to see her husband change size. Faced with making an assumption about an odd-shaped room or a shrinking husband, she chose to see the shape of the room as odd. The explanation of Cantril's report that the 'Honi' phenomenon was strongest with newly-weds and couples married for a long time is only speculative. The finding, in fact, does not seem to have been repeated.

A similar result was obtained by Wittreich (1955) for the resistance of distortion of a spouse when the observer wore distorting spectacles. There was a large individual difference in the amount of distortion produced. It was also found that junior naval ratings reported less distortion in viewing a superior officer when wearing these spectacles than when viewing each other. Asthana (1960) found that distortion was noticed quickest when viewing a disliked person; this was followed by inanimate objects, then strangers, a liked person and last of all in viewing a distorted version of oneself. Moreover, girls when viewing distorted versions of themselves report less distortion than boys. Of course, we have here the problem mentioned previously of distinguishing between perception and response: it could well be that girls are less willing to admit that they see themselves as distorted.

It is interesting that the distortion noted under these conditions, as in the experiment of Asthana, takes some time to develop fully. Because of this time factor, it is quite possible for interpretations to alter or 'gel' in different ways. It has been found, for example, that under stressful conditions it takes longer to recognise the true nature of the distorting input from an Ames Room (Block, 1961). The fact that it takes time to organise a potential input has importance where the situation is in some way unstructured. Recognition can always be viewed as a process of reconstruction, as it is by Neisser (1967), and therefore in a sense potentially ambiguous.

This ambiguity has been noticed by most people at some time or other when waiting for a friend: a stranger walking towards you is perceived as the friend you are expecting. Before the recognition that you are mistaken, there may be a period when you still see the person as your friend, but walking oddly or looking a little off-colour. Then, suddenly, the visual input no longer upholds this interpretation and the person is seen as a stranger.

From these transactionalist demonstrations, we shall now turn our attention to the stimuli generally referred to as 'ambiguous figures'. We should bear in mind, however, that though these stimuli involve only simple shapes, they may, if the transactionalists are correct, be the tip of the iceberg, suggesting that all stimuli are organisable and hence potentially ambiguous.

Ambiguity in two dimensions

Rubin (1915) devised many two-dimensional figures which contained alternative percepts. The importance of these ambiguous figures for Rubin lay in the phenomenal changes that occurred in the perception of them when part of a figure became dominant. The part of the stimulus in our attention is called the 'figure' and that part not in attention, the 'ground'. The phenomenon itself is generally known as the Figure—Ground Effect. The figure, which is uppermost in our attention, is said to be phenomenally clearer and seen differently. This can be observed if the normal colouring of a map is reversed. The brown land is normally seen

Fig 42 Rubin's ambiguous figure *Faces–Vase*

Fig 43 Yin and Yang

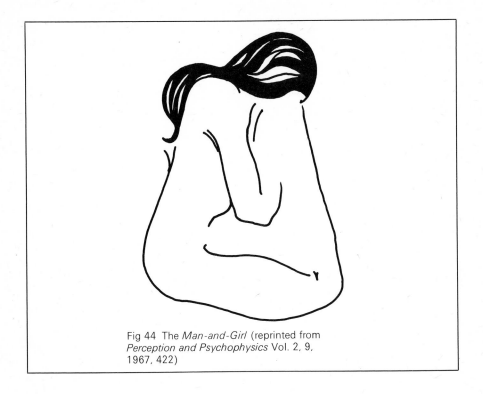

Fig 44 The *Man-and-Girl* (reprinted from
Perception and Psychophysics Vol. 2, 9,
1967, 422)

as the figure and the blue sea is seen as the ground: reversal of these
colours causes a reversal of what is normally dominant and gives rise to the
perception of shapes not noticed before.

The most famous of the ambiguous figures devised by Rubin is shown
in Fig. 42. Sometimes the faces will dominate, sometimes the vase. With
repeated viewing the fluctuations between the alternative percepts become very rapid, which may be why some people report seeing both
alternatives at once. In fact any squiggly line drawn down the centre of a
circle can produce a figure with alternative organisational properties: first
one half, then the other will become the figure. If, however, one half is
emphasised in some way, it will be harder to make the stimulus reverse;
often the white part will predominate as the figure. This does not seem to
apply to the ancient Chinese symbol of Yin and Yang (Fig. 43) which
represents the fusion of opposites. Here the two halves alternate in
attention, neither becoming dominant. Another interesting ambiguous
figure is shown in Fig. 44 and is due to Fisher (1967); he calls it the 'Man
and Girl'.

Ambiguous figures in two dimensions are in fact a special case of the
general phenomenon of the organisation of the visual input. This will be
developed further, but at this point it is enough to say that there is always a

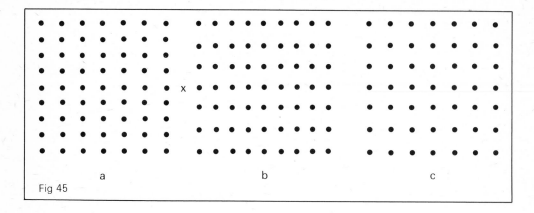

Fig 45

tendency for us to organise our perception in some way. If we look at Fig. 45, fixating between a and b, it will be seen that the dots form columns to the left of the fixation point and rows to the right. Since everyone sees it this way it is tempting to look for a nativistic explanation. However, just because everyone sees it in the same way, it is not of primary concern to us here. But what of Fig. 45c: do the dots run vertically or horizontally? The perception can be of either, from which we can deduce (in a rather circular manner) that there must be some conflicting forces in the organisational structure. Because of this, the percept will vary from time to time and from person to person. If one fixates it for some time, various groupings of dots will emerge besides rows and columns. These may be, for example, groups of four in a square. Cross shapes are also commonly seen. This reorganisation arising from the ambiguity of the stimulus can also be seen in some visual illusions.

A simple but important illusory change can occur when watching apparent motion. If four lights are arranged in a square so that diagonally opposite pairs flash together, then if the two pairs of lights are flashed out of sequence, apparent motion (page 34) will result. But the apparent motion can take one of two directions. The observer can see motion along the vertical sides of the square, one light moving up and the other down. Alternatively, he may see the lights moving horizontally and in opposite directions. These percepts will fluctuate. These two versions of the direction of motion are subjectively so different that many observers will not believe that the change is self-induced and does not result from a change in the lights themselves.

Ross (1974) quotes some interesting accounts of ambiguous perception resulting in apparent movement. Mountaineers, for example, have often noted that rocks on the skyline will appear to move in misty weather. One such incident is described by a mountaineer in the Cairngorms:

When we started on the last rise to Cairn Toul there came a wider clearance than usual. Suddenly Mortimer gripped my arm and pointed uphill through the misty chasm. 'Look!' he exclaimed, 'Two men crossing to Glen Einich.' Upon looking up at the slope I was duly surprised to see two climbers a long way ahead of us... I watched them traverse a full fifty feet from east to west across the snow-slope, one about ten yards in front of the other... we advanced and saw them halt, apparently to wait for us. At a hundred yards' range they turned out to be two black boulders.

This ambiguous movement is connected with the well-known observation that in an unstructured environment it is difficult to tell whether it is oneself that is moving or one's surroundings. This often happens when in a train standing next to another which moves off: initially it appears to be one's own train that is moving. In the example of the mountaineers, the ambiguity of the situation led to an interpretation of movement of the environment. While this ambiguity is not based on depth perception *per se*, it would seem to lead to a consideration of those perceptual experiences that are ambiguous in this respect.

Ambiguity in depth perception

We have already seen that a stimulus such as a photograph or a drawing can be interpreted in different ways. A two-dimensional figure representing three dimensions is ambiguous in that it may be the projection of many solid objects. We have seen that the retinal image may arise from various, indeed an infinite number of inputs. The Necker Cube (Fig. 46) was first described in 1832 by the Swiss crystallographer, C. A. Necker, who noticed that crystals could change in shape as he looked at them. The lines of Fig. 46 can be seen as a two-dimensional flat surface, but it is harder for most Western people to do this than to see it in three dimensions. Most people will see it as a cube with a top denoted by the corners, a, b, c, d. It is hard for some people to see in any other way (a phenomenon, as we shall see, of some interest) but for most people, after staring at the lines for some time, a different way of seeing the figure will arise: the surface marked by the corners b, c, e, f, is seen as a surface above the level of the surface denoted by the corners a, d, g, h. When seen in this manner it appears in depth as a truncated pyramid. Changing the point of fixation, or blinking, can often help to effect this change; indeed, steady fixation is sometimes a hindrance to change. This altered perception is central in origin, as shown by the fact that if the Necker Cube is seen as a stabilised retinal image (page 6) it will still reverse.

There is considerable variation in the ease with which a given individual will find the Necker Cube reversing. Frontal lesions, in particular, cause a change in reversal rate. According to Cohen (1959) this can be a slowing

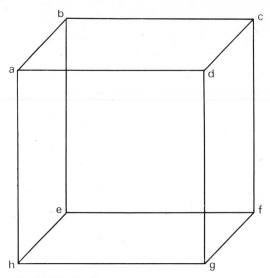

Fig 46 The Necker cube

down or a speeding up, depending on the site of the lesions.

Reversal rate has also been related, from time to time, to various personality factors. The most appealing of these theories comes from McDougall (1929). It is suggested that increasing higher brain function is accompanied by more rapid conduction at the synapses of the nervous system. However, there is in all of us some counteracting force which serves to diminish the effect of the cortex and increases the resistances at these synapses. McDougall called this biochemical factor 'substance X': the outward-going, more 'primitive' extravert has more 'substance X' than has the introvert. Because of the increased synaptic resistance of extraverts it is predicted that the fluctuation of their alternative perceptions will be carried on at a slower rate. Franks and Lindahl (1963) confirmed this hypothesis. Unfortunately others have produced different, even contradictory, results. From McDougall's hypothesis he would predict that a depressant drug would slow down reversal rate and a stimulant would increase it. But Eysenck, Holland and Trouton (1957b) found that both a depressant (amytal) and a stimulant (dexedrine) increased reversal rate. It is possible that both these drugs affected eye movements or increased blinking, and we have seen above that blinking may effect the reversal rate. However, McDougall claimed that 'substance X' was not related to blinking.

One explanation of the differences found in reversal rate may be that the extravert loses interest in this rather uninteresting perceptual task quicker than the introvert and thus 'pays less attention'. Anyway, it is certain that the reversals of the Necker Cube are not related to one single factor. Vickers (1972) has found that if observers are kept in an extremely hot room, or are strenuously exercised or subjected to violent noise, then the Necker Cube, for some reason, will reverse more rapidly. Also, anyone who has viewed the Necker Cube often will find it reversing at a very rapid rate indeed.

It might be pointed out that Necker was certainly not the first to notice the ambiguous nature of line cubes—Roman mosaics certainly testify to that. There are many other patterns which are susceptible to transpositions with respect to their perspective and these include representations of everyday objects, not simply compositions of straight lines. Such reversals of everyday objects have a long history and Boring (1942) traces the windmill reversal of Fig. 47a back to William Porterfield in 1759. The reversible silhouette shown in Fig. 47b could, as Fisher (1971) points out, have extremely serious consequences for aircraft navigation.

It is possible to create a two-dimensional object for which a three-dimensional counterpart is very unlikely. The 'prongs' shown in Fig. 48 may not be puzzling at first sight but are soon seen to be 'impossible'. If the 'impossibility' is not perceived, this is probably due to a fluctuation of attention between the left and right sides of the figure, each of which, separately, is quite possible as a two-dimensional representation of the same solid object, but not both together as viewed from the same point in space. The Dutch artist Escher has made use of 'impossible' figures in his pictures, one of which is seen in Fig. 49. The picture gives an impression of strangeness, but at first glance it is hard to see what is wrong. Quite often the paradox suddenly dawns. This sudden awareness is quite typical in the field of ambiguous perception, and the rearrangement which we accomplish is accompanied by the feeling of being taken aback when we see the 'answer'.

a   b   c

Fig 47

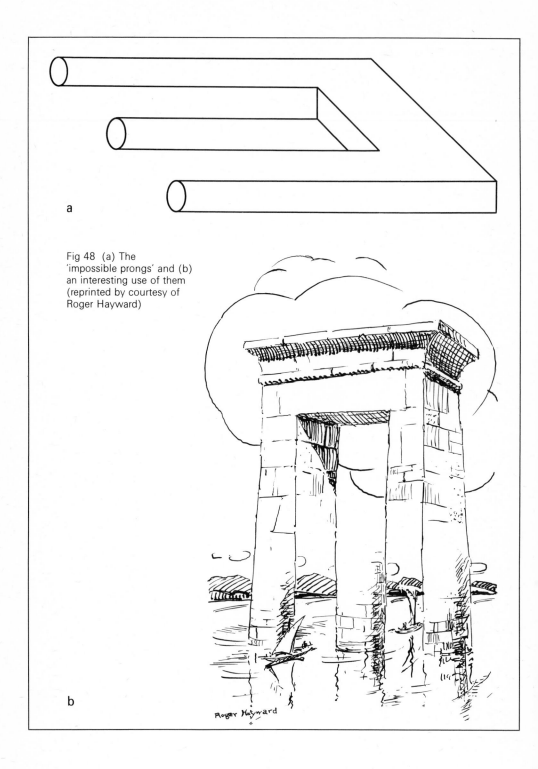

a

Fig 48 (a) The 'impossible prongs' and (b) an interesting use of them (reprinted by courtesy of Roger Hayward)

b

Roger Hayward

Fig 49 Escher's *Belvedere* makes use of the 'impossible prongs' principle to form an impossible house. The man seated at the bottom of the house seems to be having some difficulty with his Necker cube (reprinted by courtesy of the Escher Foundation)

It is not only two-dimensional drawings of cubes that reverse; it is quite possible, with a limited amount of practice, to get three-dimensional models of cubes to reverse in depth. It is true that this is accomplished more easily in the dark with luminous wire models viewed monocularly, but it can also be done under normal viewing conditions. If a three-dimensional wire cube can be reversed in depth a strange effect occurs when the observer moves his head. Viewing the cube normally, the object will remain still when the head moves and it is quite obvious that the different views obtained are from the different perspectives given by head-movement. Now, if the object is perceptually reversed, the eye perceives the same input when the head moves, but this is not compatible with the input that would be received from a truncated pyramid if the head were moved round it. To reconcile this, the object is seen to move with the observer and follow his eyes in a most uncanny fashion.

Ernst Mach, the Austrian physicist, found a similar ambiguous figure with which it is easier to verify this effect. If one takes a piece of stiff white paper, folds it in half lengthways and places it on a table like a tent viewed from above, it will look like Fig. 50. If viewed in this manner, Mach found that a reversal would occur. The fold down the centre can be seen as being below or above the rest of the figure (in order to see this reversal it may

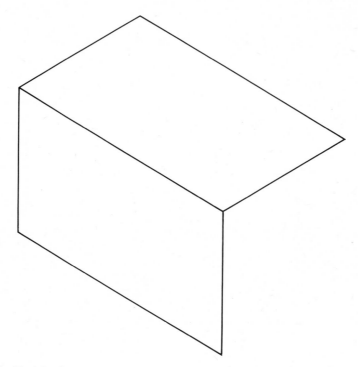

Fig 50 The Mach book

help to close one eye). Now, if instead of viewing this from above one moves back in one's chair until the near tip of the fold subtends an angle of 45 degrees to the eye, another reversal will take place and the paper will appear to stand up on end like a book that is open. In this reversed position, if the head is moved slowly from side to side the paper will appear to move back and forward, just as if it were in motion.

Another type of ambiguous depth can be seen in Fig. 51, which shows a cuneiform tablet. Here there is uncertainty about whether the marks on the tablet are below or above the plane of the page. These wedge shapes were made by pressing a stylus into wet clay, but can be seen as sticking out from the page and, when viewed in this way, the picture looks very different. Many observers see the cuneiform patterns more clearly when they see them as protruding, and this is a little odd since, as the marks are in fact indented, the original writers must have seen them more clearly in that fashion.

Generally speaking, reversible figures occur only in two-dimensional drawings. There are too many cues in most normal three-dimensional perception to give an ambiguous input. However, if an observer looks at striped wallpaper an example of ambiguity can occur which has been called the 'wallpaper effect', though perhaps a better name would be the

Fig 51 (Reprinted from *Psychology: A Study of a Science*, Koch, S. (Ed.), McGraw-Hill Book Co: 1962)

'prison bars' effect. Figure 52 shows that the stripes labelled 'a' and 'b' can be fused on a multitude of planes. Two of these are shown in the figure, one above and one below the real plane of the stimuli which is labelled 's'. This gives rise to an ambiguous depth perception in which the observer can see the stimulus at either of the two depth planes shown.

We have already mentioned the random dot stereograms of Julesz which give rise to a fused picture even though each eye receives a random input. Julesz and Johnson (1968) have constructed stereograms which give alternative percepts (Plate 4). When viewed through the stereo viewer, Anaglyphs III and IV represent unambiguous and ambiguous versions of a staircase. The unambiguous version (Anaglyph III) shows a staircase raised above the plane of the page. The ambiguous version can be either above the page, rising out of it or descending down beneath the plane of the page. The reader may care to view the ambiguous figure (Anaglyph IV) first. Unlike the Necker Cube, reversals are hard to achieve and previous viewing of the unambiguous version may prejudice any other reorganisation. It is as if, once an organisation has been achieved, there is a reluctance to relinquish it for any other.

One reason for including here the unambiguous version of the staircase is that there may be many readers who fail to achieve any fusion with these more difficult anaglyphs. Julesz suggests that about two per cent of the population are completely stereopsis-blind (stereopsis is the ability to fuse the pictures from both eyes). Perhaps the most common cause of this inability is some physical eye-defect. People with this disability are unable to see more than dots arranged at random when viewing any of the anaglyphs with the stereoviewer. A much larger group of people, estimated by Julesz at 15 per cent, have a stereopsis deficiency and have great difficulty in perceiving these pictures in depth. This is perhaps because one of the observer's eyes is very dominant. Such a person may find the ambiguous anaglyph especially difficult to fuse.

These ambiguous perceptions must rely on a different mechanism from that of the Necker Cube. The anaglyphs are seen at different depths because of differing convergence of the two eyes for each percept. Since the Necker Cube reverses as a stabilised retinal image, there must instead be some central organisational process controlling that change. If, however, a stereogram is made so that the fusion causes two surfaces which are very close together, Julesz and Johnson (1968) found that each surface comes and goes just like the differing interpretations of a Necker Cube. They used two wave (cosine) surfaces appearing to be transparently above the printed page, so close together that there was the same eye convergence for both. It was possible to see both surfaces for a brief time, but quite soon one surface would dominate and completely suppress the other; this would then reverse, and the other surface would be seen alone.

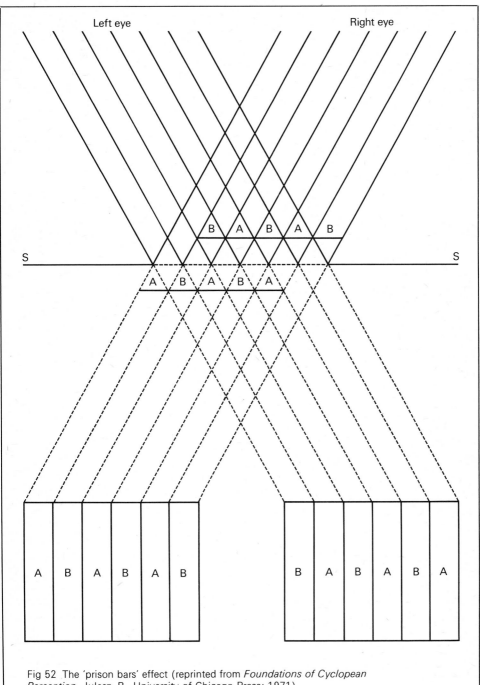

Fig 52 The 'prison bars' effect (reprinted from *Foundations of Cyclopean Perception*, Julesz, B., University of Chicago Press: 1971)

Fig 53 Detail from Dali's *Slave Market with Apparition of the Invisible Bust of Voltaire* (Collection M/MA, Reynolds Morse Salvador Dali Museum, Cleveland (Beachwood), Ohio, USA) © by ADAGP Paris, 1974

Another variable which can alter the organisation of a stimulus is viewing distance. It is possible to create a picture that is ambiguous in this respect. Dali realised this in his painting *Slave Market with Apparition of the Invisible Bust of Voltaire* (see Fig. 53). When viewed at close range the observer will see figures of people predominating. It may even be difficult to see the bust of Voltaire unless the picture is viewed from a little distance. Harmon (1970) provides a more explicit example (Fig. 54). At close range only a random collection of squares is seen; at a greater distance (or by squinting), a well-known face emerges.

Ambiguity in art and literature

In his classic work, *Art and Illusion*, Gombrich stresses the essentially ambiguous nature of even the most conventional painting. No picture can exactly copy what we see since, as Fig. 40 shows, a two-dimensional line on a flat surface can arise from an infinity of three-dimensional objects. Thus all art is to some extent ambiguous and requires active processing on the part of the observer. When we view pictures and see what they represent so easily, it is perhaps difficult to believe that the cross-cultural differences that we have noted previously really exist.

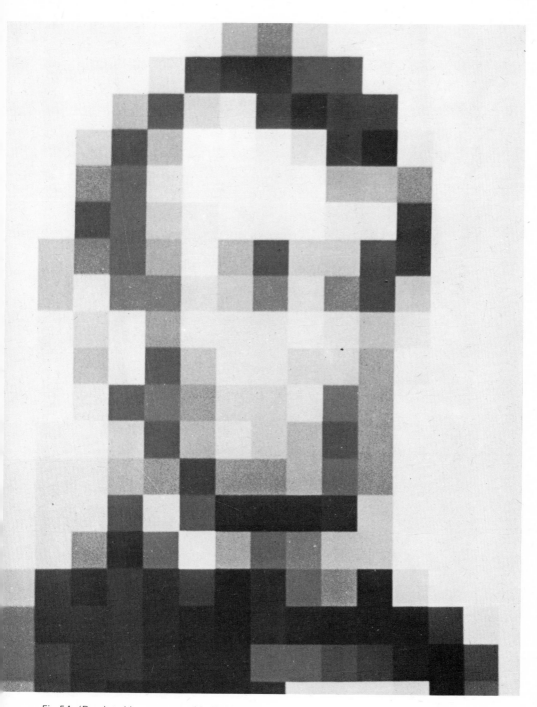

Fig 54 (Reprinted by courtesy of L. D. Harmon)

Fig 55 Aubrey Beardsley's *The Fat Woman*

Hudson (1960, 1967) has shown that many Africans find difficulty in interpreting a picture in depth. Gombrich (1960), too, quotes examples of nineteenth century Japanese and Chinese who could not appreciate Western perspective. One of the pictures Hudson used was immediately seen by someone from a Western culture as a man going up a step, because of the foreshortening drawn into the picture. However, if this drawing is not perceived in depth then there must be something very wrong with the man's leg, and this is how Hudson found many of his observers perceived the picture: they reported that the man was injured.

The principle that any pattern of retinal stimulation can arise from an infinity of inputs is also basic to the Ames Room demonstration. While Ames certainly saw the theoretical interest of such a distorted room, he cannot be credited with the building of the first such demonstration. Van de Geer and de Natris (1962) say that van Hoogstraaten, a pupil of Rembrandt, built several, and they doubt if he was the actual inventor. The speciality of van Hoogstraaten (1627–1678) was the art of *trompe l'oeil* or the visual pun. He constructed boxes into which one looked through a peep-hole. When one looks into one of his boxes, such as that in the National Gallery in London, one sees a seventeenth-century Dutch interior in three dimensions. But, in fact, only the sides and floor of the box are painted. The walls of the room in the 'picture' are painted so that they do not coincide with the sides of the box, and this gives rise to an incorrect estimate of the distance of the walls from the observer. Parts of a chair are painted on several sides of the box and fuse to form a whole chair convincingly in three dimensions. It is essential, just as in the Ames demonstration, that the head is still and that the interior of the box is viewed through a peep-hole, otherwise there would be too many other cues and the real situation would be apparent.

Fisher (1968) quite rightly points out that research workers interested in the organisation of visual input have been parasitic (perhaps unconsciously) on the work of artists. The instability of perception which Rubin called the Figure–Ground Effect was certainly known to Aubrey Beardsley. His prints in pure black and white create a tension and vibration because of the stress between parts of the figure demanding attention. Fisher points to the drawing entitled *The Fat Woman* (Fig. 55), drawn in 1894, which is thought to be a caricature of Mrs Whistler. The black area to the left of Mrs Whistler has a distinct facial effect not dissimilar to that of the Face–Vase ambiguous figure of Rubin (Fig. 42). In Beardsley's drawing there is something distinctly sinister about this face, especially since it comes and goes. It is obviously deliberate, and it has been related to the fact that at that time Beardsley was on very bad terms with Whistler.

The instability of certain patterns has been used in more recent times by many artists. We have seen that, if we look at a random series of dots, patterns will try to emerge, and even in organised stimuli such as rows of

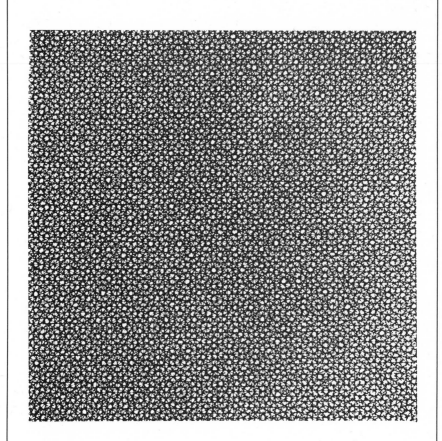

Fig 56 Screen painting *0 degrees, 22·5 degrees, 45 degrees, 67·5 degrees* by François Morellet (The Contemporaries, New York)

columns or dots a reorganisation will occur. Morellet's screen painting, *0 degrees, 22·5 degrees, 45 degrees, 67·5 degrees* (Fig. 56), achieves its aim in bewildering the observer because, while certain parts of the figure try to become dominant, they are not strong enough to do so. This gives a continuous instability while looking at the painting.

The paintings of Seurat provide another example of the ways in which the observer organises his visual input. Figure 57 shows a detail of Seurat's painting, *Sunday Afternoon on the Island of La Grande Jatte.* Usually, the observer organises this picture as presented here (out of context) in terms of the areas of brightness contrast, making shapes from the areas of similar tone. This makes for a very stable percept. However, it can also be seen as the backview of a sitting nursemaid which, in fact, is

Fig 57 Detail from *Sunday Afternoon on the Island of La Grande Jatte* by
Seurat (reprinted by courtesy of the Art Institute of Chicago)

Just as he reaches a small grassy point of land, another fish attacks him, lashing furiously with his tail.

Fig 58 A cartoon, by Verbeek, 'standing the world on its head'

what it represents in the larger context. This reorganisation may be difficult to achieve, but important perceptual changes occur when it happens.

The structure of a picture, once established, will resist change so that if an alternative percept is available this may be difficult to find. A good example of this can be seen in the cartoon of Verbeek (Fig. 58). This drawing holds two quite different scenes, as will be obvious if the page is turned upside down. In a sense, this should not be surprising, as a drawing turned through 180 degrees gives a very different input to the visual system. But there is more than a clever trick here, since it is quite easy to predict what most pictures would be like if turned upside down. The reason that it is not easy with the Verbeek cartoon must be due to the fact that we have organised the input in a certain way and it is difficult to change that organisation.

The Tachist paintings, or abstract paintings in general, can be forced into different perceptual arrangements by the viewer. This may not have been the artists' intention, but the ambiguity will always be there if there is a lack of structural clarity. There is always an attempt by the observer to make 'sense' of the visual input, that is, to organise his perception.

Artists of the Italian Schools of the fifteenth and sixteenth centuries showed how everyday objects could hide other things, especially faces. Paintings were executed of clouds, fruit and vegetables, all cunningly arranged to allow the viewer to discover a human face. In recent times many of the Surrealists, such as Ernst, deliberately allowed their art to be ambiguous so that the change from one structure to another could be emphasised. Everyday objects can themselves be ambiguous, and nobody was more aware of this than Salvador Dali. He recounts in his auto-biography, *The Secret Life of Salvador Dali* (1942), that he was impressed from boyhood by the names given by local fishermen to various rocks. One might be called a camel, and another an anvil, because they 'looked' like those objects. Dali noticed while rowing past the rock called 'the camel' that it had changed into a rooster. He says: 'What had been the camel's head now formed the comb, and the camel's lower lip, which was already prominent, had lengthened to become the beak. The hump, which had been in the middle of its back, was now all the way back and formed the rooster's tail.' Episodes like this inspired Dali to many paintings in which there was a potential ambiguity. We have already encountered one of these, *The Slave Market with Apparition of the Invisible Bust of Voltaire* (Fig. 53).

Ambiguity has been a constant theme in the art of this century. However, much of this has not been strictly perceptual ambiguity and is more con-cerned to disturb the viewer and make him re-think his prior assumptions about the world. Realistic prints of scenes of Trafalgar Square have, for instance, a pair of giant knees for the National Gallery and a lipstick in place of Nelson's Column. The ambiguity is in the curious juxtaposition, and is of a cognitive rather than a perceptual kind. Much of the Surrealists' painting falls into a similar category. Magritte's painting of an elaborate fireplace with mantelshelf has, in place of a grate, a blank board with a model steam locomotive and carriages projecting from it at right angles, suspended in mid-air, puffing smoke into the room. Here the confusion is mental rather than perceptual: there is no confusion as to what is painted.

Similarly, there is no doubt as to what is drawn in Warhol's picture of a soup-can. Deifying a common object like a soup-can as an art-object may make us look at that and all subsequent soup-cans in a different way. Quite often we do not really notice objects around us, and one repercussion of this type of art is to make us look at everyday objects more closely; quite likely, therefore, it contributes to the organisation of our perception in different ways.

There are, as one might expect, intermediate cases where one cannot decide easily whether the ambiguity is perceptual or not. Picasso's work (Fig. 59), consisting of a bicycle handle-bars and saddle fixed together to

Fig 59 *Bull's Head,1943* by
P. Picasso (photograph courtesy
of the Arts Council) © by SPADEM Paris, 1973

look like a bull's head, is certainly disturbing. There is a certain reluctance to organise the objects to form a bull's head, since the parts are so unmistakably still parts of a bicycle. An even greater instability is observed in Magritte's portrait of a female face (Fig. 60) made from parts of a human body. To make sense of the face, the pubic region must be a mouth, the breasts must be eyes and the navel a nose. There may be a reluctance to do this, but the obvious head hair surrounding these body parts tends to make the observer organise the total percept to be a face.

Ambiguity in literature, like ambiguity in art, can take many forms which are not essential for our discussion of visual ambiguity. We are primarily concerned with the possibility of changed perception through some change of processing of what is, as we have seen, perhaps always a potentially ambiguous visual input. Mistaken identity, for example, which is a recurrent theme in literature, would not generally fall within our scope. When, for instance, in *Twelfth Night,* the Duke says, 'One face, one voice, one habit and two persons', there is no question of the perception being different for one observer than for any other.

Much ambiguity in literature goes beyond questions of differing perceptions and deals with complex cognitive activity. For example, one really questions whether, when Lear acts out a trial of justice with a stool for his daughter Goneril, he actually believes that he is seeing his daughter: the 'warp'd looks' are surely metaphorical.

When the tramps in *Waiting for Godot* argue about a tree, they are not doubting each other's perceptions:

Estragon: Looks to me more like a bush.
Vladimir: A shrub.
Estragon: A bush.

Here, Beckett is stressing the essential uncertainty in communication. However, later in the play, Vladimir and Estragon argue about a pair of boots in a way that does question the ability of individuals to perceive the same event in the same manner:

Estragon: Mine were black. These are brown.
Vladimir: You're sure yours were black?
Estragon: Well they were a kind of grey.
Vladimir: And these are brown? (show)
Estragon: (Picking up a boot.) Well, they're a kind of green.

Blake castigates the evils of uncertainty in the mind of the beholder, saying: 'If the sun and moon should doubt they'd immediately go out'. However, the nature of the visual input seems to make for alternative perceptions. This we noted in the quotation at the beginning of this chapter. A very similar one, also from Shakespeare, comes from *Antony and Cleopatra.*

Le Viol by R. Magritte
(reprinted by courtesy of Mme René Magritte)
© by ADAGP Paris 1973

Sometimes we see a cloud that's dragonish;
A vapour sometime like a bear or lion,
A tower'd citadel, a pendant rock,
A forked mountain, or blue promontory
With trees upon't, that nod unto the world,
And mock our eyes with air...

There are situations, especially those of dim illumination, where people, perhaps charged with emotion, can reconstruct an environment in a multitude of ways. As Theseus puts it in *A Midsummer Night's Dream* (Act V, Scene I):

Such tricks hath strong imagination,
That, if it would but apprehend some joy,
It comprehends some bringer of that joy;
Or in the night, imagining some fear,
How easy is a bush suppos'd a bear.

Another famous incident in literature where these ambiguous circumstances arise is in Chaucer's *The Miller's Tale*, where Absolon, because of the bad light, mistakes the backside of the Miller's wife for her face and kisses it rapturously. In a perhaps similar if not so absurd way, Leonard Radcliffe in David Storey's *Radcliffe* constructs his perception:

He woke to find himself in complete darkness. He was turning on to his side as he came to his senses. Gradually the faint night glow of the estate was reflected in his window. He could still hear, however, the peculiar noise.

Reaching out he switched on the small lamp by his bed. For a while he saw nothing unfamiliar, then his gaze was directed downwards by a slight movement on the floor.

From a crack between the two ill-fitting boards emerged an enormous beetle, so large that at first he thought it must be the gleaming surface of a shoe. Then two tendrils groped forward to hoist from the crevice the remainder of its prodigious body. The sound plainly came from the crackling of its hard shell against the rough edges of the wood.

It stopped perfectly still, perhaps distracted by the light. Intermingled with the blackness was a rich crimson sheen. He stared at it in terror. It was quite close to the bed.

He moved slightly. There was no reaction from the insect. He glanced round to see where there might be others. But the floor was bare. He stretched out his arm and from the drawer beside the bed drew out the claw hammer.

He got out of bed and for a while stood gazing down at the close juxtaposition of the beetle and his bare feet. Now that it was vertically observed, the redness of its dark shell was more apparent.

He stooped forward and, his eyes closed, crushed the hammer down on to its smooth back. He felt its brittle disintegration beneath the steel head.

When he looked down he saw in fact the insect had crumbled into dust. It was a dead leaf.

The reconstruction of the visual world is a process which is known to us all. Earlier in the same novel, Storey expresses the emotional aspects of this reconstruction when it changes into recognition. The main character, Leonard Radcliffe, glanced up, 'and with a sudden repeated backward look saw a face which gradually grew into certain memorable and familiar features. The moment of recognition was like a heat pressing over his nervous body, a fur-like warmth that spread over his back and across his neck.'

Ambiguity in literature concerns more than the interpretation of the visual world; but it is with this interpretation that we shall be concerned in the next chapter.

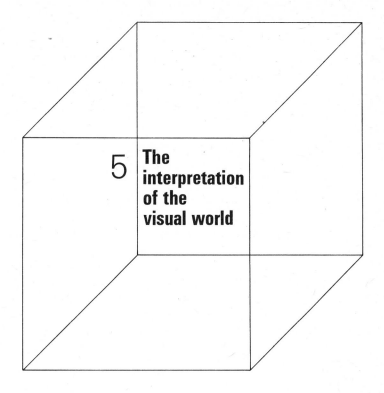

5 | **The interpretation of the visual world**

Set

The assumptions that one makes about the nature of visual input can in some circumstances alter one's perception. This influence of past experience is called the effect of 'set'.

Engel (1956) conducted experiments on binocular fusion which showed that even in this perceptually very basic activity our assumptions of set are important. If different pictures are shown to each eye, what is actually perceived is not necessarily a straight composite of the two: indeed, in some situations it is hard to get any fusion of the two pictures whatsoever. If two faces are shown, one to each eye, then in most cases the composite is found to be a more pleasant, handsome fellow than either of the faces taken separately. It therefore seems that there is a tendency to see the culturally more acceptable face, but this is not always the case, as was found by Pettigrew, Allport and Barnett (1958). In their study, conducted in South Africa, they presented pairs of faces, one to each eye. They found that Zulus saw an Indian, when an Indian was paired with a European; but Europeans saw a Zulu when the alternatives were a Zulu or another European. It was suggested that the observers saw the alternative which was most significant to them: there was selection of input according to what was important to the observer and what his experience determined.

This finding is confirmed by a study of Toch and Schulte (1961). In their study, the observer's past experience was the important variable. They took a group of observers with a substantial amount of police training and compared them with a group of people just prior to training and a control group of college students. The binocular rivalry task of Toch and Schulte consisted of presenting a violent scene to one eye and a non-violent scene to the other. The hypothesis of the experiment was that the group of people with police training would see more of the violent scene than the other groups. This was indeed found to be the case. The police-trained group saw the violent scene on approximately half the trials whereas the other two groups saw it only on a quarter.

If confronted in this way with two scenes, one of which is unfamiliar, it is found that it is hard for the unfamiliar scene to become dominant. This is because it will be only possible to organise one's perception to see one of the scenes, and the familiar scene is the easier to organise. Bagby (1957) showed this to be the case with pictures presented to observers of either Mexican or American nationality. The alternative pictures were of events such as a baseball match and a bullfight. It was found that the observers reported seeing the scene which was culturally more familiar. That this was a genuine perceptual selection rather than a response bias was claimed by Bagby because in many cases the alternative, unfamiliar scene was never (reported) at all.

Cantril (1957) mentions another stereoscopic fusion demonstration where a Madonna with Child was presented along with a naked young woman. At first there did not appear to be any fusion. An observer saw the Madonna with Child but then exclaimed 'but my God she is undressing': the Madonna changed into the naked woman. The nude then remained dominant and the observer found it impossible to see the Madonna. To another observer the exact reverse sequence occurred. This dominance of the second alternative is not usual in this situation, nor generally in the effects of set upon perception.

Figure 61, taken from Dallenbach (1951), could just as well be a nonsense drawing for its apparent lack of structure. It does in fact hide a simple well-known object, but we do not organise our perception in such a way as to see it. Prolonged concentration and alternation of the fixation point may help (the reader may wish to try this out before reading any further). In fact, it can be seen as a white cow with black ears and muzzle, and, once it has been seen as a cow, the animal will obstinately remain and the observer will not be able to return to the former lack of structure.

Another example where the input can be reconstructed is provided (unknowingly?) by the designer of the fifty rupee note from the Seychelles Islands in the Indian Ocean. Figure 62 looks straightforward enough, but if the picture is turned on its side by rotating it counter-clockwise through 90 degrees something may strike the reader. If it does not, he should look

Fig 61 (Reprinted from the *American Journal of Psychology* Vol. 64, 1951, after Dallenbach)

Fig 62 (© by the Press Association, London)

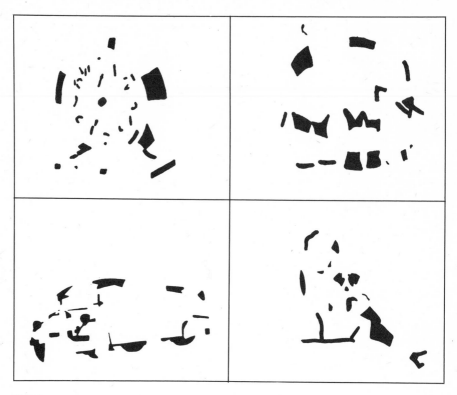

Fig 63

at the palm trees more carefully. Once the word written in the leaves of the palm trees has been seen it will not be possible to look at that picture again without organising the input in a way that makes the word immediately apparent.

Leeper (1935) showed pictures that were incomplete (see Fig. 63) in that some parts of the drawing of the figure had been omitted. Some people find these pictures hard to organise to form the common objects they represent. Even after having been told what the figures are meant to represent, some of them remain obstinately difficult to organise. The objects represented here are an alarm clock, an elephant and a bus (N.B. this experiment was done in the early 1930s). The last and most difficult picture to reconstruct will be left for the reader to organise himself: as a clue, there is a dog in it somewhere.

Telling the observer that there is a dog in the picture or a cow in Fig. 61 may not be a great help in organising the percept unless one has some idea of what sort of dog or cow is required. Each person's concept of what a 'dog' looks like will differ. In order to form a coherent percept rapidly, what we see must fit in with our already existing processes. Bartlett (1932) called these processes schemata; there seems to be 'an active organisation of past reactions or of past experiences' which strives selectively to filter incoming information to fit into the already existing schema. There has been some dispute as to whether these schemata act on the stored percept (memory) or on perception itself (Hebb and Foord, 1945; Gomulicki, 1953); but it certainly makes sense to consider the perceptual set effects demonstrated here as the bringing to bear on the visual world of our past experiences in the form of assumptions or schemata.

Külpe (1904) was the first to give experimental verification to the finding that if an observer is given explicit instructions as to what aspects of a forthcoming stimulus he should attend to, his report becomes more accurate. It was regarded in the sense of perceptual tuning, just as, when listening to the radio, reception is better if one is tuned in to the right wavelength: a more up-to-date analogy is to a computer. The output of a computer depends on more than the input—it also depends on the program to which the computer has been set. The inputs 'two, four' will give a different output according to whether it is programmed for addition or multiplication.

Haber (1966) says that to demonstrate the effect of set upon perception it is necessary to rule out peripheral mechanisms such as eye movements or scanning of the stimulus. It would be a mistake to think that instructions cannot affect these two types of behaviour, or that they are unimportant, but a clear demonstration of changes in perception without them would make it more certain that different percepts were not simply being achieved by different inputs.

A revival of interest in the effect of set in the late 1940s produced experiments such as that of Bruner and Postman (1949), in which they showed their observers playing-cards for very brief intervals of time. Mixed in with the normal cards were incongruous cards such as a two of spades coloured red, or a four of diamonds coloured black. It was argued that, since we have assumptions about how playing-cards should look, we should therefore be able to recognise cards which conform to these assumptions much more easily than the incongruous cards; this was the case.

As in most other areas of psychology, such experiments as this are seldom able to be interpreted in only one way. There are several possible causes of the effects reported in this experiment, and this has led to considerable controversy in this area of research. We have seen that we have direct contact with an observer's perception only through his verbal report. This always raises some doubt as to the extent of a one-to-one correlation between the response and the perception, and leaves room for some alternative explanation based upon verbal response bias. This might apply to the experiment of Bruner and Postman, except for some odd errors made by the observers: when viewing, for instance, a red spade,

Fig 64

they made what might be called 'compromise' responses—a red four of spades was called a four of hearts. This is understandable, and possibly a verbal slip, but how do we account for the report of a *brown* four of spades? Other responses to the red four of spades described it as purple, rusty black or black with red edges. These are unlikely to be guesses and suggest a change in the perception itself. This experiment does not seem to have been repeated, but any repetition, if obtaining the same results, would show that what we expect to see had actually led us to see differently. An observer expected red, received black as a stimulus and therefore saw purple!

What we are led to expect can alter our perception. Look first at the numbers in Fig. 64, then look at the letters: see how the 13 changes into a B.

Gregory (1970) gives an interesting example of expectation affecting perception. Figure 65a shows a recent photograph of the spiral nebula

Fig 65 The spiral nebula M51
(a) as photographed, and as seen
by the astronomers (b) Herschel
and (c) Rosse
(photos (a) and (b)
Science Museum, London; photo
(c) lent to Science Museum,
London, by the Mount Wilson
Observatory)

M51 taken with the Mount Wilson 100 inch telescope. This is undoubtedly a clearer image than the astronomer Herschel obtained in the nineteenth century. If one imagines looking at a slightly fuzzy version of (a) then it would be easy to draw it as Herschel did (Fig. 65b), especially as Herschel did not know the true spiral shape of the nebula. The astronomer Rosse, on the other hand, knew this, and his drawing of the nebula, made only seventeen years after that of Herschel, is shown in Fig. 65c. It is very likely that the shape these astronomers reported was due to their preconceptions of the true shape of the nebula. Astronomy, because of the ambiguity of the stimulus material, gives many such examples of observers seeing different things because of their set about how the Universe should look. For further examples see Gregory (1970).

A great deal of the experimentation in this area of research has endeavoured to find non-perceptual explanations, such as changes in the memory trace, to explain the effects of set. This is basically motivated by a refusal to consider the possibility of different perceptions resulting from the same perceptual input.

The uncertainty of whether the effects of set occur because of perceptual or memorial factors also arises from the type of experiment in which it is found that recognition of an object from a display is helped only when instructions as to which object to look for are given prior to seeing the display. Instructions given after the object has been shown are not so effective. It may be that prior instructions give a set to the observer which helps him to organise the subsequent input. We have seen above that this is what Külpe thought. On the other hand, it may be that instructions after the event require the observer to search for the object for which he is looking from his memory, and that this is a more difficult task.

To a large extent, the confusion between perceptual and memorial explanations of this type of experiment (prior versus subsequent instructions) has been cleared up by an experiment of Harris and Haber (1963). They show that prior instructions are effective because they can alter the order in which items from the display are encoded. Harris and Haber found that our normal coding scheme, based on language, could be improved upon in certain circumstances. If two figures such as four red stars and two blue circles are shown, they can be coded into memory either in this syntactical way or by dimensions such as red : blue; four : two; stars : circles. If the observer is to be on the lookout for one dimension, say colour (and, as in the Harris and Haber experiment, paid more for correct response concerning that dimension), then the second coding method is more efficient, because it makes it easier for the observer to retain the facts in his memory. From this experiment it can be argued that set is affecting a selection of the available information and not the clarity of the stimulus. Of course, in this situation there is no doubt as to the nature of the objects in the display, and perhaps here an explanation involving perceptual reorganisation is not needed. Not all prior instructions act on a clearly defined input, however, and in an undefined situation instructions will have a different effect.

The fact that Pillsbury (1897) noted that FOYEVER was read as FOREVER and that the the word written twice in this sentence is not easily noticed can be explained in non-perceptual terms. These arguments will not be dealt with at length here, but they are relevant to possible interpretations of an experiment by Bruner and Potter (1964). In this experiment, observers were shown a common object out of focus and then gradually the focus was increased until the picture was quite clear. Bruner and Potter asked their observers to make comments on the picture while it was changing in clarity. It was found that if the focus increased very slowly then a sharper focus was needed to recognise the object than when the focus was increased at a faster rate. Now, it could be said either that this was because there is some verbal response bias of perseveration of the initial response, or that a greater perceptual set is caused by giving the observer a long time to see an object in a manner which is in fact a misclassification. Bruner and Potter argued for the latter explanation.

Potter (1966), as mentioned in a previous chapter, conducted similar experiments with groups of children and college students showing pictures taken at various stages of 'out-of-focus'. She found that perception was generally better if the worst (the most blurred) picture was omitted, in that there would be fewer false assumptions. There was one picture, however, in which it was found that omitting the worst blur hindered recognition. It was argued that this was because this picture was subject to a very compelling wrong initial assumption which had to be rejected by a checking process. This took time, and the longer the observer could see the picture the more chance there was of a reorganisation.

The initial assumptions brought to bear upon a stimulus are important, as shown in an experiment by Hershenson and Haber (1965). A word is presented so quickly that it is not recognised. It has been found that if the word is presented several times, even though the length of time of each presentation is not increased, the word will eventually be recognised. What is the cause of this puzzling after-effect? If it is not recognised at first, why should an observer be able to recognise it later? A retinal change is out of the question. It is possible that some residual trace has been left behind from the stimulus and a build-up is consolidated upon it.

Dodwell (1971) suggests that these very fast presentations of stimuli do not give sufficient time for the brain to do the necessary computation to achieve recognition; and the known fact (Sperling, 1960) that inputs to the brain can be stored virtually intact for a short time would allow subsequent stimuli a better chance to be analysed. There is also the possibility that different parts of the stimulus are attended to and assumptions changed about the structure of the word until it 'makes sense'. The explanations are not mutually exclusive and all available methods may be used to facilitate early recognition, depending upon the nature of the display. For a review of work in this area, see Doherty and Keeley (1972).

In investigating whether the assumptions of the observer affect the way he will deal with the input, Hershenson and Haber showed their observers Turkish and English words for brief intervals. It was easier to recognise English than Turkish words, but the rate of increase of clarity of the Turkish words was greater than for the English. Hershenson and Haber held that the reason for this was that, since the observers did not know Turkish, they could not come to any prior assumptions about the nature of the word if it were Turkish. They could do this with English, and this was a nindrance when the assumption was wrong. There is no direct proof of this, but the results can be interpreted in this way and are difficult to explain except by perception based on assumptions.

Leeper (1935) conducted some interesting experiments to show that our past experience in dealing with an ambiguous figure can affect a reorganisation of the perception of a figure. In his completion experiment mentioned above, observers were tested three weeks after their original exposure to the figures. It was found that if an incomplete figure was flashed onto the screen for a hundreth of a second it stood a good chance of being recognised (68 per cent of the observers recognised the stimuli in Fig. 63). Observers without this previous experience of reconstructing the stimuli scored only 6 per cent correct in this situation. If the exposure time of the stimuli was increased to one second then prior experience made for almost perfect recognition, but only increased the naïve observers' score to 18 per cent.

The fact that experience changes the way we look at an object is shown in an experiment by Botha (1963) in which he gave his observers a reversible figure to look at. This could be seen as black on white or white on black. It was found that pre-exposure to a dominant form of either of these percepts affected nursery-school children and illiterate adults. It did not matter whether their pre-exposure was to black on white or white on black: there was a tendency to see the reversible figure in the manner of the pre-exposed form. Yet, whatever pre-exposure was given to a group of literate adults, they tended to see the reversal figure as black on white. It was suggested that the reading experience of the adult gave such a weighting to this way of seeing that it dominated, and this will explain the fact that illiterate adults and nursery-school children were influenced whatever the form of the pre-exposure.

The finding that pre-exposure can dominate perception was demonstrated in the most graphic of reversible figures—that of the 'wife and mother-in-law' (see Fig. 66) created by the cartoonist W. E. Hill. It was published in 1915 and first brought to the attention of students of perception by Boring (1930). This figure never fails to divide adults into two

Fig 66 *My Wife and My Mother-in-law* (E. G. Boring, after W. E. Hill)

groups: some see the old woman and cannot see the young woman, others just the reverse. When told what the alternative is, some observers still cannot 'see' this version even when the relevant features are pointed out. Prior exposure to the version of this figure which accentuates one set of features can make the alternative way of seeing it almost impossible. In fact, if there is a pre-exposure to such a biased version of Fig. 66, then one can even be made to see a version which is biased in the other direction with the assumptions of the pre-exposed form. In this way, a version which would normally be seen as a young woman will be perceived as an old woman, if a gradually changing series of pictures of the figure, starting with one of the old woman, is presented. Thus, again, our assumptions, this time experimentally induced, dominate our perceptual activity.

Projective tests

At all times we try to organise the perceptual field to make patterns, whether they are the rows and columns of Fig. 45 or whether they are in

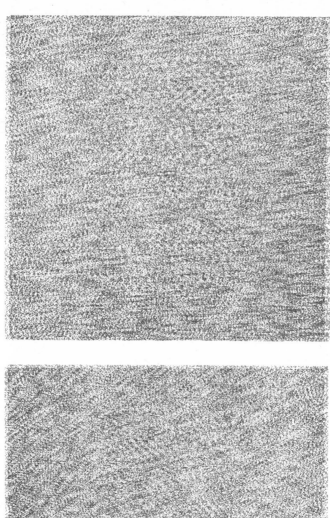

Plate 1 Anaglyphs I and II (reprinted from *Foundations of Cyclopean Perception*, Julesz, B., University of Chicago Press: 1971)

Plate 2 Rorschach Test Cards V and X (reprinted, in
reduced size for copyright reasons, from
Rorschach's *Psychodiagnostik* by permission of Verlag Hans
Huber, Bern)

terms of seeing objects instead of confusion. Because of this, if a relatively
unstructured pattern is presented, we may each, because of our individual
way of organising, scanning, or restructuring the visual world, see different
things in the unstructured pattern. This is the rationale behind the projective test.

There are many different projective tests, some of which, however, do
not involve perceptual restructuring, if a very strict definition of perception
is taken: an example is the Thematic Apperception Test, which requires a
person to invent stories based on a picture. In a clinical situation, this

Fig 67 The 'Object Relations' test (reprinted by
courtesy of the author, H. Phillipson, and
Associated Book Publishers Ltd)

differentiates between people, but the Thematic Apperception Test is a little too cognitive and divorced from the sheer reception of the stimulus to be included here. There are other, less well-known projective tests, such as the Object Relations Technique (Phillipson, 1955). Figure 67 shows an example of a stimulus from this test. The shadowy forms are ambiguous and are used to differentiate between patients with respect to their reaction to people and events. People will organise different shapes and patterns and interpret the figures in different ways.

Gombrich (1960) informs us that Botticelli maintained that by 'merely throwing a sponge full of paint at the wall it leaves a blot where one sees a fine landscape'. The fact that patterns can be interpreted in this way is incorporated in the types of projective test known as the Ink-blot Personality Tests. The best-known of these is the Rorschach Test, which consists of ten standard ink-blots (see Plate 2), five of which are coloured and five black-and-white.

The observer is asked what he sees the ink-blot to be. If, in interpreting the picture, the colour is responded to freely, it is suggested that the observer is emotionally responsive. The inhibited or depressed person will structure his responses around other aspects of the figure. Those who prefer the reds and yellows are thought to be characterised by a close relationship with the visual world, and are considered open and generally receptive to the social environment. They are found to be highly suggestible and have strong emotional feelings about other people: they tend to concentrate more on the world than on themselves. On the other hand, those people who form their responses around what Goethe called the 'negative side of the spectrum', i.e. the greens and blues, are said to have a detached attitude to the world, having a set way of reacting to the world and not usually changing when new conditions arise. Usually, they are cold and reserved in their relationships with other people, being concerned more with themselves in their interactions with the outside world. Arnheim (1954) has suggested that colour preferences found in the Rorschach Test can be seen paralleled in the mood changes of painters. He quotes as examples Rouault's preference for red, Van Gogh's for yellow, and the change in Picasso's painting from the 'blue period' to the 'pink period'.

In some cards of the Rorschach Test one is confronted with the choice of structuring the world in terms of shape or in terms of colour. If colour dominates, symmetrically placed blue rectangles may, for example, be interpreted as the sky or as forget-me-nots. This preference for colours shows the emotionally responsive personality as compared with the person who makes shapes even when the colour contradicts this interpretation. The latter is generally considered to show a person who has strong control over his impulses. In the black-and-white Rorschach cards, pattern responses are bound to dominate, but even here it is suggested that individual personalities can be differentiated. For example, use of the

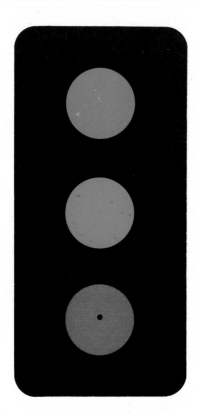

Plate 3 If the traffic light is fixated for
a minute or so and the gaze is then
transferred to the opposite page, the
colours of the traffic light will be
found to have 'righted' themselves

small white spaces between the black is said to be diagnostic of stubbornness, even of a latent paranoia. Those people who give 'form-bounded' responses have generally rather stereotyped personalities and have been differentiated on other psychological measures from those who give a more 'creative' type of response. Klein and Schlesinger (1951) considered that the form-dominated responders were intolerant of perceptual ambiguity, rejected any bizarre interpretations and tried to find something definite in the stimulus (we have already encountered this personality difference in relation to long-term differences in perception). Form-dominated responders had a smaller range for the phenomenon of apparent movement, in that there were conditions in which flickering lights were seen as static by them but as moving by people characterised as form-labile on the Rorschach Test.

Singer and Wynne (1965) have analysed responses to the Rorschach Test along a continuum of attentional disruption. The responses of the parents of various types of schizophrenic were analysed to see if the parents' attentional processes had any connection with their offspring's mental state. The patient who is diagnosed as borderline schizophrenic tends to have parents without severe attentional defects but who rather distort the interpretation of the test card. This can take the form of imagining that their response is unusual when in fact it is very typical. For example, Card V, which is often seen as a bat, was responded to by the mother of one borderline schizophrenic patient saying:

This is a weird idea, a strange idea, but it could be a bat. Bet no-one has even said or found that before, that's an unusual one.

Or again, there can be a rejection of a meaning once it has been put forward:

That could be Punch and Judy having a fight, more feminine figure seems to be having an argument. Marionettes playing some part of a play, could be a little argument.

Or again:

This could be a free-for-all over a piece of meat, two dogs having a little fight. Maybe it looks like a teddy bear.

This last example is very interesting since, though it is the reaction of the parent of a patient diagnosed as a borderline schizophrenic, it does reflect very well the ambiguity of speech-pattern of schizophrenics themselves.

Singer and Wynne have suggested that interpretations of the Rorschach cards which give as a response an object looked at from an unusual angle are found most frequently in families of fragmented schizophrenics: a fragmented schizophrenic is further along Singer and Wynne's continuum of attentional disruption. The 'bat' in Card V, for example, may be seen as a bat, but from underneath at an angle. Rorschach Card I was seen by one mother as two parachutists about to jump towards her with their heads facing each other in profile, but at the same time their bodies facing to the front. Such strange responses are not always associated with schizophrenia but need to be interpreted by the clinician along with many other factors, including the manner of response. A mother of a schizophrenic may say that a card reminds her of her 'husband's appendix' or 'the blood forces me to think of my menstruation', giving the impression that it is not her responsibility that she has organised the percept in this way but is due to some outside force for which she cannot be blamed.

Parents of patients diagnosed as severely psychotic, amorphous schizophrenics tended to give more undefined responses. To Rorschach Card VI a response given was 'some sort of species for a special occasion'. Also there is an inability to find a structure, for example: '...I dunno. It looks like it might have been the—looks like somebody started drawing and didn't finish, I think.' Again, there is the rejection of an interpretation: 'That looks like a bat. The more I look at it the less it seems to be like that, I guess. I am not sure about that bat any more.'

The responses given above are very interesting since they are not from the patients themselves, who are diagnosed as schizophrenic, but from members of their families. There seems to be a similarity in the organisation of the visual input. Even if this correlation between parental perceptual organisation and the patient's perceptual organisation is not so perfectly established for predictive purposes, it is an important line of research. The way in which a child organises his visual world is something which develops with age. We have already seen that scanning behaviour changes (Zinchenko *et al.*, 1963) as the child develops. If the organisational processes of the parent are not normal, it is not impossible that these will be transferred to the child.

The interpretations of the Rorschach Test as presented above represent only a sample of the possibilities that a clinician would have to deal with. Those presented are considered uncritically and it should be mentioned that there are workers in the field who doubt the validity of these types of test. Other more reliable tests have been designed such as the Holtzman Ink-blot Technique (for review, see Gamble (1972)). This seems to give rise to fewer alternative structurings by the observer. Eysenck (1965), however, criticised even this test, not on its reliability but on its validity with respect to the diagnosis reached.

There is even greater doubt concerning the validity of the Rorschach Test when it is given to members of different cultures. Rorschach himself even noted different response patterns within various Swiss Cantons. While there have been many investigations with the Rorschach Test in dispersed cultures, the samples used have not always been representative

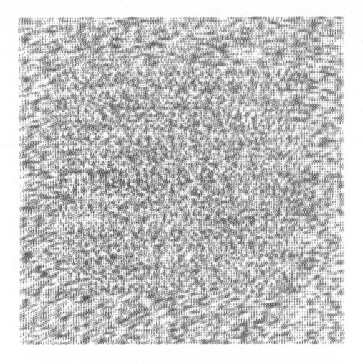

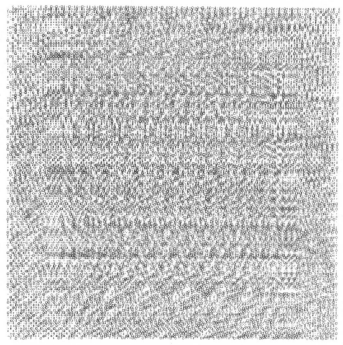

Plate 4 Anaglyphs III and IV (reprinted from *Foundations of Cyclopean Perception*, Julesz, B., University of Chicago Press: 1971)

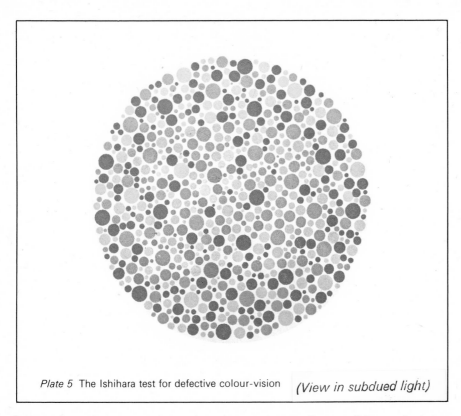

Plate 5 The Ishihara test for defective colour-vision   *(View in subdued light)*

of the population nor been large enough to allow valid conclusions. However, it is worthwhile recording some of the findings. For example, it has been noted that Moroccans give a very high proportion of responses based on small details and parts of the anatomy. The Pilaga of the Argentine Gran Chaco gave many sexual responses, and in Samoa responses to the white spaces were unusually frequent.

Whether any observer responding to the Rorschach Test by structuring shapes from the red is or is not subject to emotional outbursts, is of course an important concern for the clinician. But the diagnostic validity is not our major interest. We should like to know what are the experiential factors which contribute to any differential reorganisation, but we are a long way from that goal. The Ink-blot Tests and other projective techniques are useful because they show most powerfully that we will organise even the most unstructured input.

Ways of seeing

The attitude the observer adopts towards viewing an object is important, as was demonstrated by Benussi (1904) who found that it can affect the magnitude of an illusion. If in one case the observer adopts a 'whole-perceiving' attitude and in the other a 'part-perceiving' attitude, the effect of the Muller-Lyer Illusion (Fig. 1) will vary. The 'whole-perceiving' attitude causes an increase in illusion as compared with the 'part-perceiving' attitude. The more analytic 'part-perceiving' attitude enables the observer to isolate the lines and see them as being more equal. Benussi (1912) reinforced this finding with the discovery that if parts of the Muller-Lyer Illusion were presented sequentially, the mid-point between the arrowheads would move along the line according to the figure sequence presented. This, however, did not occur when the observer attended to the lines rather than the whole figure. We have seen that differential eye movements have been associated with the decrease of the illusory effect and these might arise because this more analytic viewing procedure is adopted.

Heaton (1968) referring to Merleau-Ponty (1962) also says that the way of looking at illusions affects their strength, but says that the Muller-Lyer Illusion arises because of viewing in an 'objective analytical manner' and that the lines appear unequal because 'they are forced into the same context and so can be compared': this is an odd use of the word 'analytic'. But one is forced to disagree even more with the explanation of why schizophrenics are said to see these illusions more strongly, according to which schizophrenics are 'intolerant of ambiguity and readily take up an analytic attitude'. It would seem that, far from being intolerant of ambiguity, the schizophrenic seems to welcome it. This tortuous reasoning would not be necessary if the finding relating degree of illusion with schizophrenia were disputed.

Generally, it is found that the person who breaks down the visual world into constituent parts sees less illusion. There may indeed be personality differences with respect to these ways of looking, but it is possible for most people to adopt any way of looking at these illusions: the adaptability of our organisational processes is very great indeed.

Another visual illusion, called the 'Auto-kinetic Phenomenon', provides us with an illustration of how an ambiguous situation can affect what the observer reports. The Auto-kinetic Phenomenon is the apparent movement of a spot of light when it is viewed in a darkened room. Even though the light remains absolutely still, it nevertheless appears to move around—an effect which can have serious implications for aviation, since crashes have been caused by aircraft pilots mistaking stars or ground lights for the lights of other moving planes. The explanation of this effect is perhaps related to some muscle imbalance in the neck or eyes resulting in a change in the felt position of the eyes.

The Auto-kinetic effect has been used in many experiments as a vehicle for determining the factors which can account for the formation and change of what is accepted to be normal. In a typical experiment, a confederate of

the experimenter planted in the room with the observer gives his assessment of the movement of the light. It is found that the observer tends to
agree with whatever the confederate says. This must be related to the
nature of the situation; since there is no real movement, the extent of the
illusory movement can be somewhat open to suggestion. Moreover, the
extent of the illusion now perceived by the observer will stabilise since, if
re-tested when he is alone, he will see the light move to the same extent as
before. A second observer placed in the room with this first observer will
agree with the first with respect to the extent of the illusion: thus the norm
of the confederate is passed on to someone who has never met him.

It has been suggested that factors isolated in this situation tell us how
the norms of a society are inculcated into its members. The ambiguous
situation of the Auto-kinetic Phenomenon may therefore be a very useful
tool for research into aspects of social psychology. This ambiguous
illusory situation provides an opportunity for a multitude of equally good
solutions or reconstructions. The social pressures, such as suggestion,
which determine our expressed opinions and decision-making can therefore be studied by the extent to which they alter our 'perceptual' judgements. However, restructuring of the normal visual world is very different
from the peculiar conditions of illusory movement seen in the Auto-
kinetic Phenomenon.

Evidence has been presented to show that, at least in certain circumstances, we may make different reconstructions from the same visual
input. Who is to know if the sightings of such supposedly extra-terrestrial
objects as flying saucers do not arise from such reorganisation? They
certainly occur most often in situations where ambiguity is likely to be
present. The more interpretation of the stimulus input that is required of
the observer, the more likely is the perception to be different. If Fig. 45 is
looked at as an art object, does it not look different from when it is considered solely as a perceptual phenomenon?

Gaffron (1962) has many interesting things to say about the way in
which our subjective experience of an event changes as our organisation
of the visual input alters. Figure 68 shows an Egyptian relief cut into the
wall of the Temple at Luxor. Gaffron suggests that there are two alternative
organisations of this and any other picture: in the first of these brightness is
dominant and in the second texture is dominant. If an observer is viewing
in the former manner, the chest shape is determined in his perception by
the cut-in border area which, together with its shadow, is seen as a
separate area between the inner chest region and the wall. The chest shape
is constructed from brightness contrasts between the areas, therefore the
observer's attention follows the regions of brightness contrast. As
Gaffron says, 'The form of the chest seems actually given in the experience
of movement, a swinging around of the border zone, similar to the way the
opening of an archway in a Baroque church appears shaped by experience

Plate 6 The visual experience of the trichromat, the red–green blind dichromat, the yellow–blue blind dichromat and the monochromat (Steve McCarroll, from *Psychology Today: An Introduction,* © 1970 by Communications Research Machines, Inc. Reprinted by permission of CRM Books, Del Mar, California, USA)

Fig 68 (Reprinted from *Psychology: A Study of a Science*,
Koch, S., Ed., McGraw-Hill Book Co: 1962)

of movement in the profiles of the side walls'. Gaffron says that if this mode
of organisation is the one the observer is experiencing, then the inner
chest region is seen as set back behind the plane of the surrounding wall.
Also, the surface appearance of the chest area is less well-defined than
that of the wall, which is seen as hard, level and smooth despite the fact
that it contains many small holes.

The region between the chest and the bent arm is again defined by the
border of brightness contrast. According to Gaffron, this perceptual unit
is not developed through movement but experienced as a change in
depth. The white page is seen not as a frame to the picture but as another
brightness zone.

If the picture is perceived in the second of the two modes above, with
texture the dominant organisational factor, the chest area appears to
represent a real object and the picture looks more familiar. The chest area
now appears to be in front of the wall and is the dominant feature of the

picture, leaving the wall as the background. The observer attends to the centre of the chest, not its border, and the surface has much more texture. The brightness gradients are now only part of the texture of three-dimensional objects and the region between the chest and bent arm has no special importance. When the picture is viewed in terms of brightness-organisation the wall is divided into parts by the regions of contrast, but in terms of texture the wall is seen as the background extending behind the objects in the picture.

The organisation of the input in terms of areas of brightness contrast is typically that used when dealing with the unfamiliar. There are reports that, when wearing spectacles that transform the visual input (page 36), brightness and colour are very much enhanced. In this situation, borders of objects are said to be seen as contrasts in brightness, and distance perception is changed. It was remarked earlier that when wearing inverting spectacles the movement of people walking seemed most unusual. The phenomenologist approach put forward here by Gaffron relates this experience to that of watching a performance of East Indian dancers: he reports that the movement seems to originate along the periphery of the dancers' moving limbs rather than from within the often motionless body. Generally, any unusual viewpoint of a scene favours an organisation in terms of brightness. This is true of a picture which is seen upside down or reversed left to right. It might also be suggested that this is the way in which a person unfamiliar with pictures, such as the African tribesmen we have considered above (page 157), would organise his perception of a photograph.

This may not be easy for us to do as we have to adopt, as Gibson (1950) says, a different kind of seeing. Gibson makes a similar dichotomy to that of Gaffron: the familiar way of perceiving which we adopt results in the *visual world*. This is the 'ordinary scene of daily life, in which solid objects look solid, square objects look square, horizontal surfaces look horizontal and the book across the room looks as big as the book lying in front of you'. But the object we know to be square, and which indeed looks square, may not present a square to the eye. If we see the world as it presents itself to our eyes we have what Gibson calls the *visual field*. This can be obtained by fixating upon some point (perhaps easier with one eye) yet not looking at that point but at the whole scene: one can then become aware of the scene as patches of colour divided up by contours. Gibson makes other clear distinctions between the visual world and the visual field. For example, the *visual world* seems to go all around us and we are not conscious of any lack of clarity in the periphery of our vision. But if the 'trick' is used of fixating a point and looking at the rest of the scene, what is now experienced, i.e. the *visual field*, has boundaries, is oval in shape and blurred at the edges. The observer's nose, even if shadowy, will occur in the visual field.

Organising one's perception in terms of the visual field, since it is unusual for us, can come as a shock or even be felt as being creative or as an inspiration. This is certainly how Heron (1955) saw his reorganisation of the view across St Ives harbour:

Suddenly, I find I am no longer looking at all this with the practical eye of one considering whether the boat is coming into anchor. Suddenly I am only conscious of a dark blue horizontal slab sitting on top of a pale blue-green strip which, in turn, rests apparently on a much larger oblong of colour—a roundish oblong of incredibly light, almost dazzling Naples yellow. Across these abstract, horizontal rectangular slabs of colour (which, you will have guessed, are simply the strips of sea, harbour water and, under those, the yellow of a nearby sand bar)—across these cut the verticals of the very near window frames and the balcony rails. Horizontal strips of colour cut up by verticals; result, a check, a pattern of square patches...

This reorganisation, no doubt, was helped by the art ideas current at that time, but shows that alternative ways of organising the visual input can be adopted.

Gibson (1968) suggests that there is a very good reason why the visual world is a stable percept. Reorganisation may be difficult to adopt because perception is a process on-going in time in which samples are successively and continuously taken from what is a stable optical array surrounding the observer. The isolation of the visual field can therefore be looked on as an 'unnatural' process.

It has been suggested that the perceptual changes that occur in meditation, occur just because these organisational processes no longer operate. One of Deikman's (1963) observers says, 'I can't settle down on any one thing... It looks like a call for attention from all over the lot of it.' And again, of the same scene, 'I didn't see the order to it or the patterning to it or anything and I couldn't impose it, it resisted my imposition of pattern'. It could even be thought that the same failing, in a more extreme form, was described in the reports of Von Senden (page 104) on perception after the removal of cataracts. Gaffron, however, suggests that this is more likely to do with a perceptual organisation by the patient in terms of brightness.

What Gaffron calls the 'texture-dominant' way of organising the visual input puts order in the picture by looking for familiar objects. Perceiving a picture in this manner makes for greater stability than if it is seen in terms of brightness contrast. If a picture is seen in terms of contrast, alternation of the dominance of parts of the picture becomes more likely. Fig. 68 shows how easily contrast can produce such a reversible figure. A picture viewed in the texture mode does not produce a reversible figure. The figure and ground will remain constant. Dali's painting *Slave Market with Apparition of the Invisible Bust of Voltaire.* (Fig. 53) can be ineffective if the contrast between the black and white sections is too severe and causes only the face of Voltaire to be seen.

It is interesting that Gaffron also suggests that the way in which a picture is scanned will affect the subjective interpretation of that picture. Here, as in all phenomenological investigations, very easily a point may be reached where individuals are in disagreement and there seems no way of deciding who is correct. It is suggested that looking along a vertical line in an upward direction causes an experience of ease and grace, whereas following the same line downwards produces an 'awkward feeling' of jerky eye movements. While the type of eye movements made can be verified, the feeling they induce can only be subjectively identified.

What we can be certain of is the difference in interpretation which is possible in organising the visual input. This applies to children as well as adults. We have referred previously to the developmental changes that occur in eye movements; this may cause different sorts of reorganisation. It is difficult for children to identify incomplete figures such as those of Fig. 63 unless more detail is added (Gollin, 1960, 1961). On the other hand, children have often been observed to 'see' things in pictures which adults cannot. Berger (1972) has found, using pictures of Christ, that children interpret pictures differently from adults. Here there was a difference between boys and girls. It is interesting that the 'ways of seeing' of children can be affected at such an early age for something so complex. However, we know that scanning and attentional processes have plenty of time to be changed before even early childhood. From the other side of the fence, Meyer and Sobieszek (1972) found that if children were dressed in an ambiguous way, so that they could appear to be either boys or girls, identical actions were interpreted by adults in different ways. If a child was considered to be a girl, an action was described as aggressive; but if the child was thought to be a boy the identical action was described in very much more favourable terms.

It could be argued that in the last example the interpretation of the visual input by the observer is not one that involves predominantly a change in a perceptual process. This, however, cannot be the case with the 'droodle' produced, according to Arnheim, by one of his students. This can be interpreted (organised) in two ways. Some observers will interpret the 'droodle' of Fig. 69 as the bottom part of a bikini, while others will see it as an olive being dropped into a martini glass. Of course, it is possible to organise the 'droodle' in both ways.

The role of the individual in interpreting the visual world has been known at least since Aristotle, who in his *Parva Naturalia* wrote:

Under the influence of strong feeling we are easily deceived regarding our sensations, different persons in different ways, as for example the coward under the influence of fear and the lover under that of love have such illusions that the former owing to a trifling resemblance thinks he sees an enemy, the latter his beloved. And the more impressionable the person is, the less is the resemblance required. Similarly, everybody is easily deceived when in anger or influenced by any strong desire, and

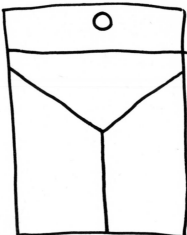

Fig 69

the more subject one is to these feelings the more one is deceived. This is the reason why men sick of a fever sometimes think they see animals on the walls owing to some slight resemblance in the figures drawn there. And this tendency to illusion at times keeps pace with the intensity of emotional experience, so that in cases where the patient is not very sick, he is still conscious of the deceptions, but where his condition is more aggravated, he even rushes upon these animals.

This restructuring of the visual world occurs for all of us but is consistently different or more pronounced in some people. Patients viewing reversible figures tend to be more dominated by one interpretation of a figure than does a non-patient. The figure—ground relationship shown in Fig. 42 is seen differently by certain people suffering from simultagnosia, which is a defect of attention in which the patient cannot attend to even two simple things at once. They see the figure in only one way, from which they find it difficult to reverse.

We all know the effect of conditions of reduced clarity of the stimulus input such as when, walking along a country lane at night, the trees take on the forms of human figures. There are individuals to whom the multiple interpretation possible from the stimulus input can cause almost constant illusory phenomena. This condition is called pareidolia and has various causes, some of which are physical in origin. Retinal haemorrhage, detached retina and optical atrophy are all conditions in which the outside world can be reconstructed to show visions of animals and people which others do not see. These differ from hallucinations in that the vision moves with the point of fixation. Also, the patient is not out of touch with reality and can be quite aware that what he is seeing is not really there. The effect of pareidolia can be experienced by anyone if the visual scene is undefined and also by patients with normal vision, as in the following example quoted from Heaton (1968):

On all the trees and bushes I saw, instead of the usual clothes, dim outlines of pantomime figures—pot-bellied fellows with thin bow legs and long thick noses, or at another time elephants with long trunks swinging. The ground seemed to swarm with lizards, frogs and toads, sometimes of portentious size. All kinds of animal forms and evil shapes seemed to surround me. Trees and bushes took on wild provoking shapes. At other times a girl's figure rode on every bush and on the trees and reeds. Girls' faces smiled from the clouds, enticing me, and when the wind moved the branches they waved at me.

In undertaking to confine our attention to those cases where the amount of non-perceptual interpretation involved is minimal, we want to avoid, for example, discussion of the memory of an event which might easily be dominated, not by an individual's perception of that event, but by those aspects he selectively retains because they fit in with his prejudices. This distinction can be seen in an experiment to investigate prejudice in which observers were given a clear picture of a white man with a knife threatening a black man. Tested for their recollection of the picture, many observers reported the picture as having been of the black man threatening the white. This is clearly a change in memory due, no doubt, to some selection in the coding of the input or in retrieval. No observer saw the picture as that of a white man being threatened by a black man when the picture was directly in front of him. While selective memory is an interesting phenomenon, it is basically not a perceptual problem and therefore is not part of the scheme of this study.

Social situations do, however, allow for variations in perception: as Ackerman and Jahoda (1950) wrote: 'For the anti-Semite, the Jew is a living Rorschach Ink-blot'. The stimulus input is amenable to interpretation by the observer and something must be said about the extent to which each of us perceives the social environment in terms of his own inter-pretation. It has been suggested that people are more accurate in their perception of the people against whom they are prejudiced. However, evidence for this is not at all clear-cut. Anti-Semites are superficially more accurate in judging whether photographs of people are of Jews or non-Jews, but this is partly, at least, because they call more people Jews. Thus, while they are more 'accurate' in their assessment of Jewishness, they are more inaccurate in their judgements of non-Jewishness. Yet one cannot deny the possibility that anti-Semites are indeed more accurate than chance guessing would predict in their assessment of who is a Jew. This is because, given that there really are physiognomic cues upon which to base a distinction, the anti-Semite may well be attuned to what cues he should attend to for a correct identification.

The transactionalists, too, realised that perception of social events could be different according to the observer involved. This was exemplified by Hastorf and Cantril (1954) when they considered the biased viewing of the sports fan. They argued that the perception of a supporter for one side is always potentially different from that of a supporter of the other, because both are sampling from the 'total matrix of events' and they will sample according to their prejudices. This is the reason why, in a boxing match, one of the contestants has to be put on the canvas in order to convince all of his fans that he was not 'robbed of the fight'. In the Thereness–Thatness Test, observers can prefer to see straight metal rods as bent rather than playing-cards of an unusual size, so it is not surprising that lines 'bend' on the tennis court to make a ball go in or out.

Hastorf and Cantril considered observers' memories and perceptions of an important football game between Princeton University and Dartmouth College. The game turned out to be a rough one, as they report in this extract:

The referees were kept busy blowing their whistles and penalising both sides. In the second quarter, Princeton's star left the game with a broken nose. In the third quarter a Dartmouth player was taken off the field with a broken leg. Tempers flared before and after the game. The official statistics of the game, which Princeton won, showed that Dartmouth was penalised seventy yards, Princeton twenty-five, not counting a few plays in which both sides were penalised.

The above quotation represents a brief résumé of the 'facts'. But how were these 'facts' seen by the supporters of both sides? It was quite clear from the students newspapers of the rival colleges that there were conflicting opinions about the game. Hastorf and Cantril therefore proceeded to investigate these discrepancies. Their first method was to get the observers to fill in a questionnaire about the fairness of each side's play; this got the expected results but did not answer the question as to whether the fans actually *saw* anything differently. Their memories might have been biased—we know that memories reconstruct themselves into patterns to be compatible with already held opinions, so the questionnaires can tell us nothing certain about their perceptions. Of greater interest, therefore, was the second method, which was to show each side's supporters a film of the event and ask for a check on the number of infringements seen. The film was taken by Dartmouth College and thus might be considered suspect in relation to some 'true' objectivity, but at least all observers saw the same film. When Dartmouth students saw the film, they saw both teams make about the same number of infringements, whereas Princeton students saw their own team make under half the infringements of Dartmouth, which in fact did correspond to the referee's opinion.

Now this shows a selectivity, perhaps of attention (though the transactionalists do not consider attentional factors) or perhaps of organisation. It is always possible, according to transactionalists, for the stimulus to be interpreted in many ways, and this is revealed here. Particularly noteworthy is an incident which occurred when the film was shipped to a group of Dartmouth alumni (old boys) who had heard about their side's dirty play and wanted to see the film for themselves. This was the telegram received by a Dartmouth College officer from the Old Boys' Association:

Preview of Princeton movies indicate considerable cutting of important part please wire explanation and possibly airmail missing part before showing scheduled January 25 we have splicing equipment.

Of course, no such cutting had taken place: as far as the Dartmouth supporters were concerned, the fouls were just not on the film. It is possible that the Dartmouth alumni had just set higher thresholds for what should be considered a foul and that they did indeed see the same as any other observer. This alternative explanation may be true, but does not seem likely from the tenor of their telegram.

Our perception depends in a large part on the assumptions we bring to the occasion. As noted above, Aristotle said that the face of the beloved looks different to the lover than it does to other people. There is always some uncertainty in the stimulus we receive. Ittelson (1962) has said that 'the exact nature of what [has] really happened cannot be determined and actually presents a misleading fiction'. This suggests that in the last analysis there is only the subjective interpretation. Even if one cannot go all the way with this, the report of the football game described above shows the possibility as well as the problems of interpretation.

Final word

As a thing the way is
Shadowy, indistinct
Indistinct and shadowy,
Yet within it is an image;
Shadowy and indistinct,
Yet within it is a substance.
Dim and dark,
Yet within it is an essence.
This essence is quite genuine.
And within it is something that can be tested.
   Lao Tzu XXI, 49 (trans. D. C. Lau)

This last example of the football game is a fitting place to stop: there has been a progression from the simple static perceptual input through to the complex moving visual event. Intuitively, we feel that, whatever the input, everybody has the same perceptions as ourselves. Indeed, this may be true for most of the time, but there are differences and this has been an attempt to document them.

It should be possible from these findings to go on to theorise on the nature of the processes which cause these differences. The reader may have been disappointed that there has been no explicit theorising on these lines. However, inevitably the observations recorded here and future observations yet to be made will test hypotheses that arise concerning the processes that make people see in different ways; it may even be that these data will be the origin of such hypotheses.

The processes that make an adult view an object differently from a child may well not be the same as those processes that cause differences in visual perception between adults. Certainly, the processes that can make a grey object appear virtually any colour are different from those that made the Princeton and Dartmouth supporters see different football games when watching the same match. It would seem that, at the moment, no one theory could hope to explain more than a few of the enormous variety of differences in visual perception that are known to exist; and even when considering some specific difference we find that the processes involved, while generally becoming a little clearer, are still essentially mysterious.

This is not a prognosis of despair. Even though a full understanding of how the person deals with the visual input is a long way off, it is bound to be more complex than processing peas. However, if the reader feels himself to have come to any conclusions concerning differences in visual perception, then that in itself will be enough justification for the existence of this work.

Bibliography

Abercrombie, J. M. L. (1960) *The Anatomy of Judgment.* London: Hutchinson.

Ackerman, N. W. and Jahoda, M. (1950) *Anti-Semitism and Emotional Disorder.* New York: Harper.

Adam, J., Gibb, M. and Freeman, I. (1966) Effects of luminance contrast factors upon figural after-effects induced by short fixation periods. *Percept. mot. Skills.* **22**, 535.

Allport, G. W. (1947) *Personality: A Psychological Interpretation.* New York: Holt.

Allport, G. W. and Pettigrew, T. F. (1957) Cultural influences on the perception of movement: the trapezoidal illusion among Zulus. *J. abnorm. soc. Psychol.* **55**, 104.

Ames, A., Jr (1951) Visual perception and the rotating trapezoid window. *Psychol. Monogr.* **65**, No. 14 (Whole No. 324).

Ames, E. W. and Silfan, C. K. (1965) Methodological issues in the study of age differences in infants' attention to stimuli varying in movement and complexity. Paper presented at the meetings of the Society for Research in Child Development, Minneapolis.

Andersson, A. L., Nilsson, A., Ruuth, E. and Smith, G. J. W. (1972) *Visual After-effects and the Individual as an Adaptive System.* Lund: Gleerup.

Annis, R. C. and Frost, B. (1973) Human visual ecology and orientation anistropies in acuity. *Science.* **182**, 729.

Arieti, S. (1962) The microgeny of thought and perception. *Arch. gen. Psychiat.* **6**, 454.

Arnheim, R. (1954) *Art and Visual Perception.* London: Faber & Faber.

Arnheim, R. (1970) *Visual Thinking.* London: Faber.

Asher, H. (1961) *Experiments in Seeing.* New York: Basic Books.

Asthana, H. S. (1960) Perceptual distortion as a function of the valence of perceived objects. *J. soc. Psychol.* **52**, 119.

Atkinson, J., Braddick, O. and Braddick, F. (1974) Acuity and contrast sensitivity in infant vision. *Nature.* **247**, 403.

Attneave, F. (1971) Multistability in perception. *Scient. Am.* **225**, December, 62.

Bagby, J. W. (1957) A cross-cultural study of perceptual predominance in binocular rivalry. *J. abnorm. soc. Psychol.* **54**, 331.

Baldwin, A. L. (1955) *Behaviour and Development in Childhood.* New York: Dryden Press.

Barnet, A. B., Lodge, A. and Armington, J. C. (1965) Electroretinogram in newborn human infants. *Science.* **148**, 651.

Bartlett, F. C. (1932) *Remembering: A Study in Experimental and Social Psychology.* London: Cambridge Univ. Press.

Bartley, S. H. (1972) *Perception in Everyday Life.* New York: Harper & Row.

Bayer, C. A. and Pressey, A. W. (1972) Geometric illusions as a function of pigmentation of the fundus oculi and target size. *Psychon. Sci.* **26**, 77.

Beloff, J. and Beloff, H. (1961) The influence of valence on distance judgements of human faces. *J. abnorm. soc. Psychol.* **62**, 720.

Benussi, V. (1912) Stroboskopische Schienbewegungen und geometrischoptische Gestaltausscheinungen. *Arch. ges. Psychol.* **24**, 31.

Berger, J. (1972) *The Listener.* 13 January.

Berry, J. W. (1966) Temne and Eskimo perceptual skills. *Int. J. Psychol.* **1**, 207.

Berry, J. W. (1971) Muller-Lyer susceptibility. Culture, ecology or race? *Int. J. Psychol.* **6**, 193.

Berry, W. and Imus, H. (1935) Quantitive aspects of the flight of colours. *Am. J. Psychol.* **47**, 449.

Beveridge, W. M. (1935) Racial differences in phenomenal regression. *Br. J. Psychol.* **26**, 59.

Beveridge, W. M. (1939) Some racial differences in perception. *Br. J. Psychol.* **30**, 57.

Binet, A. (1895) La mesure des illusions visuelles chez les enfants. *Rev. philosoph.* **40**, 11.

Birch, H. G., Belmont, I. and Karp, E. (1967) Delayed processing and extinction. *Brain.* **90**, 113.

Blakemore, C. and Campbell, F. W. (1969) Adaptation to spatial stimuli. *J. Physiol.* **200**, 11.

Blakemore, C. and Cooper, G. F. (1970) Development of the brain depends on visual environment. *Nature.* **228**, 477.

Blakemore, C. and Julesz, B. (1971) Stereoscopic depth after-effect produced without monocular cues. *Science.* **171**, 286.

Blakemore, C. and Sutton, P. (1969) Size adaptation: a new after-effect. *Science.* **166**, 245.

Block, D. (1961) The effect of anxiety on the resolution of a perceptual conflict. In *Perceptual Changes in Psychopathology.* Ittelson *et al.* (eds). New Brunswick: Rutgers Univ. Press.

Blumenthal, R. and Meltzoff, J. (1967) Social schemas and perceptual accuracy in schizophrenia. *Br. J. soc. clin. Psychol.* **6**, 119.

Boersma, F. J., Muir, W., Wilton, K. and Barham, R. (1969) Eye movements during embedded figure tasks. *Percept. mot. Skills.* **28**, 271.

Bond, E. K. (1972) Perception of form by the human infant. *Psychol. Bull.* **77**, 225.

Boring, E. G. (1930) A new ambiguous figure. *Am. J. Psychol.* **42**, 444.

Boring, E. G. (1942) *Sensation and Perception in the History of Experimental Psychology.* New York: Appleton.

Botha, E. (1963) Practice without reward and figure–ground perceptions of adults and children. *Percept. mot. Skills.* **16**, 271.

Bower, T. G. R. (1964) Discrimination of depth in pre-motor infants. *Psychon. Sci.* **1**, 368.

Bower, T. G. R. (1965) Stimulus variables determining space perception in infants. *Science.* **149**, 88.

Brennen, W. S., Ames, E. W. and Moore, R. W. (1966) Age differences in infants' attention to patterns of different complexities. *Science.* **151**, 354.

Brown, R. W. and Lenneberg, E. H. (1954) A study in language and cognition. *J. abnorm. soc. Psychol.* **49**, 454.

Bruner, J. S. (1969) Early skill acquisition as problem solving. Paper presented at XIX International Congress of Psychology, London.

Bruner, J. S. and Postman, L. (1949) On the perception of incongruity: a paradigm. *J. Personality.* **18**, 206.

Bruner, J. S. and Potter, M. C. (1964) Interference in visual recognition. *Science.* **144**, 424.

Brunswik, E. (1955) Representative design and probabalistic theory in a functional psychology. *Psychol. Rev.* **62**, 93.

Buchsbaum, M., Pfefferbaum, A. and Stillman, R. (1972) Individual differences in eye-movement patterns. *Percept. mot. Skills.* **35**, 895.

Campbell, F. W. and Kulikowski, J. J. (1966) Orientational selectivity of the human visual system. *J. Physiol.* **187**, 437.

Campbell, F. W. and Maffei, L. (1971) The tilt after-effect: a fresh look. *Vision Res.* **11**, 833.

Cantril, H. (1957) Perception and interpersonal relations. *A. J. Psychiat.* **114**, 119.

Carmichael, L. and Dearborn, W. E. (1947) *Reading and Visual Fatigue.* Boston: Houghton Mifflin.

Caron, R. F. and Caron, A. J. (1968) The effects of repeated exposure and stimulus complexity on visual fixations in infants. *Psychon. Sci.* **10**, 207.

Champreys, F. H. (1881) Notes on an infant. *Mind.* **6**, 104.

Chapman, J. (1966) The early symptoms of schizophrenia. *Brit. J. Psychiat.* **112**, 225.

Claridge, G. S. (1967) *Personality and Arousal.* Oxford: Pergamon.

Claridge, G. S. and Herrington, R. N. (1963) An E.E.G. correlate of the Archimedes Spiral after-effect and its relationship with personality. *Behav. Res. Ther.* **1**, 217.

Cohen, L. (1959) Rate of apparent change of a Necker cube as a function of prior stimulation. *Am. J. Psychol.* **72**, 327.

Cohen, S. (1964) *Drugs of Hallucination: The Uses and Misuses of Lysergic Acid Diethylamide.* London: Secker & Warburg.

Cohen, W. (1957) Spatial and textural characteristics of the Ganzfield. *Am. J. Psychol.* **70**, 403.

Cook, W. M. (1931) Ability of children in color discriminations. *Child Dev.* **2**, 303.

Cooper, L. A. and Weintraub, D. J. (1970) Delboeuf-type circle illusions, interaction among luminance, temporal characteristics and inducing figure variations. *J. Exper. Psychol.* **85**, 75.

Coren, S. and Girgus, J. S. (1972) Illusion decrement in intersecting line figures. *Psychon. Sci.* **26**, 108.

Crews, S. J., James, B., Marsters, J. B. and West, C. H. (1970) Drugs and nutritional factors in optic neuropathy. *Trans. opthal. Soc. U.K.* **90**, 773.

Critchley, M. (1951) Types of visual perseveration: 'Paliopsia' and illusory visual spread. *Brain.* **74**, 267.

Critchley, M. (1953) *The Parietal Lobes.* London: Arnold.

Critchley, M. (1964) The problem of visual agnosia. *J. neurol. Sci.* **1**, 274.

Critchley, M. (1965) Acquired anomalies of colour perception of central origin. *Brain.* **88**, 711.

Dali, S. (1942) *The Secret Life of Salvador Dali.* New York: Dial Press.

Dallenbach, K. M. (1951) A puzzle picture with a new principle of concealment. *Am. J. Psychol.* **54**, 431.

Dannenmaier, W. D. and Thumin, F. J. (1964) Authority status as a factor in perceptual distortion of size. *J. soc. Psychol.* **63**, 361.

Davies, P. (1972) Classically conditioned visual after-images. Paper read at the Conference of the British Psychological Society, London.

Dawson, J. L. M. (1967) Cultural and physiological influences upon spacial perceptual processes in West Africa—Part I. *Int. J. Psychol.* **2**, 115.

Day, R. H. (1969) *Human Perception.* Sydney: Wiley.

Deikman, A. J. (1963) Experimental meditation. *J. ner. ment. Dis.* **136**, 329.

Dember, W. N., Mathews, W. D. and Stefl, M. (1973) Backward masking and enhancement of multisegmented visual targets. *Bull. psychon. Sci.* **1**, 45.

Dember, W. N. and Purcell, D. G. (1967) Recovery of masked visual targets by inhibition of the masking stimulus. *Science*. **157**, 1335.

Deregowski, J. B. (1972) Pictorial perception and culture. *Scient. Am.* **227**, November, 82.

Deregowski, J. B., Muldrow, E. S. and Muldrow, W. F. (1972) Pictorial recognition in a remote Ethiopian population. *Perception*, **1**, 417.

Deregowski, J. B. and Serpell, R. (1971) *Performance on a Sorting Task with Various Modes of Representation: A Cross-Cultural Experiment.* Human Development Research Unit: University of Zambia.

Deutsch, J. A. and Deutsch, D. (1963) Attention: some theoretical considerations. *Psychol. Rev.* **70**, 80.

Dimmick, F. L. and Hubbard, M. R. (1939) The spectral location of psychologically unique yellow, green and blue. *Am. J. Psychol.* **52**, 242.

Dixon, N. F. (1971) *Subliminal Perception: The Nature of a Controversy.* London: McGraw-Hill.

Dixon, N. F. and Dixon, P. M. (1966) 'Sloping water' and related framework illusions: some informal observations. *Quart. J. exper. Psychol.* **18**, 369.

Dixon, N. F. and Miesels, L. (1966) The effect of information content upon perception and after-effects of a rotating field. *Quart. J. exp. Psychol.* **18**, 310.

Dodwell, P. C. (1971) On perceptual clarity. *Psychol. Rev.* **78**, 275.

Doherty, M. E. and Keeley, S. M. (1972) On the identification of repeatedly presented visual stimuli. *Psychol. Bull.* **78**, 142.

Donchin, E. and Lindsley, D. B. (1965) Retroactive brightness enhancement with brief paired flashes of light. *Vision Res.* **5**, 59

Doob, L. W. (1964) Eidetic images about the Ibo. *Ethnology.* **3**, 357.

Doob, L. W. (1966) Eidetic imagery: a cross-cultural will-o'-the-wisp? *J. Psychol.* **63**, 13.

Duke-Elder, W. S. (1954) *Text Book of Ophthalmology.* Vol. 6. London: Henry Kimpton.

Ebert, P. C. and Pollack, R. H. (1972) Magnitude of the Muller-Lyer illusion as a function of lightness contrast, viewing time and fundus pigmentation. *Psychon. Sci.* **26**, 347.

Efstathiou, A. and Morant, R. B. (1966) Persistence of the waterfall illusion after-effect as a test of brain damage. *J. abnorm. Psychol.* **71**, 300.

Engel, E. (1956) The role of content in binocular resoltuion. *Am. J. Psychol.* **69**, 87.

Epstein, W. (1967) *Varieties of Perceptual Learning.* New York: McGraw-Hill.

Eriksen, C. W., Becker, B. B. and Hoffman, J. E. (1970) Safari to masking land: a hunt for the elusive U. *Percept. Psychophys.* **8**, 245.

Ettlinger, G. (1967) Visual alexia. In *Models for the Perception of Speech and Visual Form.* W. Wathen-Dunn (ed.). Cambridge, Mass.: MIT Press.

Eysenck, H. J. (1963) The biological basis of personality. *Nature.* **199**, 1031.

Eysenck, H. J. (1965) Review of the Holtzman inkblot technique. In *The Sixth Mental Measurements Year Book.* O. K. Buros (ed.). London: Gryphon Press.

Eysenck, H. J. (1967) *The Biological Basis of Personality.* Springfield, Ill.: Charles C. Thomas.

Eysenck, H. J., Granger, G. W. and Brengelmann, J. C. (1957) *Perceptual Processes and Mental Illness.* London: Oxford Univ. Press.

Eysenck, H. J., Holland, H. and Trouton, D. S. (1957a) Drugs and personality. III. The effects of stimulant and depressant drugs on visual after-effects. *J. ment. Sci.* **103**, 650.

Eysenck, H. J., Holland, H. and Trouton, D. S. (1957b) Drugs and personality. IV. The effects of stimulant and depressant drugs on the rate of fluctuation of a reversible figure. *J. ment. Sci.* **103**, 656.

Fagan, J. F. (1974) Infant color perception. *Science.* **183**, 973.

Fantz, R. L. (1958) Pattern vision in young infants. *Psychol. Rec.* **8**, 43.

Fantz, R. L. (1961) The origin of form perception. *Scient. Am.* **204**, May, 66.

Fantz, R. L. (1964) Visual experience in infants: decreased attention to familiar patterns relative to novel ones. *Science.* **146**, 668.

Feinbloom, W. (1938) A quantitative study of the visual after-image. *Arch. Psychol.* **33**, No. 233.

Festinger, L., White, C. W. and Allyn, M. R. (1968) Eye movements and decrement in the Muller-Lyer illusion. *Percept. Psychophys.* **3**, 376.

Fisher, G. H. (1967) Preparation of ambiguous stimulus materials. *Percept. Psychophys.* **2**, 421.

Fisher, G. H. (1968) Who overlooks the fat woman? *Br. J. Aesthetics.* **8**, 394.

Fisher, G. H. (1971) Why do we see the world as we do? *Aspects Educ.* **13**, December, 63.

Flament, C. (1959) Ambiguïté du stimulus, incertitude de la réponse et processes d'influence sociale. *Année psychol.* **59**, 73.

Franks, C. M. and Lindahl, L. E. H. (1963) Extraversion and rate of fluctuation of the Necker Cube. *Percept. mot. Skills.* **16**, 131.

Frenkel-Brunswik, E. (1949) Intolerance of ambiguity as an emotional and perceptual variable. *J. Personality.* **18**, 108.

Friedman, S. (1972) Newborn visual attention to repeated exposures of redundant and novel targets. *Percept. Psychophys.* **12**, 289.

Frisby, J. P. (1972) Real and apparent movement—same or different mechanisms. *Vision Res.* **12**, 1051.

Frith, C. D. (1967) The interaction of noise and personality with critical flicker fusion performance. *Br. J. Psychol.* **58**, 127.

Frith, C. D. (1973) Abnormalities in perception. In *Handbook of Abnormal Psychology.* H. J. Eysenck (ed.). London: Pitman Medical.

Gaffron, M. (1962) In *Psychology: A Study of a Science.* Vol. 4, 562. New York: McGraw-Hill.

Gamble, K. R. (1972) The Holtzman inkblot technique: a review. *Psychol. Bull.* **77**, 172.

Gardner, R. W., Holtzman, P. S., Klein, G. S., Linton, H. and Spence, D. P. (1959) Cognitive control. *Psychol. Issues.* **1**, No. 4.

Gardner, R. W. and Long, R. I. (1962) Control, defence and centration effect: a study of scanning behaviour. *Br. J. Psychol.* **53**, 129.

van de Geer, J. P. and de Natris, P. J. A. (1962) Dutch distorted rooms from the seventeenth century. *Acta Psychol.* **20**, 101.

Geldard, F. A. (1972) Vision—from a wide mantel. *Percept. Psychophys.* **11**, 193.

Gerrits, H. J. M. and Timmerman, G. J. M. E. N. (1969) The filling-in process in patients with retinal scotomata. *Vision Res.* **9**, 439.

Ghent, L. (1961) Form and its orientation: a child's eye view. *Am. J. Psychol.* **74**, 177.

Ghent, L. (1963) Stimulus orientation as a factor in the recognition of geometric forms by school-age children. Paper presented at the meeting of the Eastern Psychological Association, April.

Ghent-Braine, L. (1968) Asymmetries of pattern perception in Israelis. *Neuropsychol.* **6**, 73.

Gibson, E. J. (1969) *Principles of Perceptual Learning and development.* New York: Appleton-Century-Crofts.

Gibson, J. J. (1950) *The Perception of the Visual World.* Boston: Houghton Mifflin.

Gibson, J. J. (1968) *The Senses Considered as Perceptual Systems.* London: Allen & Unwin.

Gibson, J. J. and Radner, M. (1937) Adaptation, after-effect and contrast in the perception of tilted lines. I. Quantitative studies. *J. exper. Psychol.* **20**, 453.

Gilbert, J. A. (1894) Researches on the mental and physical development of school children. *Stud. Yale psychol. Lab.* **2**, 40.

Gogel, W. C. and Newton, R. E. (1969) Depth distortions in binocular fields. *Percept. mot. Skills.* **28**, 251.

Gollin, E. S. (1960) Developmental studies of visual recognition of incomplete objects. *Percept. mot. Skills.* **11**, 289.

Gollin, E. S. (1961) Further studies of visual recognition of incomplete objects. *Percept. mot. Skills.* **13**, 307.

Gombrich, E. H. (1960) *Art and Illusion.* New York: Phaidon Press.

Gombrich, E. H. (1965) Visual discovery through art. *Arts.* November.

Gomulicki, B. R. (1953) The development and present status of the trace theory of memory. *Br. J. Psychol. Monogr. Suppl.* No. 29.

Graham, C. H. (1965) *Vision and Visual Perception.* New York: Wiley.

Graham, C. H. and Hsia, Y. (1958) Color defect and color theory: studies on normal and color blind persons including a unilaterally dichromatic subject. *Science.* **127**, 675.

Graham, C. H., Hsia, Y. and Stephen, F. F. (1963) Visual discriminations of a subject with acquired unilateral tritanopia. *Science.* **140**, 381.

Granger, G. W. and Ikeda, H. (1968) Drugs and visual thresholds. In *Drugs and Sensory Functions*. A. Herxheimer (ed.). London: Churchill.

Gregory, R. L. (1966) *Eye and Brain*. London: Weidenfeld & Nicolson.

Gregory, R. L. (1970) *The Intelligent Eye*. London: Weidenfeld & Nicolson.

Grosz, H. J. and Zimmerman, J. (1965) Experimental analysis of hysterical blindness. *Arch. gen. Psychiat.* **13**, 255.

Haber, R. N. (1966) Nature of the effect of set on perception. *Psychol. Rev.* **73**, 335.

Haber, R. N. (1969) Eidetic imagery. *Scient. Am.* **220**, April, 36.

Hakerem, G., Sutton, S. and Zubin, J. (1964) Pupillary reactions to light in schizophrenic patients and normals. *Ann. N.Y. Acad. Sci.* **105**, Art 15, 820.

Hamilton, V. (1972) The size constancy problem in schizophrenia: a cognitive skill analysis. *Br. J. Psychol.* **63**, 73.

Harmon, L. D. (1970) Some aspects of recognition of human faces. *Fourth Kybernetic Kongress Berlin, 1970.* Heidelberg: Springer.

Harrington, T. L. (1965) Adaptation of humans to coloured–split field glass. *Psychon. Sci.* **3**, 71.

Harris, C. S. (1965) Perceptual adaptation to inverted, reversed and displaced vision. *Psychol. Rev.* **72**, 419.

Harris, C. S. and Haber, R. N. (1963) Selective attention and coding in visual perception. *J. exper. Psychol.* **65**, 328.

Hartmann, H. (1958) *Ego Psychology and the Problem of Adaptation.* New York: International Univ. Press.

Harway, N. I. (1963) Judgement of distance in children and adults. *J. exper. Psychol.* **65**, 385.

Hastorf, A. H. (1950) The influence of suggestion on the relationship between stimulus size and perceived distance. *J. Psychol.* **29**, 195.

Hastorf, A. H. and Cantril, H. (1954) They saw a game. A case study. *J. abnorm. soc. Psychol.* **29**, 129.

Hay, J. and Pick, H. (1966) Visual and proprioceptive adaptation to optical displacement of the visual stimulus. *J. exper. Psychol.* **71**, 150.

Hayward, R. (1968) Blivets: research and development. *Worm Runner's Dig.* **10**, December, 89.

Heaton, J. M. (1967) Depth. *Confinia. Psychiat.* **10**, 211.

Heaton, J. M. (1968) *The Eye: Phenomenology and Psychology of Function and Disorder.* London: Tavistock.

Hebb, D. O. and Foord, E. N. (1945) Errors of visual recognition and the nature of the trace. *J. exp. Psychol.* **35**, 335.

Hecht, S., Schlaer, S. and Pirenne, M. H. (1942) Energy, quanta and vision. *J. gen. Physiol.* **25**, 819.

Heckenmueller, E. G. (1965) Stabilization of the retinal image: a review of methods, effects and theory. *Psychol. Bull.* **63**, 157.

Heider, E. R. and Olivier, D. C. (1972) The structure of the color space in naming and memory for two languages. *Cognit. Psychol.* **3**, 337.

Held, R. (1965) Plasticity in sensory motor systems. *Scient. Am.* **213**, May, 84.

Held, R. and Bossom, J. (1961) Neonatal deprivation and adult re-arrangement: complementary techniques for analysing plastic sensory-motor co-ordinations. *J. comp. Physiol. Psychol.* **54**, 33.

Held, R., Efstathiou, A. and Greene, M. (1966) Adaptation to displaced and delayed visual feedback from the hand. *J. exper. Psychol.* **72**, 887.

Held, R. and Gottleib, N. (1958) A technique for studying adaptation to disarranged hand–eye co-ordination contingent upon re-afferent stimulation. *Percept. mot. Skills.* **8**, 87.

Held, R. and Shattuck, S. R. (1971) Color and edge-sensitive channels in the human visual system: tuning for orientation. *Science.* **174**, 314.

Helson, H. (1938) Fundamental problems in colour vision: the principle governing changes in hue, saturation and lightness of non-selective samples in chromatic illumination. *J. exper. Psychol.* **23**, 439.

Helson, H. (1964). *Adaptation Level Theory: An Experimental and Systematic Approach to Behaviour.* New York: Harper.

Hepler, N. (1968) Color: a motion contingent after-effect. *Science.* **162**, 376.

Heron, P. (1955) Inspiration for the painter. *New Statesman and Nation.* 1 January.

Herrington, R. N. and Claridge, G. S. (1965) Sedation threshold and Archimedes spiral after-effect in early psychosis. *J. psychiat. Res.* **3**, 159.

Hershenson, M. (1964) Visual discrimination in the human newborn. *J. comp. Physiol. Psychol.* **28**, 270.

Hershenson, M. and Haber, R. N. (1965) The role of meaning in the perception of briefly exposed words. *Can. J. Psychol.* **19**, 42.

Hess, E. H. (1965) Attitude and pupil size. *Scient. Am.* **212**, April, 46.

Hieatt, D. J. and Tong, J. E. (1969) Differences between normals and schizophrenics on activation-induced change in two flash fusion thresholds. *Br. J. Psychiat.* **115**, 477.

Hiler, H. (1946). Some associative aspects of color. *J. Aesthet. Art Crit.* **4**, 203.

Hochberg, J. and Brooks, V. (1962) Pictorial recognition as an unlearned ability: a study of one child's performance. *Am. J. Psychol* **75**, 624.

Hockey, G. R. J. (1970) Effect of loud noise on attentional selectivity. *Quart. J. exp. Psychol.* **22**, 28.

Holland, H. C. (1965) *The Spiral After-effect.* Oxford: Pergamon.

Holmstedt, B. and Lindgren, J. E. (1967) Chemical constituents and pharmacology of South American snuffs. *Psycho-active Drugs.* Workshop Series A Pharmacology, NIMH, No. 2 Washington DC: US Govt. Printing Office.

Horowitz, F. D. (1969) Learning, developmental research and individual differences. *Adv. Child Dev. Behav.* **4**, 83.

Hubel, D. H. and Wiesel, T. N. (1962) Receptive fields, binocular interaction and functional architecture in the cat's visual cortex. *J. Physiol.* **160**, 106.

Hudson, W. (1960) Pictorial depth perception in sub-cultural groups in Africa. *J. soc. Psychol.* **52**, 183.

Hudson, W. (1967) The study of the problem of pictorial perception among unaccultural groups. *Int. J. Psychol.* **2**, 90.

Hume, E. M. and Krebs, H. A. (1949) Vitamin A requirements of human adults. *Spec. Rep. Ser. med. Res. Coun.* No. 264.

Ikeda, H. and Obanai, T. (1955) Studies in figural after-effects: IV The contrast-influence illusion of concentric circles and the figural after-effect. *Jap. psychol. Res. J.* **2**, 17.

Ittelson, W. H. (1962) In *Psychology: A Study of a Science.* Vol. 4, 660. S. Koch (ed.). New York: McGraw-Hill.

Ittelson, W. H., Kutash, S. B., Abramson, L. and Seidenberg, B. (eds) (1961) *Perceptual Changes in Psychopathology.* New Brunswick: Rutgers Univ. Press.

Jahoda, G. (1966) Geometric illusions and environment: a study in Ghana. *Br. J. Psychol.* **57**, 193.

Jahoda, G. (1971) Retinal pigmentation, illusion susceptibility and space perception. *Int. J. Psychol.* **6**, 199.

Jahoda, G. and Stacey, B. (1970) Susceptibility and geometrical illusions according to culture and professional training. *Percept. Psychophys.* **7**, 199.

James, W. (1890) *Principles of Psychology.* New York: Holt.

Jaspers, K. (1962) *General Psychopathology.* Trans. J. Hoenig and M. W. Hamilton. Manchester: Manchester Univ. Press.

Judd, C. H. (1902) Practice and its effect on the perception of illusions. *Psychol. Rev.* **9**, 27.

Julesz, B. (1964) Binocular depth perception without familiarity cues. *Science.* **145**, 356.

Julesz, B. (1971) *Foundations of Cyclopean Perception.* Chicago: Univ. Chicago Press.

Julesz, B. and Johnson, S. C. (1968) Stereograms portraying ambiguously perceivable surfaces. *Proc. natn. Acad. Sci.* **61**, 437.

Kagan, J. (1972) Do infants think? *Scient. Am.* **226**, March, 74.

Kahneman, D. (1968) Method, findings and theory in studies of visual masking. *Psychol. Bull.* **70**, 404.

Kasamatsu, A. and Hirai, T. (1966) An electroencephalographic study of Zen meditation (Zazen). *Folia. psychiat. neurol. Jap.* **20**, 315.

Katz, P. A. (1963) Effects of labels on children's perception and discrimination learning. *J. exper. Psychol.* **66**, 423.

Kenkel, F. (1913) Untersuchungen über den Zusammenhang zwischen Erscheinungsgrösse und Erscheinungsbewegung bei einigen sogenannten optischen Täuschungen. *Z. Psychol.* **67**, 358.

Kenny, D. T. and Ginsberg, R. (1958) The specificity of intolerance of ambiguity measures. *J. abnorm. soc. Psychol.* **56**, 300.

Kenyon, F. C. (1898) A curious optical illusion with an electric fan. *Science.* **8**, 371.

Kilbride, P. L. and Robbins, M. C. (1968) Linear perspective, pictorial depth perception and education among the Baganda. *Percept. mot. Skills.* **27**, 601.

Kilpatrick, F. P. (1954) Two processes in perceptual learning. *J. exper. Psychol.* **47**, 362.

Kinsbourne, M. and Warrington, E. K. (1963) A study of visual persever-ation. *J. Neurol. Neurosurg. Psychiat.* **20**, 468.

Klein, G. S. (1954) in *Nebraska Symposium on Motivation.* M. R. Jones (ed.) Lincoln: Univ. Nebraska Press.

Klein, G. S. (1970) *Perception, Motives and Personality.* New York: Knopf.

Klein, G. S. and Schlesinger, H. J. (1951) Perceptual attitude towards instability: 1. Prediction of apparent movement experiences from Rorschach responses. *J. Personality.* **19**, 289.

Kline, P. (1972) *Fact and Fantasy in Freudian Theory.* London: Methuen.

Kling, J. W. and Riggs, L. A. (eds) (1971) *Woodworth and Schlosberg's Experimental Psychology.* London: Methuen.

Klüver, H. (1928) *Mescal: The Divine Plant and its Psychological Effects.* London: Kegan Paul, Trench, Trubner.

Kohler, I. (1962) Experiments with goggles. *Scient. Am.* **206**, May, 63.

Köhler, W. (1920) *Die Physischen Gestalten in Ruhe und im Stationärem Zustand.* Braunschweig: Vieweg.

Köhler, W. and Wallach, H. (1944) Figural after-effects: an investigation of visual processes. *Proc. Am. phil. Soc.* **88**, 269.

Kolers, P. A. (1963) Some differences between real and apparent visual movement. *Vision Res.* **3**, 191.

Korte, A. (1915) Kinematoskopische Untersuchungen. *Z. Psychol.* **72**, 193.

Kravitz, J. H. and Yaffe, F. (1972) Conditioned adaptation to prismatic displacement with a tone as the conditioned stimulus. *Percept. Psychophys.* **12**, 305.

Kravkov, S. V. (1941) Colour vision and the autonomic nervous system. *J. opt. Soc. Am.* **31**, 335.

Krill, A. E., Alpert, H. J. and Ostfeld, A. M. (1963) Effects of a hallucino-genic agent in totally blind subjects. *Arch. Ophthal.* **69**, 180.

Külpe, O. (1904) Versuche über Abstraktion. International Congress of Experimental Psychology, Berlin.

Laing, R. D. (1959) *The Divided Self.* London: Tavistock.

Lambert, W. W., Solomon, R. L. and Watson, P. D. (1949) Reinforcement and extinction as factors in size estimation. *J. exper. Psychol.* **39**, 637.

Land, E. H. (1959) Experiments in color vision. *Scient. Am.* **200**, May, 84.

Lantz, D. and Stefflre, V. (1964) Language and cognition revisited. *J. abnorm. soc. Psychol.* **69**, 472.

Leeper, R. W. (1935) A study of a neglected portion of the field of learning—the development of sensory organization. *J. genet. Psychol.* **46**, 41.

Lefton, L. A. (1973) Metacontrast: a review. *Percept. Psychophys.* **13**, 161.

Leibowitz, H. W. and Judisch, J. M. (1967) The relation between age and magnitude of the Ponzo Illusion. *Am. J. Psychol.* **80**, 105.

Levy, P. and Lang, P. J. (1966) Activation, control and the spiral after-movement. *J. pers. soc. Psychol.* **3**, 105.

Lloyd, B. B. (1972) *Perception and Cognition: A Cross-cultural Perspective.* London: Penguin.

Lovegrove, W. J. and Over, R. (1973) Colour selectivity in orientation masking and after-effect. *Vision Res.* **13**, 895.

Luborsky, L., Blinder, B. and Schimek, J. (1965) Looking, recalling and G.S.R. as a function of defense. *J. abn. Psychol.* **70**, 270.

Luria, A. R. (1973) *The Working Brain.* London: Penguin.

Luria, A. R., Karpov, B. A. and Yarbus (1966) Disturbances of visual perception in frontal lesions. *Cortex.* **2**, 202.

Mackay, D. M. (1957) Moving visual images produced by regular stationary patterns. *Nature.* **180**, 849.

Mackworth, N. H. and Bruner, J. S. (1970) How adults and children search and recognize pictures. *Human Dev.* **13**, 149.

Malinowski, B. (1923) The psychology of sex and the foundation of kinship in primitive societies. *Psyche.* **4**, 98.

Masland, R. H. (1969) Visual motion perception: experimental modification. *Science.* **165**, 819.

Mayhew, J. E. W. and Anstis, S. M. (1972) Movement after-effects contingent on colour, intensity and pattern. *Percept. Psychophys.* **12**, 77.

McArthur, R. (1967) Sex differences in field dependence for the Eskimo. Replication of Berry's findings. *Int. J. Psychol.* **2**, 139.

McClelland, D. C. and Liberman, A. M. (1949) The effect of need for achievement on recognition of need-related words. *J. Personality.* **18**, 236.

McCollough, C. (1965a) Color adaptation of edge detectors in the human visual system. *Science.* **149**, 1115.

McCollough, C. (1965b) The conditioning of color-blindness. *Am. J. Psychol.* **78**, 362.

McDougall, W. (1929) The chemical theory of temperament applied to introversion and extraversion. *J. abnorm. soc. Psychol.* **24**, 293.

McGhie, A. (1969) *Pathology of Attention.* London: Penguin.

McKinney, J. P. (1963) Disappearance of luminous signs. *Science.* **140**, 403.

McKinnon, R. and Singer, G. (1969) Schizophrenia and the scanning cognitive control. A reevaluation. *J. abn. Psychol.* **74**, 242.

McLaughlin, R. J. and Eysenck, H. J. (1966) Visual masking as a function of personality. *Br. J. Psychol.* **57**, 393.

Meldman, M. J. (1965) The quantitive analysis of anxiety and depression. *Psychosomatics.* **6**, 8.

Meldman, M. J. (1970) *Diseases of Attention and Perception.* Oxford: Pergamon.

Merleau-Ponty, M. (1962) *Phenomenology of Perception.* Trans. C. Smith. London: Routledge & Kegan Paul.

Metzger, W. (1930) Optische Unterschungengen am Ganzfeld: II Zur Phänomenologie des Homogenen Ganzfelds. *Psychol. Forsch.* **13**, 6.

Meyer, J. W. and Sobieszek, B. I. (1972) Effect of a child's sex on adult interpretation of its behaviour. *Dev. Psychol.* **6**, 42.

Miller, N. E. (1948) Theory and experiment relating psychoanalytic displacement to stimulus-response generalisation. *J. abnorm. soc. Psychol.* **73**, 155.

Miranda, S. B. and Fantz, R. L. (1973) Visual preferences of Down's Syndrome and normal infants. *Child Dev.* **44**, 555.

Mishkin, M. and Forgays, D. G. (1952) Word recognition as a function of retinal locus. *J. exper. Psychol.* **43**, 43.

Mitchell, D. E., Freeman, R. D., Millodot, M. and Haegerstrom, G. (1973) Meridional amblyopia: evidence for modification of the human visual system by early visual experience. *Vision Res.* **13**, 535.

Morant, R. B. and Efstathiou, A. (1966) The Archimedes spiral and diagnosis of brain damage. *Percept. mot. Skills.* **22**, 391.

Moskowitz, H., Sharma, S. and McGlothlin, W. (1972) Effect of marihuana upon peripheral vision as a function of the information processing demands in central vision. *Percept. mot. Skills.* **35**, 875.

Mundle, C. W. K. (1971) *Perception: Facts and Theories.* London: Oxford Univ. Press.

Murch, G. M. (1970) Perception of rotary movement. *J. exper. Psychol.* **86**, 83.

Neall, J. M. and Cromwell, R. C. (1969) Preference for complexity in acute schizophrenia. *J. consult. clin. Psychol.* **33**, 245.

Neisser, U. (1967) *Cognitive Psychology.* New York: Appleton-Century-Crofts.

Okonji, M. O. (1969) The differential effects of rural and urban upbringing on the development of cognitive styles. *Int. J. Psychol.* **4**, 293.

Orbach, J. (1967) Recognition of English and Hebrew words in the right and left visual fields. *Neuropsychol.* **5**, 127.

Over, R., Broerse, J., Crassini, B. and Lovegrove, W. (1974) Orientation-specific after effects and illusions in the perception of brightness. *Percept. Psychophys.* **15**, 53.

Over, R. and Over, J. (1967) Detection and recognition of mirror-image obliques by young children. *J. comp. Physiol. Psychol.* **64**, 467.

Oxbury, J. M., Oxbury, S. M. and Humphrey, N. K. (1969) Varieties of oculi. *Psychon. Sci.* **8**, 83.

Pantle, A. and Sekuler, R. W. (1968) Contrast responses of human visual mechanisms sensitive to orientation and detection of motion. *Vision Res.* **9**, 397.

Pastore, N. (1952) Some remarks on the Ames oscillatory effect. *Psychol. Rev.* **59**, 319.

Pettigrew, T. F., Allport, G. W. and Barnett, E. O. (1958) Binocular resolution and perception of race in South Africa. *Br. J. Psychol.* **49**, 265.

Phillipson, H. (1955) *The Object Relation Technique.* London: Tavistock.

Piaget, J. (1961) *Les Mechanismes Perceptifs.* Presses Univ. de France. (Translated by Seagrim G. N. as *The Mechanisms of Perception.* London: Routledge & Kegan Paul, 1969.)

Piaget, J. and Lambercier, M. (1944) Essai sur un effet d' 'Einstellung' survenant au cours de perceptions visuelles successives (effet Usnadze). *Arch. Psychol., Genève.* **30**, 139.

Piaget, J. and Vinh-Bang (1961a) Comparison of the eye movements and fixations of children and adults. *Arch. Psychol., Genève.* **38**, 167.

Piaget, J. and Vinh-Bang (1961b) L'evolution de l'illusion des espaces devisés (Oppel-Kundt) en présentation tachistoscopique. *Arch. Psychol., Genève.* **38**, 1.

Pick, A. D., Christy, M. D. and Frankel, G. W. (1972) A developmental study of visual selective attention. *J. exper. Child Psychol.* **14**, 165.

Pick, H. L. (1964) Perception in Soviet psychology. *Psychol. Bull.* **62**, 21.

Pick, H. L. and Pick, A. D. (1970) Sensory and perceptual development. In Carmichael's *Manual of Child Psychology*. P. H. Mussen (ed.). New York: Wiley.

Pickford, R. W. (1949) Total colour blindness of hysterical origin. *Br. J. med. Psychol.* **22**, 121.

Pickford, R. W. (1951) *Individual Differences in Colour Vision*. London: Routledge & Kegan Paul.

Pickford, R. W. (1964) A deuteranomalous artist. *Br. J. Psychol.* **55**, 469.

Pillsbury, W. B. (1897) A study in apperception. *Am. J. Psychol.* **8**, 315.

Pollack, R. H. (1963) Contour detectability thresholds as a function of chronological age. *Percept. mot. Skills.* **17**, 411.

Pollack, R. H. (1964) Simultaneous and successive presentation of elements of the Muller-Lyer figure chronological age. *Percept. mot. Skills*, **19**, 303.

Pollack, R. H. (1966) Temporal range of apparent movement. *Psychon. Sci.* **5**, 243.

Pollack, R. H. (1969) Some implications of ontogentic changes in perception. In *Studies in Cognitive Development: Essays in Honour of Jean Piaget*. D. Elkind and J. H. Flavell (eds). New York: Oxford Univ. Press.

Pollack, R. H. and Silvar, S. D. (1967) Magnitude of the Muller-Lyer illusion in children as a function of the pigmentation of the fundus *Growth*. J. S. Bruner, R. R. Olver, P. M. Greenfield *et al.* New York:

Postman, L., Bruner, J. S. and McGinnies, E. (1948) Personal values as selective factors in perception. *J. abnorm. soc. Psychol.* **43**, 142.

Potter, M. C. (1966) On perceptual recognition. In *Studies in Cognitive Growth*. J. S. Bruner, R. R. Olver, P. M. Greenfield *et al.* New York: Wiley.

Preyer, W. (1888) *The Mind of the Child. Part II: The Development of the Intellect*. Trans. H. W. Brown. New York: Appleton.

Rice, T. (1930) Physical defects in character. II. Near-sightedness. *Hygeia*. **8**, 644.

Robinson, D. N. (1966) Disinhibition of visually masked stimuli. *Science*. **154**, 157.

Robinson, J. O. (1972) *The Psychology of Visual Illusions*. London: Hutchinson Univ. Library.

Robinson, J. S. (1955) The effect of learning verbal labels for stimuli on their later discrimination. *J. exper. Psychol*. **49**, 112.

Rock, I. (1966) *The Nature of Perceptual Adaptation*. New York: Basic Books.

Rock, I. and Harris, C. S. (1967) Vision and touch. *Scient. Am*. **216**, May, 96.

Ross, H. E. (1974) *Behaviour and Perception in Strange Environments*. London: Allen & Unwin.

Rubin, E. (1915) *Synoplevede Figurer*. Copenhagen: Gyldendalske.

Salapatek, P. (1969) The visual investigation of geometric patterns by the one and two month old infant. Paper presented at the meeting of the American Association for the Advancement of Science, Boston. December.

Sandström, C. I. (1951) *Orientation in the Present Space*. Stockholm: Almqvist & Wiksell.

Savage, C. (1955) Variations in ego feeling induced by D-lysergic acid diethylamide (LSD 25). *Psychoanal. Rev*. **42**, 1.

Segall, M. H. and Campbell, D. T. (1963) A reply to H. H. Spitz. *Science*. **140**, 422.

Segall, M. H., Campbell, D. T. and Herskovitz, M. J. (1963) Cultural differences in the perception of geometric illusions. *Science*. **139**, 769.

Segall, M. H., Campbell, D. T. and Herskovitz, M. J. (1966) *The Influence of Culture on Visual Perception*. Indianapolis: Bobbs-Merrill.

Segers, J. E. (1936) Nouvelles observations relatives à la perception des couleurs chez l'enfant. *Arch. Belg. Sci. Educ*. **2**, 52.

Sekuler, R. W. (1965) Spatial and temporal determinants of visual backward masking. *J. exper. Psychol.* **70**, 401.

Sekuler, R. W. and Ganz, L. (1963) After effect of seen motion with a stabilised retinal image. *Science.* **139**, 419.

Sekuler, R. W. and Pantle, A. (1967) A model for after-effects of seen movement. *Vision Res.* **7**, 427.

von Senden, M. (1960) *Space and Light. The Perception of Space and Shape in the Congenitally Blind Before and After Operation.* Trans. P. Heath. London: Methuen.

Serpell, R. (1971) Preference for specific orientations of abstract shapes among Zambian children. *J. cross-cult. Psychol.* **2**, 225.

Serpell, R. (1972) How perception differs among cultures. *New Society.* 20 June.

Shakow, D. (1962) Segmental set. *Arch. gen. Psychiat.* **6**, 1.

Shakow, D. (1966) Contributions from schizophrenia to the understanding of normal psychological function. Paper presented to the Eastern Psychological Association, April.

Sharma, S. and Moskowitz, H. (1972) Effect of marihuana on the visual autokinetic phenomenon. *Percept. mot. Skills.* **35**, 891.

Shrauger, S. and Altrocchi, J. (1964) The personality of the perceiver as a factor in person perception. *Psychol. Bull.* **62**, 289.

Siegel, I. M. and Arden, G. B. (1968) The effects of drugs on colour vision. In *Drugs and Sensory Functions.* A. Herxheimer (ed.). London: Churchill.

Silverman, J. (1964) The problem of attention in the research and theory of schizophrenia. *Psychol. Rev.* **71**, 352.

Singer, J. L. (1952) Personal and environmental determinants of perception in a size constancy experiment. *J. exper. Psychol.* **43**, 420.

Singer, M. T. and Wynne, L. C. (1965) Thought disorder and family relations of schizophrenics: IV Results and implication. *Arch. gen. Psychiat.* **12**, 201.

Slack, C. W. (1956) Familiar size as a cue to size in the presence of conflicting cues. *J. exper. Psychol.* **52**, 194.

Slack, C. W. (1959) Critique on the interpretation of cultural differences in the perception of motion in Ames's trapezoidal window. *Am. J. Psychol.* **72**, 127.

Smith, G. J. W. and Henriksson, M. (1955) The effect of an established percept of a perceptual process beyond awareness. *Acta. psychol.* **11**, 346.

Smith, G. J. W., Spence, D. P. and Klein, G. S. (1959) Subliminal effects of verbal stimuli. *J. abnorm. soc. Psychol.* **59**, 167.

Smith, O. W. and Smith, P. L. (1966) Developmental studies of spatial judgements by children and adults. *Percept. mot. Skills.* **22**, 3.

Snyder, F. W. and Pronko, N. H. (1952) *Vision with Spatial Invertion.* Wichita, Kans: McCormick-Armstrong.

Somekh, P. E. and Wilding, J. M. (1973) Perception without awareness in a dichoptic viewing situation. *Brit. J. Psychol.* **64**, 339.

Spears, W. C. (1964) Assessment of visual preference and discrimination in the four month old infant. *J. comp. Physiol. Psychol.* **57**, 361.

Spears, W. C. (1966) Visual preference in the four month old infant. *Psychon. Sci.* **4**, 237.

Sperling, G. (1960) The information available in brief visual presentations. *Psychol. Monogr.* **74** (11, Whole No. 498).

Spitz, H. H. and Blackman, L. (1958) The Muller-Lyer illusion in retardates and normals. *Percept. mot. Skills.* **8**, 219.

Spitz, H. H. and Blackman, L. (1959) Studies in mental retardation: I. A comparison of metal retardates and normals on visual figural after-effects and reversible figures. *J. abnorm. soc. Psychol.* **58**, 105.

Stannard, R., Singer, G. and Over, R. (1966) The effect of information feedback on size judgements of schizophrenic patients. *Br. J. Psychol.* **57**, 329.

Staples, R. (1932) The responsiveness of infants to colour. *J. exper. Psychol.* **15**, 119.

Steinberg, H., Legge, D. and Summerfield, A. (1961) Drug-induced changes in visual perception. *Neuro-psychopharmacology.* **2**, 392.

Stewart, V. M. (1973) Tests of the 'carpentered world' hypothesis by race and environment in America and Zambia. *Int. J. Psychol.* **8**, 83.

Stratton, G. M. (1896) Some preliminary experiments on vision without inversion of the retinal image. *Psychol. Rev.* **3**, 611.

Stratton, G. M. (1897) Upright vision and the retinal image. *Psychol. Rev.* **4**, 182.

Stratton, G. M. (1917) The mnemonic feat of the 'Shass Pollack'. *Psychol. Rev.* **24**, 244.

Stromeyer, C. F. (1969) Further studies of the McCollough effect. *Percept. Psychophys.* **6**, 105.

Stromeyer, C. F. (1970) Eidetikers. *Psychol. Today.* **4**, 76.

Stromeyer, C. F. (1971) McCollough effect analogs of two-color projections. *Vision Res.* **11**, 969.

Stromeyer, C. F. and Mansfield, R. J. W. (1970) Color after-effects produced with movng edges. *Percept. Psychophys.* **7**, 108.

Stromeyer, C. F. and Psotka, J. (1970) The detailed texture of eidetic images. *Nature.* **225**, 346.

Stutterheim, W. A. (1937) *Eyestrain and Convergence.* London: H. K. Lewis.

Taylor, J. G. (1962) *The Behavioural Basis of Perception.* New Haven, Conn.: Yale Univ. Press.

Tecce, J. I. (1970) Attention and evoked potentials in man. In *Attention.* D. Mostofsky (ed.). New York: Appleton-Century-Crofts.

Teuber, H-L. (1968) Alteration of perception and memory in man: reflections on methods by Milner, B. and Teuber, H-L. In *Analysis of Behavioural Change.* L. Weiskrantz (ed.). London: Harper & Row.

Teuber, H-L., Battersby, W. S. and Bender, M. B. (1960) Visual field defects after penetrating missile wounds of the brain. Cambridge, Mass: Harvard Univ. Press.

Teuber, H-L. and Weinstein, S. (1956) Ability to discover hidden figures after cerebral lesions. *Arch. Neurol. Psychol.* **76**, 369.

Theodor, L. and Miller, R. D. (1972) The effect of marihuana on visual signal detection and the recovery of visual acuity after exposure to glare. In *Cannabis: A Report of the Commission of Inquiry into the Non-medical Use of Drugs.* Ottawa: Information Canada.

Thomas, E. L. (1968) Movements of the eye. *Scient. Am.* **219**, August, 88.

Thouless, R. H. (1932) Individual differences in phenomenal regression. *Br. J. Psychol.* **22**, 216.

Thouless, R. H. (1933) A racial difference in perception. *J. Soc. Psychol.* **4**, 330.

Tinker, M. A. (1958) Recent studies of eye movements in reading. *Psychol. Bull.* **55**, 215.

Toch, H. H. and Schulte, R. (1961) Readiness to perceive violence as a result of police training. *Br. J. Psychol.* **52**, 389.

Tolman, E.C. and Brunswik, E. L. (1935) The organism and the causal texture of the environment. *Psychol. Rev.* **42**, 43.

Tomkins, S. S. and Miner, J. B. (1959) *The Tomkins-Horn Picture Arrangement Test.* New York: Springer.

Treisman, A. (1969) Strategies and models of selective attention. *Psychol. Rev.* **76**, 282.

Trevor-Roper, P. D. (1959) The influence of eye disease on pictorial art. *Proc. R. Soc. med. Ophthalmol.* **52**, 721.

Trevor-Roper, P. D. (1970) *The World through Blunted Sight.* London: Thames & Hudson.

Trincker, D. and Trincker, I. (1955) Die ontogenetische Entwicklung des Helligkeits- und Farbensehens beim Menschen. I. Die Entwicklung des Helligkeitssehens. *Albrecht v. Graefes Arch. Ophthal.* **156**, 519.

Tronick, E. and Clanton, C. (1971) Infant looking patterns. *Vision Res.* **11**, 1479.

Tyrwhill, J. (1960) In *Explorations in Communication.* E. Carpenter and M. McLuhan (eds). Boston, Mass: Beacon Press.

Urbantschitsch, V. (1907) Über Subjektive Optische Anschauungsbilder. Leipzig and Wien: Deutricke.

Vernon, P. E. and Straker, A. (1943) Distribution of colour-blind men in Great Britain. *Nature.* **152**, 690.

Venables, P. H. and Wing, J. K. (1962) Levels of arousal and subclassification of schizophrenia. *Arch. gen. Psychiat.* **7**, 114.

Vickers, D. (1972) A cyclic decision model of perceptual alternation. *Perception.* **1**, 31.

Vurpillot, E. (1968) The development of scanning strategies and their relation to visual differentiation. *J. exper. Child Psychol.* **6**, 622.

Wachtel, P. L. (1967) Conceptions of broad and narrow attention. *Psychol. Bull.* **68**, 417.

Wagener, H. P., Smith, H. L. and Nickerson, R. W. (1946) Retrobulbar neuritis and complete heart block caused by digitalis poisoning. *Arch. Ophthal.* **36**, 478.

Walk, R. D. (1966) The development of depth perception in animal and human infants. In Concept of Development. H. W. Stephenson (ed.) *Monogr. Soc. Res. Child. Dev.* **31** (5, Serial No. 107), 82.

Walk, R. D. and Gibson, E. J. (1961) A comparative and analytical study of visual depth perception. *Psychol. Monogr.* **75**, No. 519.

Walker, J. T. (1972) A texture-contingent visual motion after-effect. *Psychon. Sci.* **28**, 333.

Wallace, J. G. (1956) Some studies of perception in relation to age. *Br. J. Psychol.* **47**, 283.

Wallach, H. and Frey, K. J. (1972) Adaptation in distance perception based on oculomotor cues. *Percept. Psychophys.* **11**, 77.

Walls, G. L. (1960) Land! Land! *Psychol. Bull.* **57**, 29.

Walls, G. L. and Matthews, R. W. (1952) *New Means of Studying Color Blindness and Normal Foveal Color Vision.* Los Angeles: Univ. California Press.

Warren, R. M. (1969) Visual intensity judgements: an empirical rule and a theory. *Psychol. Rev.* **75**, 16.

Warrington, E.K. and James, M. (1967) Disorders of visual perception with localized cerebral lesions. *Neuropsychol.* **5**, 253.

Wapner, S. and Werner, H. (1957) *Perceptual Development.* Worcester, Mass: Clark Univ. Press.

Weber, C. O. (1939) The relation of personality trends to degrees of visual constancy correction for size and form. *J. applied Psychol.* **23**, 703.

Weckowicz, T. E. (1957) Size constancy in schizophrenic patients. *J. Mental Sci.* **103**, 432.

Weckowicz, T. E. (1960) Perception of hidden figures by schizophrenic patients. *Arch. gen. Psychol.* **2**, 521.

Weintraub, D. J., Tong, L. and Smith, A. J. (1973) Muller-Lyer versus size/reflectance—contrast illusion: Is the age related decrement caused by a declining sensitivity to brightness contours? *Dev. Psychol.* **8**, 6.

Weisstein, N. (1969) What the frog's eye tells the human brain: single cell analyzers in the human visual system. *Psychol. Bull.* **72**, 157.

Werner, H. (1935) Studies on contour. *Am. J. Psychol.* **47**, 40.

Werner, H. and Strauss, A. (1941) Pathology of figure background relation in a child. *J. abnorm. soc. Psychol.* **36**, 236.

Wertheimer, Max. (1912) Experimentelle Studien über das Sehen von Bewegung. *Z. Psychol.* **61**, 161.

Wertheimer, M. and Herring, F. H. (1968) Individual differences in figural after-effects. Some problems and potentials. *J. Psychol.* **68**, 211.

White, B. L. and Castle, P. W. (1964) Visual exploratory behaviour following post natal handling of human infants. *Percept. mot. Skills.* **18**, 497.

Wickelgren, L. (1967) Convergence in the human newborn. *J. exper. Child. Psychol.* **5**, 74.

Williams, M. (1970) *Brain Damage and the Mind.* London: Penguin.

Witkin, H. A. (1959) The Perception of the upright. *Scient. Am.* **200**, February, 50.

Witkin, H. A. (1966) Cultural influences in the development of cognitive style in cross cultural studies in mental development. Symposium 36 XVIII International Congress of Psychology, Moscow.

Witkin, H. A., Lewis, H. B., Hertzman, M., Machovew, K., Meissner, P. B. and Wapner, S. (1954) *Personality Through Perception.* New York: Harper.

Witkin, H. A., Dyk, R. B., Faterson, H. F., Goodenough, D. E. and Karp, S. A. (1962) *Psychological Differentiation.* New York: Wiley.

Wittreich, W. J. (1955) The influence of simulated mutilation upon the perception of the human figure. *J. abnorm. soc. Psychol.* **51**, 493.

Wittreich, W. J. (1959) Visual perception and personality. *Scient. Am.* **200**, April, 56.

Wober, M. (1967) Adapting Witkin's field independence theory to accommodate new information from Africa. *Br. J. Psychol.* **58**, 29.

Wohlgemuth, A. (1911) On the after-effects of seen movement. *Br. J. Psychol. Monogr.* 11.

Wohlwill, J. F. (1963) The development of 'overconstancy' in space perception. In *Advances in Child Development and Behaviour,* Vol. 1, 205. L. P. Lipsitt and C. C. Spiker (eds). New York: Academic Press.

Wohlwill, J. F. (1965) Texture of the stimulus field and age as variables in the perception of relative distance in photographic slides. *J. exper. Child Psychol.* **2**, 163.

von Wright, J. M. (1968) Selection in visual memory. *Quart. J. exper. Psychol.* **20**, 62.

Wright, W. D. (1952) The characteristics of tritanopia. *J. Opt. Soc. Am.* **42**, 509.

Yarbus, A. L. (1967) *Eye Movements and Vision.* New York: Plenum Press.

Zahn, T. P., Rosenthal, D. and Lawlor, W. (1963) G.S.R. orienting reactions to visual auditory stimuli in chronic schizophrenic and normal subjects. *Psychophysiol. Newsl.* **9**, 43.

Zeigler, H. D. and Leibowitz, H. (1957) Apparent visual size as a function of distance for children and adults. *Am. J. Psychol.* **70**, 106.

Zinchenko, V., Chzhi-Tsin and Tarakanov, V. V. (1963) The formation and development of perceptual activity. *Sov. Psychol. Psychiat.* **2**, 3.

Zubek, J. P. (1964) Prolonged sensory and perceptual deprivation. *Br. med. Bull.* **20**, 1.

Index